MY NINE LIVES:

AN EXUBERANT ADVENTURE

MY NINE LIVES:

AN EXUBERANT ADVENTURE

BEN LIN

atmosphere press

*dedicated to the memory of my father Peter
and mother Priscilla*

TABLE OF CONTENTS

My family (from left): brothers David, me, Harry, Henry, mother Priscilla and father Peter Lin

As Barbara Walters' TV guest demonstrating Chinese cooking

As Jade Palace's head chef

As V.C. Zhang (left) with Keenan Shimizu in the play *The Imposter*

As Wu Tsing in the play *The Joy Luck Club*

Manufacturing won ton soup at the Venice Maid Factory

A scroll ("Unparalleled Authority on Taste") for Craig Claiborne on occasion of Jade Palace's one-year anniversary celebration

FOREWORD

For most of my life, behind the façade of a mentally healthy, self-assured man, in reality I suffered from a most profound, pervasive inferiority complex, a result of sibling rivalry. Lasting from the birth of my younger brother till I was in my mid-50s, it destroyed my self-confidence, crippled my relationship with women, darkened my outlook of the future, and made me an emotional wreck. Ironically, the liability also turned out to be a positive force, a redemption that inspired me to try harder to overcome adversities, turn weakness into strength, and pursue the impossible dream—without which I could not have embarked on my exuberant journey of diversified endeavors, my "nine lives."

In the ensuing pages I detail my career as an entrepreneur who, despite overwhelming odds, commercialized America's first packaged won ton soup that was distributed nationally and internationally; my ignominy of having flunked English composition for foreign students that shamed and stimulated me into becoming a writer; the trial and tribulations of being a restaurateur while turning the establishment into one of the most celebrated restaurants in Philadelphia, my PR effort to invite the renowned food writer Craig Claiborne to be the guest of honor and made a media plash; the untold story of MSG and my challenge to unveil the mystery; my long trek to become an actor; and my role as an enlisted man who fought the army all the way to the Pentagon over an unjust order and won.

CHAPTER ONE (1957–1959)

Army Escapade

Reading in the army library, I heard a stranger's voice: "Lin, I want to talk to you."

I looked up and it was none other than the highest-ranking officer—and the most inaccessible person—at my military base: our commanding general. I had never seen him at close range. A few times when his chauffeur-driven car emblazoned with a one-star red flag passed by, I knew the general was inside, and I saluted as all soldiers were required to. But I didn't know what he really looked like.

Now seeing him for the first time, I had no trouble identifying him. He had a one-star insignia on each side of his shoulders, indicating his rank as brigadier general and a name tag: HAROLD WALMSLEY. He looked somber and intimidating, seemingly not an easy man to please.

He obviously knew not only who I was but also when and where he could find me at that precise moment as he sought me out purposefully. I instantly rose and stood at attention. My first thought was one of unspeakable terror: "What did I do wrong?" "Did I bug out from work too early?" "Is he going to punish me for some misdeeds that I absentmindedly committed?"

I felt much better when General Walmsley asked: "How is your piano going?" But I had no idea how he found out I was a pianist, or why he took interest in little me, the lowest ranking GI in the army hierarchy. Even if my piano playing was progressing badly I could only reply perfunctorily "Fine," adding "I play at the chapel's antechamber where there is a grand piano."

Seemingly a music devotee he asked, "Are you able to play freely?" I was reluctant to answer. The Catholic chaplain there never hid his dislike of me for disturbing his peace, even when there was no service. I didn't really want to bad-mouth him, but somehow I mentioned that my playing seemed to antagonize the chaplain a little.

"Let's go there now." He continued to surprise me and told me to ride with him in his car with the red flag. On our way there, soldiers left and right were saluting the general, and I had the vicarious sensation of being a big shot, enjoying the respectful protocol. Remaining serious, he made no attempt to be sociable: no inquiries concerning my musical background or words about anything else as I rode in dead, uncomfortable silence for the three-minute trip.

In the antechamber General Walmsley briefly inspected the piano keyboard but did not strike any notes to determine the tone or action, and was satisfied it seemed to be in good working order. We next met with Captain Splaine, the Catholic chaplain, a grumpy man who always looked at me with a frown. After an exchange of greetings the general told him, "I'd like to help Lin with his piano. Unless he interferes with your service please let him play as often and as long as he wants to."

"Of course."

He next told me, "I want you to audition for me tomorrow. How about 17:30?"

"Yes, sir."

The turn of events was totally unexpected. I had no idea what he was up to but was too afraid to ask. A few possibilities floated in my head. Perhaps he wanted me to perform in the Officers' Club or a private gathering. As we parted company I was still a little shook up and amazed by what had transpired in the last 15 minutes.

At the appointed hour I played Chopin's "Fantaisie-Impromptu," exalting in the virtuoso passages and plumbing the depths of my emotions in the hauntingly beautiful slow middle section (adapted for the popular song "I'm Always Chasing Rainbows"). When this theme reappeared near the end in the bass, I concluded with a lyrical flourish. The general listened with rapt attention before commenting: "Excellent." He next revealed his true intention. "I want to give you time off from duty to practice. How much time do you need?"

This question puzzled me. In retrospect, most likely he had scrutinized the F.B.I.'s dossier on me and discovered all about me including the fact I was an aspiring concert pianist turned chemist but still doggedly trying to practice every chance I had. At any rate, I was put on the spot. I would be too naive to ask for too little time, but I might incur his displeasure by asking for too much. With no time to think I blurted out "Two hours."

He consented instantly and said, "Starting tomorrow you can leave your lab at 14:30." Walmsley took off immediately. Much to my regret I didn't even have a chance to thank him.

Early next morning Colonel Miller, the military chief of my lab, came to see me. I had never dealt with him directly, and the few times I met him he was friendly, treating me as a professional chemist and not a military subordinate. He was now ever so gracious and all smiles, happy to bring good tidings to what appeared to be his top superior's new protege.

"General Walmsley just called me. From now on you are off at 14:30 every day."

"Thank you, sir."

From that day to my remaining days in the service I promptly headed for the chapel without fail at that hour. General Walmsley never checked on my progress or made me perform. He just disappeared as mysteriously as he appeared. And I never saw him again.

I was curious as to why the good general showered so much largesse on me. I found out some facts without many details: He grew up in a musical family. His mother was a professional singer, and he had seriously contemplated a career as a concert pianist. As he was about to perform in public one day, he got nervous about facing the crowd. He retreated in a hurry and gave up his aspiration.

I never learned how he became a general. As commander of the Army Chemical Center, America's most elite military base where most of the soldiers were scientists, he had to have an illustrious background and might well have been a West Pointer and earned a chemistry degree. If so, it was quite a coincidence that we both set out to pursue a musical vocation but became chemists instead. Whatever the case, that he would go out of his way to treat a lowly private with such concern and magnanimity was a stupendous surprise that earned my eternal gratitude.

My connection with the army had begun in 1957, about one and a half years before I met him.

Badly, very badly.

It was absolutely the worst day in my life. I thought I had already reached my nadir. In my quest to be a concert pianist I developed an injured right index finger from over practicing. It was like a vegetable. When I tried to strike a note on my Steinway that finger had so little strength that virtually no sound came out. When I played a scale, the piano sounded like it had one missing key.

I was hoping the problem was temporary. It was not, despite my frantic efforts to remedy with physical therapy and medical treatments. I was 24 years old and music was the only thing I had lived for, my sole purpose in life. With the onslaught of my finger atrophy I stayed away from the piano, hating it. As I was steeped in despondency and didn't think anything worse could happen, I got an "invitation" requesting the pleasure of my company from the Selective Service.

In the 1950s conscription was in effect, and any man between the ages of 18 and 25 was subject to military service unless he had a deferment. Initially I had a college deferment because I was a music major at Columbia while studying the piano with a Juilliard teacher. But after realizing I lacked the tools to be a piano virtuoso, I sadly resolved to do the next best thing: use my hands as a surgeon, and I enrolled in a pre-med program with a major in chemistry at Penn.

Upon graduation, with my acceptance at the Jefferson Medical College, I was able to continue my military deferment. But an unexpected happening changed all that. During the seven months before my entry to Jefferson I became increasingly overcome by my first love, my passion for music, so deeply rooted that it overpowered all other considerations. Inevitably I felt I was destined after all to be a concert pianist and that I could not be happy otherwise. As I re-embraced my earlier aspiration, I began to commute weekly from my Philadelphia home to New York for my lessons with noted pedagogue Madam Olga Stroumillo.

After informing Jefferson of my decision I forgot my draft status had become 1-A, the highest eligibility classification. That's how I was conscripted.

From movies and novels like *From Here to Eternity* and *The Naked and the Dead*, I came to view the army as pure hell. I loathed the idea of regimentation, loss of freedom, individuality and dignity, and the terror of drill sergeants. It was a two-year prison term in the prime of my life.

On December 2, 1957, I duly arrived at Fort Jackson for

basic training, without realizing music not only did not desert me but would play an important role during my tour of duty. Named after President Andrew Jackson and located in Columbia, South Carolina, Fort Jackson was the largest and the most active initial entry training (IET) ground occupying some 5,000 acres. It turned disparate civilians' lives upside down and remarkably transformed men into disciplined, professional soldiers in eight grueling weeks.

Except I was just a little different from the others. With my head shaved like a Buddhist monk and wearing an incongruous army uniform I looked odd, feeling strange and out of place. I was the only Asian in the entire company. Some of the guys jokingly asked me if I was a Chinese soldier in the wrong army.

Just a few years before the United States ended the Korean War fighting the Communist Chinese. Unjustifiably, there was a great deal of hostility toward Chinese-Americans. In addition, we were saddled with a historical, deeply rooted racism that was still widespread. In point of fact, I had experienced two such recent incidents. 1. Driving in Boston I was confused by the traffic cop at an intersection and didn't know what to do. He looked at me with disdain and screamed: "THIS IS AMERICA!" 2. On a Greyhound bus with few passengers, my friend Mai and I were talking in Chinese near the rear, bothering nobody. A woman, who was obviously offended by the sound of our alien tongue, accosted us, kicked Mai in the shin, and walked away. Hence, I wondered how I would fare in the days to come—with more than a little apprehension. Fortunately, the army, ever a bastion of tolerance, treated everyone equally without regard to race, color, or creed and allowed no discrimination from its troops. Thus, I encountered no overt bigotry. But I didn't mind a little harmless teasing from my fellow trainees.

They comprised draftees and volunteers. The former had

the letters "US" preceding their serial numbers, while the latter, "RA." These letters appeared on our fatigues and field jackets, so one could easily tell to which group each person belonged.

There was a natural antagonism between the two. It was beyond the understanding of the "US" why anyone in his right mind would enlist during peace time: Probably they had nothing better to do, or couldn't find a civilian job, or out of desperation, willingly sacrificed their precious freedom for the sake of job security from which they could not be laid off or fired.

On the other hand, the "RA" looked down on the "US" for our total lack of patriotism, our abhorrence to being of service to our country for two short years, our distaste for the great institution of the army, without which we couldn't have enjoyed the freedom and democracy that we did, and for our snobbery and being sissy. The two disparate groups often bantered with each other and had a good laugh.

In the late '50s and early '60s we enjoyed a rare period of peace. I didn't have to worry about the brutality of battle: maimed limbs, post-traumatic stress disorder, or the loss of life. The one concern every trainee did have were the frequent threats from the drill sergeant: "If you flunk basic training you have to spend another eight weeks repeating it."

Otherwise our drill sergeant did not fit the stereotypical image of a military tyrant. On the contrary he was a relatively benign fellow. A tobacco-chewing, slow-speaking Southerner, he might bellow once in a while but never abused us physically (not allowed anyway) or verbally. The one officer who frequently dealt with us was Second Lieutenant Lomax, who had probably just gotten his single gold bar from Officer Candidate School or ROTC (Reserve Officers Training Corps). About my age, he impressed us with his perennially neatly starched and pressed uniform and his love for raw onion, which he eagerly gnawed on every time he appeared. No complaint about him either; he was a gentleman and behaved civilly.

A typical day in basic training began with wakeup call at 5:00 A.M. We had very little time to wash up and make our beds before physical training at 5:30. If a bed was not made so tightly that a quarter did not bounce, the drill sergeant would tear it apart. The rest of the day was devoted to a rigorous program of military training. The exercises were demanding physically and mentally, meant to toughen our muscles, sharpen our minds, challenge our ability to think and gain knowledge quickly. In the evening the sergeant was free to do whatever he saw fit to train us further. At 8:30 we got a little time to ourselves before lights off at 9:30.

The full schedule took a while to get used to. Speedily my foreboding of boot camp dissipated. I made up my mind to make the most of everything and began to see things in a different light. The training was quite interesting and enlightening. It included such subjects as:

- Uniform code of military justice including court martial.

- Nuclear warfare, chemical warfare (e.g. agents like nerve, mustard and blister gases) and biological warfare (agents such as fungi, virus, bacteria to kill or incapacitate).

- Rifle marksmanship, not just target practice but learning to take apart and reassemble an M-1 within a few minutes.

- The ABCs of physical readiness, military etiquette, and the role of the Inspector General to whom we could redress our grievances.

All of which became applicable to me in one way or another.

As a musician, I found special resonance in the cadences that accompanied our marching and running and were intended to improve our stamina and uplift our spirits. The most typical was: "SOUND OFF, 1-2, SOUND OFF, 3-4; CADCENCE COUNT, 1-2-3-4, 1-2-3—4." Others were simple melodies with rhyming verses, often poignant or humorous. Two examples as remembered by ex-soldier Steve, who had spent seven years at Ft. Jackson, are quoted here in part:

> 1. I don't know but I've been told
> Eskimo pussy mighty cold.
> I don't know but I heard rumor
> My first sergeant wearing bloomers.
>
> First sergeant, first sergeant, can't you see
> All this running is a-killing me.
> MP, MP, can't you see
> You can't spell wimp without MP.
>
> 2. Fe-ee fi-fo fum
> I smell the blood of some commie scum.
> Be he live or be he dead
> I'll pay him for the blood he's shed.

Our drill sergeant would sing one line at a time, and we would repeat after him. He might not have been a Pavarotti, but his heart was in the right place and the singing sounded cute. To this day his vocal style still echoes in my ear.

Our harshest training exercises were 1) crawling with a rifle amid loud explosions, the closest thing to a battle situation. For the faint-hearted it could be a terrifying experience. If he veered from the prescribed path he could be seriously injured or killed. And 2) trying to put on a gas mask in a room filled with toxic, choking gas. There was no escape from inhaling some of the gas no matter how fast we tried. By treating the exercises as fun and games I actually had a good time and delighted in the excitement.

I had greater enjoyment on the firing range. During my younger days in China I was fond of the slingshot with which I could hit distant objects with great accuracy, in particular, birds. (But I gave up this cruel sport after—to my great re-morse—I killed one.) Apparently, my eye for target shooting stayed with me as I hit enough bull's eyes on my M-1 to earn the marksman medal.

Less fun was going to the mess hall. We invariably had to do push-ups and/or chin-ups before entering. It was stren-uous but not beyond our limits except for one poor trainee. A chopstick-thin weakling, he was unable to do the simplest exercise and stayed away from the mess hall—secretly. He survived only with package after package of food from home.

As for me, a foodie who would one day be a Chinese restaurant critic, chef, and cooking teacher, I needed many adjustments to live on a Yankee diet, with its tendency to overcook vegetables, its lack of textural delight, and the ab-sence of soy sauce, something I couldn't do without for long. Mess hall chow nevertheless was nutritious. Always hungry, I frequently had two bottles of milk, double portions of steak and other entrees. I fattened myself so much that I weighed the heaviest in my life, bloating from 167 pounds to 185.

Early on I found a grand piano in the servicemen's hall, and I could not resist the temptation of tickling the keys. Initially I was fearful of opening my old wound, reliving my pain and frustration from my injured finger. Gingerly I tried to play. The finger was still feeble, but it seemed to be better. I began to spend more and more time on the piano. Miracu-lously with passing days my bad finger showed signs of life. It was still a little weak, but by pressing harder I could produce a passable sound. Before long I could play almost normally. I was overjoyed. I wondered if my piano playing could be of any service to me.

One question uppermost on everyone's mind was where we would be sent after basic training. The least desirable—but most likely—place was infantry, the largest army branch where they needed people the most. During wartime, the infantry-man was the first to face the enemies and sustain casualties. In peacetime, he had to be combat ready and constantly undergoing training. Other alternatives included administrative and maintenance duties or the Officer Candidate School. I qualified for the latter but turned down the opportunity because it would prolong my army tour.

It was common knowledge the best possible assignment was Special Services. It would be a gravy job with very light duties and a good possibility of being stationed in Europe where I longed to travel to. So I called on Special Services. The man in charge was a non-commissioned officer. He was unassuming and quite accessible.

"I'm a pianist. I wonder if I might join the Special Service."

"Possibly. I need to hear you play."

"Right now?"

"If you are ready."

My fingers were not nimble then, being out of practice. But I decided to wing it. After warming up a little on Bach I played Chopin's "Fantaisie-Impromptu in C Sharp Minor." The sergeant was highly pleased, giving me a mark of 92 or 93.

"You qualified. As a matter of fact, you would definitely be in Special Services because we enjoy priority over all other assignments. You will be going to Europe, most likely Germany. You will get your order when you finish boot camp. Congratulations!"

The thought of spending my two years entertaining the troops—perhaps playing a little dance music while stationed in Germany and traveling all over Europe—buoyed my spirits. If I had any options, Germany would positively be my first choice. I chose German as a second language in college;

enjoyed the original text of Friedrich Schiller's play *Maria Stuart;* studied the piano with a wonderful teacher from Frankfurt, Lonny Epstein; and adored the three Bs of Bach, Beethoven, and Brahms, and the legendary pianist Walter Gieseking. How I would love to converse well in that language and deepen my appreciation for its culture!

In the meantime, I had to face what was to be the toughest training: bivouacking miles away from our base and then marching back. It was in the dead of winter. When we arrived at the campsite the frigid weather chilled us to the bone. It would be a brutal, long night sleeping on icy-cold, hard ground. After setting up our individual tents I thought I had to wear a lot of clothes to keep warm. Our sergeant, however, told us to wear very little, because our body would generate enough heat under a heavy blanket. He was right.

But no counseling from him could allay our fears about what lay just ahead. As we woke up before daybreak, our next rigorous task was the dreaded daylong march with shoulder-breaking backpacks from the camping ground back to our base. The marches could alternate between regular paced and running, sometimes over difficult terrain. The march would be the severest test of my basic training—I was never strong physically—and I wondered how I could survive.

But my guardian angel must have been watching over me. After a hasty breakfast as we were pulling out, a jeep arrived. The driver caught me just in time. He told me he had a directive from Special Services that superseded my training schedule and nullified the marching order.

"The director wants you to perform on the piano tomorrow on TV," he said. "He doesn't want you to look haggard. He also wants to give you time to practice."

Hallelujah! To the envy of everyone I was driven back to the base and given the rest of the day off. As a lowly buck private, to be treated so royally and in such a dramatic, Hollywood fashion was beyond my wildest dreams.

I spent the whole day in the servicemen's hall playing the piano to my heart's content. In late evening the soldiers returned to the barracks from their long march. One look at them and I realized how fortunate I was to be spared the ordeal. It took a very heavy toll on them; I never saw a more disheveled, defeated, exhausted, sad-looking group of young men. My heart went out to them, and I was especially touched by the sight of a lanky colleague, Don Rhinehardt, who was quietly crying.

There were no other hardships to endure and eight weeks went by quickly. I became stronger, sharpened my mental acuity, lost the excess weight I had amassed, gained valuable experience and knowledge, and learned to appreciate the army almost as much as the RAs. Everyone was glad and proud to have passed the crucial, initial entry training, and no one had to repeat it. For our graduation, we marched in fine precision around the parade ground resplendent in our dress uniforms, while top officers watched us on the review stand. When the army band concluded with some rousing march, I couldn't help but get a little emotional on this auspicious occasion.

When announcements of our assignments were made I fully expected the words "Benjamin Lin, US 52-454-151, Special Services." But to my utter disbelief and disappointment, I was ordered to report to the Army Chemical Corp in Edgewood, MD, as a chemist. I rushed to the Special Services director to find out why. He told me it was a surprise to him, too. While Special Services enjoyed top assignment priority, he just found out that the army had recently initiated a new program to utilize recruits' scientific backgrounds. And that new initiative trumped even the priority of Special Services.

I had long forgotten I was a pre-med with a bachelor's degree in chemistry and had worked at Merck, the pharmaceutical giant, just before being drafted. Resigning to my fate

I bade farewell to Ft. Jackson with fond memories.

The army gave us a few days' liberty to go home. Home was in West Philadelphia, abutting the University of Pennsylvania, my alma mater. My leave passed all too swiftly. I didn't have quite enough time to lap up Mother's delicious cooking that I missed so much, read up on Chinese newspapers, and renew my love affair with my Steinway. As I was getting ready to report for duty at the Army Chemical Center, just a two-hour drive from Philadelphia and 20 miles northeast of Baltimore, I had the happy thought that I could return home on weekends possibly every week.

The Army Chemical Center (ACC) was under the command of General Harold Walmsley, who was to be my unexpected benefactor as mentioned earlier. Edgewood was small and the only military post where chemical warfare was studied. Its agents pertained to a group of gases intended to kill, maim, disable, or irritate. And the deadliest was nerve gas (years later the United Nations classified it as a weapon of mass destruction and the Chemical Weapons Convention outlawed its production and use).

When I first arrived, what struck me was the open-air stockpile of nerve gas in steel containers. They looked menacing and someone soon told me about it. When exposed, the victim would suffer convulsive spasms, then suffocation, and die within minutes. Colorless and odorless, the gas could strike without warning as detection was exceedingly difficult. That's why ACC kept pigeons all around the storage area. If they were suddenly dying it denoted a gas leak. For anyone near the area the only remedy was to instantly self-inject an antidote, atropine sulfate. And a few people in the past had to resort to it and escaped death only by their vigilance and quick action.

Like me, most soldiers there had bachelor's degrees in various branches of science and mathematics. No doubt the most exclusive group of servicemen in the States, they worked in the labs under civilian supervisors. The atmosphere was relaxed and unmilitary-like. No physical exertion, no sergeants breathing down their necks. Everyone was taking long coffee and lunch breaks, doing little work and looking for ways to bug out. To keep the semblance of the military and for a change of pace there was very painless military training on Friday afternoons, consisting of lectures and nothing else. And once a year there was target practice with a carbine.

Since these scientists/soldiers were recent graduates more than a few treated ACC as a college campus, and the more assertive and naughty ones behaved like fraternity boys, not unlike the characters in the movie *Animal House*. They scrawled "FTA" all over the place, prompting investigations by intelligence officers, who thought FTA was some subversive organization before discovering the true meaning: FUCK THE ARMY. It was the common way to demonstrate the rebellion and revenge of being drafted.

Reportedly one enlisted man poured sugar into the gas tank of an officer's car, a sure way to disable it. Another ordered bags of fertilizer to be dumped on an officer's lawn. Two soldiers boldly tried to drive into the base with naked women but got caught by the military police at the gate. Things got so out of hand that top brass went ballistic and castigated us for defacing government property and other unlawful, disrespectful acts, and warned that anyone misbehaving again would be ruthlessly punished. Indeed, one such soldier was summarily thrown into the stockade for getting into a fracas with an officer. The punishment worked as no one dared doing anything out of line after that.

Before the scientific personnel could begin work they had to have security clearance because the jobs were highly classified. Dutifully, I filled out a long questionnaire concerning detailed facets of my life including my three high schools (in Chunking and Hong Kong) and four colleges (Wayland Baptist College, Columbia, Juilliard Music School, and Penn), full- and part-time jobs (totaling about a dozen), people who had known me well, organizations I had joined, questions intended to ascertain my loyalty and integrity. My complicated background was further compounded by my having been born and raised in China where I still had numerous relatives under the Communist regime which was our enemy during the Korean war.

While other ACC scientists all got their clearance quickly, mine understandably was slow and deliberate. I kept waiting and waiting. The long vetting process turned out to be a blessing, a paid vacation (about $80 monthly) in disguise. After the morning ritual of reveille, breakfast, and muster everyone went to his respective lab. Since I had no security clearance and therefore no place to report for work, I was left to my own devices, free to do whatever I pleased from 8:00 A.M. to 4:30 P.M. And the authorities didn't seem to care about—or bother to find out—how I spent the day.

To my great delight I found a grand piano in the chapel's antechamber. Not unexpectedly I spent hours upon hours there. It was not always convenient due to interruptions by the service or preemptions by other pianists. But elsewhere I found an old upright piano in an empty hall where nobody ever came near. Frequently I found a small dog, seemingly a music lover. It sat quietly next to me, attentively listened to my playing and lavished its affection for me by licking me. Now I had two pianos to while away the hours, with an appreciative audience of one.

When not luxuriating in piano playing I repaired to several haunts. One was reading in the well-stocked library. My loving perusal of newspapers, magazines, and Tolstoy's *War and Peace* possibly sowed the seeds of my latent interest in writing. Another was the servicemen's club where duplicate bridge was the chief attraction. Having been an avid player since high school, I honed my skill by reading books by Charles Goren and others, playing frequently, and practiced on auto-bridge. I was good in theory but often poor in execution, because I had a weak memory for cards, a fatal fault in bridge. So when I won a puny quarter of a Master Point, I had a pleasant surprise and treasured it all the more.

Going to the ACC theater was another pleasing pastime, and it cost only a quarter to see the newest movies before they were even released. I have been an inveterate movie lover since I was a teenager in Shanghai, entranced by such classics as *Great Expectations,* which made me helplessly in love with Jean Simmons; *Captains Courageous*; *Gaslight*; *The Picture of Dorian Gray; Fantasia*, my favorite segment being Paul Dukas' "Sorcerer's Apprentice" starring my beloved cartoon icon, Mickey Mouse; and especially *A Song to Remember,* the story of Chopin. (Movie theaters those days had rental earphones that provided simultaneous Chinese translations. So, despite my lack of English comprehension, I was able to understand the dialogue.)

Occasionally I drove my old Ford to Baltimore to splurge on a good Viennese dinner at the Hausner restaurant, where the wiener schnitzel was quite good, or roamed around East Baltimore Avenue, a red-light district, or to see a burlesque show.

Back on the base I was glad to strike up a friendship with the director of Special Services who was also a horn player. It was he who introduced me to "Brahms' Horn Trio, Op. 40" for piano, horn, and violin. Brahms wrote it to commemorate the death of his mother. The director and I occasionally talked about playing the masterpiece with a violinist but were thwarted by the difficulty of finding one. The trio has four movements. The third, marked *Adagio mesto* (meaning mournful), is considered one of Brahms' most impassioned, sorrowful, and heartfelt slow movements. It was truly an eloquent and inspired tribute that resonated with me, especially after the death of my own mother.

On Friday afternoons, right after our military lectures, I never failed to go home, and not even a weekend kitchen police duty (KP) could deter me. I would follow the common practice of "selling" my KP. That meant paying someone $15 to work in my place. The army didn't seem to mind this mild bending of the rules, and there was never a shortage of men to take up my offer.

Since I had loads of time on my hands waiting for security clearance, and with my right index finger fully regaining its use, I came up with a fresh idea: Why not capitalize on the proximity of Baltimore to study the piano? This town was known not only for its great crab houses and the inimitable journalist H. L. Mencken, but also its music institute, the Peabody Conservatory, ranked then along with a few others like the New England Conservatory, and the Eastman School of Music perhaps just below the Curtis Institute and the Juilliard School of Music. So I made an audition appointment.

My auditor was Reginald Stewart, the Conservatory director, conductor of the Baltimore Symphony, and a prestigious pianist (identified by the *New York Times* upon his demise in 1984 as one "who had an excellent international recital career," who during his Peabody tenure "brought such luminaries as Igor Stravinsky and Leonard Bernstein to the school").

For the audition I played Bach's "Prelude and Fugue in G Major" from his *Well-Tempered Clavier*, Book One. Of the 24 fugues this was my favorite, with its ingenious thematic development, contrapuntal beauty, fluidity, and propulsive force thrusting forward to a magnificent climatic close.

Stewart reacted enthusiastically and said, "You are accepted."

"Am I able to get a scholarship?"

"Go ahead and fill out an application with the financial aid department."

It was a golden opportunity.

Before committing myself I carefully analyzed my situation. I certainly couldn't be a full-time student. Nor did I think the army would let me leave the base to take weekly lessons. Also, I felt my security clearance was imminent. If I were assigned to lab work it might be hard to rigorously pursue my piano studies. So I regrettably gave up the plan.

But my clearance was not forthcoming. It was certainly no cause for complaint as I continued to merrily enjoy my "paid vacation."

While my days always went smoothly, my nights were a different matter. Unbeknownst to me I had a terrible anti-social problem about which I had to find out the hard way. Asleep one night I felt suddenly airborne, floating in space and in motion as if I was blissfully on a magic carpet. When I opened my eyes, I could make out in the dark that four of my barrack-mates were holding my cot and walking. I suspected the men were up to no good, most likely playing a prank on me.

"What the hell are you doing?" I shouted.

They said my snoring was so thunderous nobody could sleep. They decided to do something drastic about it. Short of murdering me they swore to remove the source of their insomnia in an insidious but ingenious way: to carry me carefully and slowly—so as not to wake me—out of the barrack to the adjoining Day Room. I was livid and cursed them at the top of my lungs. This fury made them give up their conspiracy and move me back.

They told me to sleep on my stomach, which was one way to stop snoring, but it didn't work for me. No matter how hard I tried to lie in this uncomfortable position, as soon as I fell asleep I became a noise-making factory. Someone immediately would jab me awake. But that never lasted long. I soon returned to my dreamland and began my wood sawing. Again someone would jolt me. It became a never-ending vicious cycle that began that night and lasted the balance of my army tour. I don't believe I ever enjoyed a single good night's sleep. As a result I suffered the most debilitating sleep deprivation.

My snoring turned out to be the outward manifestation of a very serious, deeper problem: sleep apnea. I didn't discover this until many years later when the Jefferson Sleep Disorder Center revealed that I stopped breathing 685 times a night, sometimes up to a minute at a time. As my airways became blocked by my collapsed throat muscles, I had to struggle constantly between breathing and non-breathing. The potential dangers varied from stroke, to heart attack, to hypertension. On a long-term basis, the deprivation of oxygen could damage my brain cells and shorten my life span. Fortunately, the best cure for me was CPAP, an acronym for continuous positive air pressure, a breathing device that forcibly opened my airways and allowed me to breathe unobstructed. I have been wearing CPAP and sleeping like a baby ever since 1990 thereby ending both my snoring and apnea. Had I worn CPAP during my army tenure I could have avoided my untold agony and the horror of making so many enemies. There was one problem though: CPAP was not invented until over two decades after my army discharge.

One day two men in civilian clothes, apparently from the F.B.I., visited me as part of the security clearance process. They were concerned about my Chinese origins and had questions about my allegiance. They wondered if I was still sympathetic to the old country and needed assurance that my loyalty to the U.S. was not outweighed by my cultural and emotional ties to China. I was reminded of the forced internment of Japanese-Americans during World War II because there were doubts about their allegiance.

The F.B.I.'s uncertainty about me was understandable in

light of the Korean War. Initially it was a conflict between North Korea and the combined allied forces of America and South Korea supported by UN forces and led by General Douglas MacArthur. But when MacArthur ignored the warning of China not to approach the Yalu River, which is on the border between North Korea and China, the latter poured a massive human wave of infantrymen into the war. It got so escalated that the U.S. was seriously considering deploying atom bombs on North Korea and China. But President Harry Truman eventually decided to limit the scope of the war, fearing it might lead to the participation of Russia and the precipitation of World War III. When MacArthur openly opposed and criticized this strategy, Truman fired him for his insubordination and blatant indiscretion. This war, which started in 1950, resulted in an estimated 34,500 American deaths and concluded in 1953. It was also during the height of the McCarthy Era during which anyone suspected of being a Communist or Communist sympathizer was hunted down and persecuted.

I told the two investigators that my parents and I abhorred the odious, totalitarian regime of Communist China. We were grateful to find refuge in this land of freedom, justice, and opportunity. If anything, I was probably more loyal with more appreciation than many native sons because I chose to be an American. I took great pride in being a citizen and had an abiding love for America. There should be no question about my fidelity whatsoever.

Furthermore, my oldest brother, Dr. David Lin, a gifted surgeon, volunteered to serve in the U.S. army during the Korean War. Commissioned a captain, he headed the First Evacuation Hospital near the fighting front, literally risking his life. Once while photographing a Chinese POW he was spat on for his seeming betrayal to China, his country of birth, and his loyalty to the U.S. For David's valor, dedication, and sacrifice (once he operated continuously for 72 hours), he won the

Bronze Star Medal and South Korea's Presidential Citation.

Undoubtedly the agents already knew my family history well. In any case, whatever doubts they had before the interview seemed to have disappeared as they nodded in satisfaction and departed with smiles. I felt that my long delay for clearance would soon end.

But I still waited in vain for positive news. Incredibly my limbo lasted some four long months. Finally, the verdict came: I was denied clearance. The reason: my older brother Harry, also a medical doctor, was living in China. The security people feared that the Chinese government might hold him hostage to exact confidential information from me. It was a risk they did not want to take. At this point, ironically Harry was mercilessly persecuted by the Communist regime for his patriotic criticisms. After exhausting all means to emigrate Harry took his own life at the age of 29, just a few months after my clearance denial.

Without this hindsight, the army stripped me of my scientist's status and ordered me to report to Fort Bragg, NC. I knew very little about Ft. Bragg except it was home of the 82nd Airborne Division, the training ground for paratroops where life was severe. It made me highly apprehensive, and I anticipated a difficult time; however, I had no choice but to resign myself to my fate. No guardian angel to save me this time, no last-minute reprieve.

As I made preparations to leave, I felt sad to say goodbye to ACC, my home away from home, my "paid vacation," my two pianos, and my two close friends, both of whom I've kept up with to this day: Morty Rosen, a detachment clerk who later became an attorney, and Tom Jurcich, a fellow chemist who later worked as a civil servant.

Five days before my departure one evening, a new GI entered the chapel where I was playing the piano. He had just transferred from Ft. Bragg. He told me it was the most combat ready and military active base in the whole country, an absolute horror and sheer hell for anyone unfortunate enough to be sent there. It was the closest thing to going to war, as everyone underwent constant training and military exercises. He did not go much into detail. I could only visualize that it would be a hundred times worse than my boot camp experience, possibly the kind of punishments marine recruits had to endure in Parris Island (which resulted in a well-covered death). Fort Bragg would break my bones and crush my spirits. In no time this young man succeeded in scaring the daylights out of me. I was mired in gloom and doom.

The following day I chanced to meet a stranger and asked how he was doing.

"Great! I'm getting discharged tomorrow."

"Where were you working?" There were jobs for both scientists and non-scientists, and he was one of the latter.

"In a lab."

"Which lab?"

"The only one that didn't require security clearance."

I was getting not only curious but a little excited.

"Are there any vacancies?"

"Yes. They were looking for a chemist."

As soon as he told me who was in charge of placement, I rushed to see him, a Captain Faulkner (if memory serves).

"I hear you have an opening for a chemist."

"Yes, we do."

"I understand it doesn't require clearance."

"That's right."

"Well, I have a scientist's MOS (an army code that defined soldiers' specialties) and I was a chemist before I was drafted. I would like to apply for this job."

After inquiring about my background and confirming my MOS, he gave me the news that sent me to high heavens: "We could use you."

25

But there was a possible obstacle. I said, "I already got an order to report to Fort Bragg."

"Could you change my order?"

"No, once a military order is issued nobody can change it."

In other words, military orders were sacrosanct and immutable. He regretted his inability to place me and told me I had no choice but to report to Fort Bragg.

Before my journey to North Carolina, with just four days remaining at ACC, an idea struck me. I remembered the army telling us during boot camp that if we had any legitimate complaint, we had the right to take it up with the inspector general (IG). May be there was a ray of hope. Whether my complaint had legitimacy, I had nothing to lose by visiting him. But I had a disastrous beginning. Before I uttered a single word about my predicament, I committed a faux pas that seemed to doom my quest. In retrospect it was comical.

When an enlisted man called on the IG there was rigid protocol to follow. I should find out whom I would be talking to before knocking on his door. When asked to enter I should salute, followed by saying solemnly: "Private Benjamin Lin requests permission to speak to Inspector General So and So." When the request was granted I could approach him but had to stand at full attention until he gave me permission to sit down.

I did none of that.

I had been living the life of a pseudo-civilian for too long; I had forgotten all about various military formalities and etiquette. When I stood outside the IG's office, I didn't try to find out his name or rank, which was Colonel J. N. Granade. Noticing his office was open I simply barged in and shuffled toward him without being invited. Next, I extended my hand and said: "Hi, I'm Ben Lin. Can I talk to you?" and was on the verge of sitting down without being asked.

He was flabbergasted and refused to shake my hand.

Clearly, he bristled at my abominable behavior. Sternly he reminded me of the protocol and told me to start all over again. Embarrassed and feeling stupid, I backed out. The second time around I did everything perfectly, although I feared I might have lost his good graces and blown my chance for any possible salvation.

Soon I realized Colonel Granade was an amiable, helpful IG. He listened patiently and sympathetically. My main complaint: "If the army is serious about utilizing its scientific draftees, why waste my talents as a chemist when there is a job for which I am qualified? Why ship me to Fort Bragg? It doesn't make sense."

He agreed with my logic but reiterated what Captain Faulkner had told me: "You are stuck with your order and nobody can help you. It's too bad."

As I was dejectedly leaving I thought of a remote possibility on the spur of the moment.

"What about complaining to the person who gave me the order?" I asked.

This question surprised him. It was a Pentagon man, a civilian, he said. This civilian chief, I thought, no doubt boasted a top position, which towered above the military. Hoping against hope I begged him, "Could you please find out who he is and make an appointment for me?"

If my impudence did not annoy him too much he was nevertheless not persuaded. "It would be useless. Why waste time?" Indeed, my proposed mission seemed to be an exercise in futility that was destined to fail. But I continued to press my luck. Apparently touched by my earnest pleading and proving he was a man of compassion he did exactly what I requested. There was no time to waste; it was a Thursday and I was due at Fort Bragg the upcoming Monday. So I was grateful he made a Friday morning appointment and gave me special permission to leave the post.

Word quickly spread among my colleagues that I was going to the Pentagon on an improbable mission. There was no lack of well-wishers, but everyone was skeptical about my prospects. In fact, I needed no reminder that "You can't fight city hall," much less a quest that was tantamount to an unprecedented, epic battle waged against the mighty institution of the army. Besides, I was cursed with having the proverbial "Chinaman's chance." (My apologies to those offended by this racist slur.)

My meeting at the Pentagon was short. My tormentor, the man who gave me my hateful order, was serious, impassive, and very busy with papers all over his desk. Most likely he had never met any recipient of his order, let alone one who tried to change his order. Selfishly and immaturely, I should have realized his job was to fill vacancies, juggle positions, and issue military orders without regard to the personalities involved. Furthermore, he was doing me a great favor by granting the interview in the first place. Instead of behaving courteously and appreciatively I was very rude and startled him with a complaint: "I am a victim of injustice."

Obviously a man of infinite grace and refinement, he didn't seem to be offended by this brash, rebellious young private. Without saying a word he let me present my case. He made no comments and reacted with no emotion. Instead, he instantly picked up a phone and dialed. After identifying himself he said, "Captain Faulkner, I have Private Benjamin Lin here with me. He says he talked to you a few days ago and that you have a job opening for him that doesn't require clearance. Please confirm this."

He next told me, "I'm going to send two telegrams: one to Fort Bragg to say you won't be reporting there on Monday. I'll send another telegram to the Army Chemical Center with a new order. You're getting your MOS back, and you'll report there for work on Monday."

Once again my guardian angel saved me in the nick of time. God works in mysterious ways.

Upon my return to ACC my friends cheered me boisterously as a hero, a baseball star who hit a home run to clench the World Series title. This Friday, unlike any other Fridays, was not just a happy time to go home, but the greatest day of my army life.

My new lab job comprised mainly the testing of gas mask components, such as measuring the tensile strength of the rubber strips. I worked under a civilian supervisor and shared the lab with another civilian and an enlisted man, none of whom were chemists. The duty was light and easy, with no pressure, no deadline, working at a leisurely pace. To make things even more pleasant, I worked only six hours daily with two hours off to practice the piano, courtesy of General Walmsley.

Adding a little responsibility as a way to repay the army, I volunteered to be one of the military lecturers mandated every Friday afternoon. It was not an easy undertaking. As an immigrant whose command of English was still poor, whose accent was heavy and whose preparation for the lectures was laborious, I was, nonetheless, happy to give something back to the army. Besides, I had studied public speaking in college and enjoyed it enormously. So I welcomed the opportunity of talking to a captive audience and was richly compensated. It helped build my self-confidence and improve my English. Moreover, this experience may well have influenced my decision to be a teacher and stage actor.

One evening I met a new arrival in the chapel. As we exchanged background he intrigued me with his story. He was Jewish but not a practitioner of Judaism. Instead he was an atheist, which was stated on his military record and the word "atheist" was inscribed on his dog tag. He didn't think his nonbelief mattered one way or another until this discovery: The

Army Regulations had a special dispensation for Jewish personnel who were entitled to three days off for Rosh Hashanah, the Jewish New year. All they had to do was to make a simple request. This fellow wasted no time in changing his religious affiliation officially to that of Jewish.

His conversation reminded me of a related story. At ACC there were a good many Jewish soldiers. When Rosh Hashanah was approaching, our detachment sergeant was so flooded with applications for three-day passes that he hardly bothered to scrutinize. He just signed the passes as quickly as possible. Once, a naughty Irishman with a very Irish name decided to try his Irish luck. As expected his request was buried among his Jewish colleagues'. To his surprise and delight he got his pass. And the sergeant was none the wiser.

With the approach of Chinese New Year, the story triggered my imagination, spurring me to try out my Chinese luck, not by subterfuge but by legitimate means. On a wing and a prayer I visited Sergeant Smith of my detachment. He was a gruff career non-commissioned officer who never smiled.

No protocol was required when a soldier called on a sergeant in his office. I just came straight out with my request.

"I'd like to put in for a for a three-day pass."

"What for?"

"Chinese New Year."

"Get the hell out of here," he bellowed. "You're wasting my time!"

"If Jewish people can get a three-day pass for their New Year why can't I get one for my Chinese New Year?"

"I never heard of such a ridiculous thing. The Army Regulations have provisions for Jewish New Year. But nothing for Chinese New Year. This is not the Chinese army. Now get out."

Not one to give up easily, I searched my mind for a solution. I thought my best hope was to appeal to Major Jongewaard, a

Protestant chaplain whom I met when playing the piano at the chapel. Unlike the Catholic chaplain, he always greeted me warmly and seemed helpful with any problem I might have.

"Chinese New Year is coming up," I said. "Like your Christmas, it's the most important occasion for the Chinese. That's when close relatives gather for a reunion and celebrate the holidays together." He nodded in sympathy.

"Sergeant Smith just turned down my request for a three-day pass. Could you do something about it?"

Major Jongewaard kindly obliged and phoned Sargent Smith. Outranked by this officer and bowing to the power of the chaplain, Smith had no choice but to cooperate. But as he was handing me the pass he looked disgusted and scornful. But no matter, I happily spent the occasion with my family.

If we enlisted men had little individuality with everyone being equal, luckily, I seemed to be more equal than the others. The army had been treating me in a blessed way for which I was grateful. It made my military stint easy, memorable, and even enjoyable. Certainly, I was also helped by my boundless persistence and chutzpah. They were not inborn traits but the result of my historical inferiority complex stemming from sibling rivalry. I was motivated to try harder to contravene my sense of low esteem, to overcome whatever adversities stood in the way. Ultimately, however, it was the army's graciousness that gave me the needed push. To me the army was no longer a hard-nosed, cold, impersonal institution, but one humanized by the benevolence of people like General Walmsley, Inspector General Granade, the Pentagon civilian chief, and Chaplain Jongewaard.

I would be an ingrate if I did not I resolve to be a good, law-abiding soldier, and the last thing I wanted to do was anything untoward. But my absentmindedness proved to be my undoing. One Friday when I went home as usual I had a surprise. Typically, I returned to the base at four o'clock

Monday morning and tried to grab a little sleep. Shortly after reveille at 6:00 A.M. my detachment sergeant confronted me and shook me up with these scary words: "You were AWOL (Absent Without Official Leave.)" I couldn't think of anything that merited his accusation.

"I did no such thing," I protested.

"You were supposed to pull KP. Where were you?"

I should have checked our bulletin board frequently to find out what was going on, especially notices concerning our assigned duties. But before going home that Friday I forgot all about it. The order on the bulletin board clearly called for my KP duty that Saturday or Sunday. So I was guilty as charged.

For the more serious AWOL, the consequences, as stipulated in the Military Code of Justice, could be court martial followed by doing time in the stockade and/or dishonorable discharge. Fortunately, my infraction was a mild one. I got Article 15, a non-judicial army punishment. Beginning that Monday, I had to spend all my non-working hours in the barracks for seven days. There was no enforcement of my penalty; it's strictly an honor system with no one guarding or checking up on me. I would have been terribly bored but since I could watch TV and read in the adjoining Day Room I tolerated my punishment not too painfully.

(Incidentally, for anyone pulling KP one of the jobs was to peel potatoes. The standard procedure: place them in a machine to do the initial peeling. Then complete the process by hand. One wise guy thought of a labor-saving device: He left the potatoes purposely in the twirling machine for a long time until the skins were completely gone without using his hands. So the potatoes ended up well peeled but the size of ping pong balls. When discovered by the mess hall sergeant, he got a break. Instead of Article 15 as punishment he got a tongue lashing.)

Commiserating on my Article 15 punishment was my best

friend Mort Rosen, who possibly could have prevented me from going AWOL. As a company clerk he was privy to inside information, knew what was on the bulletin board, and would have alerted me about my KP. The only problem: we were in two different detachments.

From my earliest days at ACC, Rosen and I hit it off because 1. Jews and Chinese seemed to have a natural affinity for each other, both being the world's oldest civilizations with cultural similarities. 2. We shared an appreciation for the arts. And 3. I admired his erudition in English literature, which was his college major and a source of my growing interest. He initially aspired to be a writer, but after realizing the futility of trying to emulate D. H. Lawrence, one of his idols, he became discouraged. That was one of the reasons he gave up this ambition. Eventually he became one of New York's top real estate attorneys.

During our R&R, rest and recuperation, he invited me to go to Europe with him and another colleague. We could fly for free on the Military Air Transport Service. But despite my long wish to visit that continent, at this juncture I fell in love with the piano once again and didn't want to lose any time practicing and regretfully missed this valuable opportunity.

When I asked Rosen to attend a Van Cliburn concert in Philadelphia with me it was his turn to reject my invitation. In 1958 Cliburn had just stunned the world by capturing first prize in the quadrennial International Tchaikovsky Piano Competition in Moscow during a period of cold war between the U.S and U.S.S.R. New York gave him a ticker-tape parade, and he was mobbed like a rock star. His concerts were sold out way in advance.

He was about to repeat his winning program by playing Tchaikovsky's "B Flat Minor Concerto" in Philadelphia. I had a special reason to attend this concert: I knew Cliburn personally. When I enrolled in Juilliard's summer session in 1951, he was my classmate in the Master Piano Class. His genius was already evident as one of the frequent performers. We also shared something else in common: He was from Texas where I had just spent my first year as an immigrant in a Baptist college.

Since Rosen and I didn't have tickets and a full house was expected, realistically he didn't want to spend five hours on a round trip wild goose chase. I was a dreamer, saying, "If we try really hard we might find spare tickets due to sickness or conflict. It has worked for me before." Very, very reluctantly he came along. We headed for Philadelphia immediately after he got off from work. (I was still free daily at 2:30 P.M.)

It was before 7:00 P.M. when we reached the Academy of Music. As people began to drift in I asked everyone for spare tickets and told Rosen to do the same. He did not try too hard or was too shy to follow my advice which was understandable; after all it was like begging and required a thick skin and a lot of patience. Indeed, despite my strenuous effort I had no success initially. But my persistence and diligence paid off; eventually I got a ticket. While Rosen continued to be helpless, I doubled up my effort to pinch-hit for him and as the hour drew near 8:00 P.M. I finally got him a ticket just before the house lights dimmed.

Now listening to Cliburn in a different venue I, like everyone else, was transfixed by this lanky, bushy-haired young man. He started his concert with his own arrangement of "The Star-Spangled Banner." It was a grandiloquent statement, full of big chords and strong colors. He played with a patriotic fervor as if he was still in an international competition. He then plunged into the concerto and brought the house down.

I wanted to congratulate him, but it was very difficult with a thick crowd gathered outside the Academy of Music. After a long wait I reached him. I last saw him eight years prior. Now looking more urbane, well-poised but still unassuming, he easily recognized me and gave me a bear hug. He went on to fulfill his promise as a superstar and returned often to Russia where he was adored as much as in the U.S. How remarkable it was to capture the hearts and minds of two cold war enemies and forge their mutual friendship through the magic and sheer talent of one lone individual!

My two-year tour of duty came to an end sooner than I had realized. I was discharged on December 1, 1959, with the rank of specialist fourth class. But my connection with the army was far from over. I was in army reserve with mandatory refresher courses and training in Indiantown Gap, PA, every summer. Because of my scientist's MOS I was also subject to recall for active duty way past the recruitment age until my 40s in case of national emergency or war. But the following summer the army had a change of heart and freed me of all military obligations. I became a civilian 100 percent. But my army tour will always stand out as an indelible part of my crucible in this journey of ours called life. I would not exchange it for anything in the world.

CHAPTER TWO (1974–1979)

Jade Palace

Growing up in Shanghai, I first discovered the thrill of dining out from food vendors. They were skilled culinary artists who plied their trade in alleys and on side streets, offering a diverse array of appetizer-like specialties. While most of the merchants were stationary, some roamed from place to place in search of customers with a portable kitchen—complete with a coal burning stove, cooking and dining utensils—slung over their shoulders. Typically, the vendors specialized in just a single selection. As such it was so worked over, lavished with such care, that the results were nothing short of spectacular.

They varied from juicy pork-filled buns graced with a crispy bottom and topped with sesame seeds, ultra-tender tofu enhanced with an inimitable sauce, crusty scallion cake that elevated the humble green onion to a truffle-like tastiness, to "stinking bean curd" which emitted a pervasive stench detectable several blocks away, repulsive to the uninitiated but utterly irresistible to the cognoscenti. As a youngster predisposed with a culinary bent, my favorite after-school pastime was to splurge my allowance on these treats, much to the dismay of my parents for spoiling my dinner appetite.

My parents grew up under very difficult economic circumstances. The son of an impoverished Protestant minister,

Father never ate well and lacked decent clothing. Mother's dad was frequently unemployed, so the family had to cope with starvation on occasions. Eventually Mom went on to be a gourmand and great cook while Dad never shared her passion for food.

Ironically, in the late 1940s when Father gained prominence and influence as a banker, he spent most evenings entertaining—and being entertained—in Shanghai's top restaurants. My brothers and I often tagged along, which turned out to be quite a revelation with far-reaching consequences. It introduced me to the joys of restaurant dining, made a believer out of me, and helped shape my perennial craving for all things tasty.

In subsequent years after I migrated to the U.S. and came of age, my enthusiasm for Chinese restaurants continued to soar. In time I turned into a most ardent patron who dined out as often as possible. At my most extreme, when I went to New York I would often go to two restaurants in Chinatown for a single meal, capitalizing on the specialties of the house. I also delighted in the pursuit of newer and better culinary oases and enjoyed exchanging intelligence with my Chinese friends; one of them introduced me to a restaurant that would become a turning point in my life: the Jade Palace.

As an extension to my dining interest I was drawn increasingly to the cooking itself, and in particular, the dramatic technique of stir-frying, and the contrasting tastes and textures, contrapuntal effect and aesthetic appeal achieved by the judicious blending of ingredients. And under the tutelage of Mother in the mid-1950s I became an avid cook, culminating in my being a cooking instructor and executive chef years later.

While wokking it up is a lot of fun, the ultimate dining pleasure indisputably lies with superior restaurants. There is no better way to enjoy a relaxed meal among other contented guests, to have the luxury of choosing from multitudes of

selections including those too arduous or impossible to duplicate at home, be fussed over by attentive servers—and no
cleanup afterward. More importantly, talented chefs can not
only dazzle the senses and ingratiate one's well-being but also
instill a lingering sense of euphoria unmatched by other
counterparts. Offering invaluable assistance is the powerful,
high temperature gas range (90,000 BTU). It enables the chefs
to accomplish instant cooking thereby sealing the flavor,
retaining the succulence, and preserving the texture.

After becoming a Chinese restaurant reviewer I had a
chance to gain a deeper insight into this intriguing institution.
And so, my affection for it took on a new dimension as I
developed a longing to be an owner myself, changing from a
passive role to an active one of serving, setting the menu, and
calling the shots. To provide quality nourishment to the public
seemed to be a noble, inspiring, and artistic calling from which
one could derive enormous pride and a sense of fulfillment.
My longing grew so obsessively that I could not get it off my
mind, and I felt life would not be complete without becoming
a restaurateur. As a result I went all out to pursue my dream.

Luckily, I didn't have to try too hard. It so happened I had
just reviewed the Jade Palace for the *Philadelphia Collegiate
Guide,* and in the course of my interview I discovered the
owners were thinking of selling it. The upshot: I not only raved
about it but showed the ultimate approval of a critic by buying
it in early September 1974.

Located in Northeast Philadelphia at 2222 Cottman
Avenue, the Jade Palace did not have the most ideal location.
People tended to equate Chinatown as the mecca of Chinese
restaurants and thought their counterparts elsewhere could
not be as good. Furthermore, Northeast Philly was a hinterland, an inconvenient distance from downtown. It did, however, have one advantage: a Jewish neighborhood, and Jews
were commonly known to be the best patrons of Chinese

restaurants. On the other hand, more than a few Chinese restaurateurs expressly chose that location for the same reason and so competition was fierce. Two rivals, Bamboo House and Lee, were in the immediate vicinity; several others were not far away.

It was not the most propitious time for me to take on another challenge. I was doing graduate work in journalism, running my food company (founded in 1962, two-and-one-half years after my army discharge—see chapter on "Won Ton Entrepreneur") and teaching cooking in Philadelphia and New York. Nevertheless, I was confident by managing my time efficiently I could wear several hats and devote enough effort to my new venture. But if I should fail, at least I would get the bug out of my system.

Before acquiring the Jade Palace I had to find a replacement for the current head chef (and co-owner) Mrs. Seeying Liang, whose talents were so prodigious it would be difficult to fill her shoes. Top-notch chefs were always much in demand and none were known to me. One possible source was employment agencies in New York's Chinatown. But I doubted I would get the best talent. Plus, I was averse to taking a chance on someone with whom I might not get along.

By coincidence a friend of Father's introduced me to a chef by the name of Che So Yi. A Northern Chinese endowed with an illustrious background, he studied cooking at the age of 15 with his uncle, 70, who had been the imperial chef to the Empress Dowager. He furthered his studies with Beijing's best-known chefs, and by his 20s commanded a repertoire of over 700 dishes. With the Communist takeover in China he migrated to South American where he became one of the most celebrated chefs in Uruguay and Argentina. Seeking his fortune in the U.S. he had just opened a restaurant not far from the Jade Palace.

After dining there a few times I was impressed. But few

others shared my enthusiasm. Soon he was out of business (proving that good restaurants without the proper publicity might not always succeed) and became my prime candidate. Since chefs were notorious for being ill-tempered and demanding, I wanted to make sure my choice would be a sensitive, considerate, and mild-mannered person. Che struck me as just such a gentleman, always smiling and polite, and seemingly an easy man to work with during the little time I had known him.

So I made him an offer that he readily accepted. Knowing that kitchen personnel were highly transitory I let him invest a small sum in the business as an incentive to maintain a long-term relationship. I also hired his wife Susan as the cashier and acceded to his request to provide an apartment.

Until my *Collegiate Guide* review and another for *Philadelphia* magazine in 1970, the Jade Palace (JP), had never received any other publicity. However, it did have a small but loyal following and a viable business (owner Stanley Liang actually let me scrutinize his receipts when I was considering buying). After my purchase, to ensure a smooth transition I decided to make no changes initially and kept the same menu and all the employees. For two weeks just before the JP changed hands Mrs. Liang generously taught Che gratis the uncommon dishes in the menu. A quick study, Che mastered them all. Hence, I was expecting to have a seamless transition and enjoy positive cash flow right from the start. With excitement and anticipation, I embarked on my culinary journey that would prove to be a highlight—with also some unexpected miseries—in my life.

At the outset everything was going well and no patron ever inquired whether there had been a change in management. To devote sufficient time to my journalism studies and teaching I showed up only from Wednesday to Sunday evenings but never for lunch when business was slow.

When the time was ripe Che and I worked jointly to devise

a new menu. We kept some of Mrs. Liang's specialties such as shrimp with pine nuts, beef with three types of mushrooms, and such standard Cantonese fare as egg foo yang, shrimp with lobster sauce, and pepper steak to appeal to the conservative clientele. For the adventurous we filled the menu with spicy-hot Sichuan entrees like General Tso chicken, yue hsiang eggplant, and bean curd with minced pork, and northern Chinese classics like Peking duck and mou shu pork, plus a host of Che's favorites including sweet and pungent whole fish and sautéed king crab garnished with meat and vegetables. Another feature was multi-course banquets for larger parties. I wrote an introduction in the menu and described all the newer dishes for easier ordering.

In taking the JP in a new direction I knew the great risks involved. If it did not resonate with the public my business would surely be doomed, and it would be difficult to reverse a losing trend. On the other hand, President Nixon's highly publicized visit to China in 1972 with heavy coverage of the banquets did wonders to liberalize the taste of Americans for Chinese food. They became more open-minded and willing to try different alternatives. Moreover, Philadelphia was experiencing a restaurant renaissance in the early '70s with the opening of numerous new and sophisticated dining spots in the downtown area.

So it might not be a bad time to subject the JP to the litmus test of a review. However, with a plethora of restaurants, food writers were reluctant to come simply on the strength of a polite invitation. Fortunately, when I was promoting my won ton soup business I learned much about public relations and became well acquainted with Elaine Tait, food editor of the *Philadelphia Inquirer*. When asked she helpfully sent a colleague of hers, Bill Collins, to review.

The review was so laudatory and carried so much weight that the JP became an overnight sensation and our business got a tremendous boost with a long line stretching outside during weekends. In subsequent months every area newspaper large and small came to review and heaped encomiums on us. The *Philadelphia Daily,* for example, called the JP an "excellent Chinese place," South Jersey's *Courier-Post* gave it the highest rating, Montgomery County's *Times Chronicle* touted the JP as "a Chinese gem" and in another review by Bill Collins, he extolled it as "the crown jewel of the city's Oriental dining rooms."

Way before all this transpired I had my first giant headache which threatened to put me out of business due to our problem with food inspections. As the nation's fourth largest city Philadelphia had only 27 inspectors to cover some 5,000 restaurants plus catering businesses and cooking schools. Logistically it was impossible. So they limited their scrutiny to a select few: the best-known ones and restaurants that had recently received good publicity.

Just a few days after the *Inquirer* review a young inspector showed up. He looked stern and intimidating. Wearing a pair of white gloves, at one point he crawled on the floor looking for grease and dirt under everything imaginable. Before finishing he meticulously checked out every inch of the JP and wrote up a sesquipedalian list of violations—all of which I inherited from my predecessor—and gave us a deadline to correct.

I did everything within my power to comply: getting rid of the omnipresent grease which had been accumulated for years; making sure all the pots, pans, and every other cooking utensil were in pristine shape; repairing any indentations and cracks on the walls no matter how small; hiring an exterminator to kill off the omnipresent roaches; placing mouse traps all over the place; scrubbing the kitchen tiles on my hands and knees, etc. In subsequent inspections we fared better, but there were always some violations. The hard truth: any restaurant that was doing any business at all could not possibly keep everything immaculate. Sadly, I was ordered to appear in a municipal court, where the judge told me I might have to shut down the JP and face the possible humiliation of seeing its name in the newspapers among other restaurants unlucky enough to be similarly closed.

Now I was certainly in favor of health department's sacred mission to ensure cleanliness, sanitation, and public safety and many of the violations cited in the JP were totally justified. But the temptation for inspectors to abuse their power was also great, not just in Philadelphia but elsewhere. In New York, for instance, I read that many restaurateurs had to repeatedly bribe the inspectors to stay in business. Despite efforts to clamp down on the corruption, rampant briberies remained. A waiter of mine told me his father was a food inspector in Hong Kong where he and his colleagues also commonly took bribes.

In order to keep the JP in operation I sought out the district health department's supervisor and did something I abhorred: I gave him a $100 gift certificate. It worked like magic. When he noticed we had already corrected all the critical violations he suggested a few minor changes, took the JP off the blacklist, and gave us a new lease on life. And that was the best money I spent on the JP. In future inspections while there were always a few things wrong they were easily correctible and I never repeated the horrible experiences of prior inspections.

Before the JP was a few months old it was once again mired in turmoil, a heart-wrenching misery that came close to ending my tenure as a restaurateur. Chef Che, who first impressed me as such an affable, courteous man turned out to be anything but. Indeed, he had the worst temper of any person I had ever associated with, treating me shabbily and getting violently angry with the slightest disagreement. It was one of the most agonizing periods of my life and I wanted to end our partnership.

By coincidence, a would-be savior appeared. Mr. Chao, a famous chef in Taiwan, where he was a cooking teacher of mine, had just relocated to Philadelphia. He offered his service if I should need it. That he could handle the duties and continue my success was beyond question, and I doubted lightning would strike again with another temperamental chef. So my easy way out was to replace Che with Chao. But being fair-minded and in deference to his contributions I was willing to give him the right of first refusal: to take over the JP and buy me out or step down. He chose neither. Instead, he became a model of contrition, vowing to rein in his bad disposition, change his ways of dealing with me, and begging me to let him stay.

Against my better judgment I bowed to my soft-heartedness and gave in. Initially I was overjoyed that Che did become a different person; he was kind, gentle, and treated me with respect. But true to the axiom "jiang shun yi gai, ben xin nan yi," or "one can easier change mountains and rivers than one's nature," Che typified it. After a short while he transformed from a temporary Dr. Jekyll back to a permanent Mr. Hyde, and I was back to square one. By this time Chao, the Taiwanese chef, was no longer available for he had opened his own restaurant. Lacking other connections I decided to forgo the arduous and time-consuming process of finding a suitable replacement. The alterative was to retain Che, learn to live with him, and pray I would not go insane. I was not in the restaurant for the long haul anyway as my aspiration then was to be a journalist and I had started to take writing courses at Temple University.

In the meantime I felt I could accomplish much with my marketing and PR skills to take the JP to a new level, which kept my spirits up. I came up with a slogan for the JP: "imperial cooking that turns a meal into a sensuous revelation." To celebrate its first anniversary I wanted to do something spectacular, to create a publicity event that in all likelihood no other restaurateurs ever considered or thought possible: by inviting America's most eminent and influential food editor, Craig Claiborne of the *New York Times*, to be the guest of honor at an elegant banquet. He was known for his unsurpassed passion for Chinese food with frequent columns on the cuisine, restaurants, and chefs. Indeed, more than anyone else he had advanced the popularity of Chinese restaurants and raised America's consciousness about this cuisine.

Translating my celebration quest into reality, however, was fraught with difficulties. Not long before he was embroiled in a controversy that made international news and invited scathing condemnations: a $4,000 meal. It was a charity auction sponsored by American Express. Claiborne's successful $300 bid allowed him to dine in any restaurant in the world with a friend and no limit on the cost. He chose Pierre Franey, a renowned French chef, as his companion and dined at a famous Paris restaurant, Chez Denis, racking up a $4,000 bill on a 31-course, nine-wine meal. When he wrote about this in the *Times* it provoked outrage from the readers for his extravagance. Even Pope Paul VI denounced the dinner as "stupid and scandalous waste."

So my timing was poor; he would probably have little stomach for another extravagant dinner and any publicity that might arise from it. Worse, there was no inducement for a distinguished journalist to take time off from his busy schedule and travel all the way from his East Hampton, NY, home to Northeast Philadelphia for the dubious honor I was hoping to offer.

It helped that we were not total strangers, for our paths had crossed briefly on a few occasions. The first time occurred when I asked him to do a possible story on me as an entrepreneur, the first person to have ever commercialized packaged won ton soup. Giving him some additional angles, I attached my magazine article "One from Column A" in which I tried to interject some humor, plus some publicity about me including a *Philadelphia Daily News* clipping, which excerpted a comedy that I had penned, *Mr. Wong: Or How I learned to Love the White House.* Claiborne politely declined, saying he was on the verge of retiring from the *Times.*

The second time happened at midnight. I was already in bed when the phone rang. I thought it had to be a crank call or wrong number. Instead, it was none other than our esteemed hero. Without apologizing for the late hour, he identified himself and went straight to the point:

"I need your help desperately. The New York Chinese Restaurant Association is honoring me for my service and for advancing their business. I have to give a speech tomorrow, and I need a good Chinese joke." I was flabbergasted. In his capacity as the dean of America's food writers he must have a wide circle of friends, witty acquaintances whom he could turn to. Yet, he chose me whom he had never met and at such an uncivil hour. Apparently from the perusal of the attachments I had sent him earlier he concluded I was a funny guy who could help provide some comic relief for his Chinese audience.

Well, I happened to enjoy collecting and telling jokes. And so for the next 30 minutes I told him all the good Chinese jokes I knew, including:

> • The Chinese are of course known as the inventors of the compass. What's unknown is that they were the first ones to discover America. With this navigation tool, a captain sails on the high seas on a junk and comes upon this land of ours. As the ship is approaching the shore he notices native Indians dancing, all naked from the waist up.

"Let's go back to China," the captain tells his crew. "We have no future here; no laundry business for us here."

• An American is about to make his first parachute jump and is understandably nervous. His Chinese instructor consoles him: "Don't you worry. If things should go wrong just say 'Buddha save me, Buddha save me.' And He will help you. But remember, there is no god, only Buddha." As the American leaps out of the airplane he pulls the parachute cord but it doesn't open. He tries to open the reserve parachute but it also fails. Tumbling down at rapid speed, he is scared stiff but remembers what his instructor tells him. So he calls out "Buddha save me, Buddha save me." And a big Buddha hand catches him in its palm. In great jubilation he says, "Thank God I'm saved." Thereupon the palm turns upside down.

• A Caucasian tourist goes to a Chinatown gift shop and buys a paper fan. Later when he uses the fan it breaks. Angrily, he returns and complains to the owner.

"I fanned myself only a few times and it broke."

"That's too bad," commiserates the proprietor. "How much did you pay for the fan?"

"A dollar and twenty-five cents."

"How did you use the fan?"

This question provokes the irate customer further. "What do you mean how did I use the fan? I used it like everybody else." Holding the fan in one hand, he fans himself the customary way.

"Ah! For a dollar twenty-five cent fan you don't fan like that; you fan like this," the Chinese demonstrates by holding the fan completely still in front of his face while repeatedly swaying his head from side to side.

I had told this joke as the emcee at a convention attended by several hundred Chinese. It brought down the house with thunderous cheers and applause. But I had no idea how Claiborne reacted to it or any of my other jokes. He thanked me perfunctorily and our conversation ended at 12:30 A.M. as strangely as it began. I didn't think our paths would ever cross again, and in time I forgot all about this incident.

One day I read in the *Philadelphia Inquirer* that Claiborne, who had come out of his retirement and returned to the *New York Times*, was coming to a Philadelphia department store to promote a Chinese cookbook he had co-written with Virginia Lee. I was loath to chase after celebrities and initially had no intention to go but was persuaded otherwise by Dr. Y. H. Ku, a close family friend, at the eleventh hour. I arrived late when the reception was already over and he was leaving.

"My name is Ben Lin," I volunteered. "You probably don't remember me."

"Of course I remember you. I just told your fan joke," he said warmly, flashing a broad smile and shook my hand. After a brief exchange of pleasantries I wished him luck and we parted company.

To celebrate Jade Palace's first anniversary I thought there was no better way than to invite Claiborne as my guest of honor. Though I knew my chances of success were extremely slim I wrote him a letter of invitation, subtly reminding him of the "debt" he owed me for the fan joke and set November 29, 1975, as D-Day. I knew he would not accept any honorarium. Instead, I offered him an all-expense paid trip. Expressing appreciation for the honor, he said he could not commit himself because of his "uncertain schedule," which was probably as polite a way of turning me down as he could muster.

I persisted with letters, hoping my sincerity would somehow move him. My persistence eventually brought me a ray of hope. He said when the time came he would come but *only if* he had no conflict or other urgent business. But this conditional acceptance put me in a quandary. How would I plan an elaborate affair with such uncertainty? I decided to take a positive attitude, kept my fingers crossed, and proceeded full steam ahead.

Among the guests I invited were the *Inquirer*'s food writers Elaine Tait, Marilynn Marter, and John Bull, the managing editor and suburban restaurant reviewer; *Philadelphia* magazine's Jim Quinn; George Perrier, owner-chef of the great French restaurant Le Bec-Fin; and Jack Rosenthal, former president of the Culinary Institute of American.

To plan a dinner worthy of the occasion, chef Che So Yi devised a 12-course regal feast culled from the secret recipes that he had learned from his uncle, the imperial chef to Empress Dowager (one of the greatest gourmets in China's history; her every meal consisted of 75 dishes) on the solemn promise that he would not divulge them to another soul.

The anniversary menu would comprise:

1. Crystalline crab (king crab with preserved duck eggs).

2. Kwei Fei shark fin (named after a Tang dynasty empress, the fin is stewed with pheasant and preserved ham).

3. Hundred flower abalone (mollusk in the shape of chrysanthemum).

4. Roaming dragon frolicking phoenix (a duo of lobster and chicken).

5. Eight jewel duck (boned fowl stuffed with eight ingredients).

6. Royal bird's nest soup (a glorified version of this famous soup accentuated with pheasant sauce).

7. Jade pillar scallop (dried mollusk heightened with shrimp).

8. Steamed Buddha's hand (vegetables and meats in the shape of a hand).

9. Five hue shrimp (crustacean with five colorful garnishes).

10. Eight immortals feast (a blend of seafood).

11. Empress Dowager chicken (poultry which is marinated, deep fried, and then steamed).

12. Five treasure soup (a dessert accentuated with logan, a tropical fruit, and lotus seeds).

With everything in place and the press eager to do a story on this unprecedented extravaganza I was like an ant on a hot iron wok still unable to get a commitment from Claiborne. Worse came to worse, I would just have to suffer the profound embarrassment of calling the whole thing off and notifying my invited guests with great apologies. It was only about 10 days before the gala that he finally relieved me of my suspense and agony. Refusing my reimbursements for his travel expenses he told me he would come to Philadelphia by train, check in at the Latham Hotel in downtown Rittenhouse Square, and arrive at the restaurant by taxi, a good 40-minute ride.

Chef Che started preparation a week earlier. Sticking to his vow of total secrecy he worked only late at night when the restaurant was closed with the kitchen all to himself. On this festive day he stayed up till the wee hours. A great cause of concern to me was that he had not prepared a similar imperial dinner for years. What if he was out of practice or lost his touch? Moreover, it's a meal I had never tasted and therefore had no idea how it would fare. However, there was no use worrying; I just had to have complete faith and trust him to meet the challenge.

At the appointed hour on Nov. 29 the great man appeared, natty in glen plaid among admiring eyes and the popping of flash bulbs (from my good friend and photographer Joan Ruggles). There was palpable excitement in the air and warm greetings between Claiborne and his close friend George Perrier, the world class French chef. I served champagne but cut short the reception so we could commence with the three-plus-hour feast.

With the free flow of additional champagne, delicate jasmine tea, fiery 90-proof sorghum wine, and a rare South African red wine, courtesy of Jack Rosenthal, the banquet began with crystalline crab. It was a stunning success and augured well for the remaining courses which were served at a leisurely pace to allow for slow savoring and relaxed conversations. Normally I would play the role of the gracious host, in total command of the situation, regaling my guests with anecdotes, commenting on the subtleties of Chinese cuisine, and whatnot. On this occasion I felt tongue-tied in such august company and my attempt to engage Claiborne in some food topics only met with his stern remark "no shop talk."

Actually what everyone wanted to ask him about—but dared not—was the $4,000 dinner that he wrote about only two weeks ago in the *New York Times*. To excerpt Lesley Kruhly's account in the *Evening Bulletin*:

> "Finally, gourmet cook and teacher Julie Dannenbaum, a longtime friend of Claiborne's, broached the subject.
>
> "Claiborne rubbed his eyes, sighed and with the air of a man who has heard the question too many times, said 'don't ask. Just don't ask.'
>
> "Claiborne did divulge, however, that in response to the letters of outrage, a column that he had done

about white truffles ($400 a pound) had been cancelled, and on his current promotional tour of a new book, *Craig Claiborne's Favorites from The New York Times,* he has faithfully promised his editors 'not to take on the Pope,' who had lodged one of the most vehement protests against the extravagance of the meal."

Once the forbidden subject was out of the way, conversation eased as the diners swapped stories, jokes, and favorite drink recipes from Harry's American Bar in Paris. Kruhly concluded with: "the dinner, just as Lin had hoped, turned out to be an event of people who knew and cared about food celebrating a celebration, a meal even the dowager would have been proud of."

At the end of the dinner I should have given a short speech honoring Claiborne, but sidetracked by all the last-minute details and worries I regretfully forgot to prepare one. Instead, I just introduced him as the man "who has articulated most eloquently the joys of Chinese dining" and presented him with a scroll emblazoned with the Chinese characters "Pin Wei Quan Wei," or "Unparalleled Authority on Taste," written by a noted calligrapher living in New York city.

As expected the event generated a whale of publicity. In addition to Kruhly's story there were two other lengthy articles. Bill Collins observed in the *Inquirer*: "it's doubtful that President Ford will dine any more sumptuously." Ellen Shaw of the *New Paper* termed my effort "one of the splashiest public relations gambits." And Harry Harris, TV columnist of the *Inquirer*, told me: "You put the Jade Palace on the map."

Not surprisingly, Claiborne did not write about this gala; I certainly did not expect or ask him to. However, local press coverage—and the subsequent ripple effects—elevated the JP to the top ranks of the city's best-known restaurants and made me a celebrity, all of which could not have materialized had it not been for my little fan joke.

A few months later marked the arrival of Chinese New Year. It inspired me to come up with a good plan to attract customers: a multi-course banquet. Such a feast, considered the most desirable way of enjoying an intricate meal, normally required a party of eight or more because of the complexity in preparation. I devised a weekend special, a prix fixe menu of 10 fanciful courses for parties of only two or more. To minimize logistics in the kitchen and maximize participation I required patrons to make reservations at one of the three seatings: at 6:00, 8:00, or 10:00 P.M. I did not have to advertise at all. By inviting key food writers to be my guests I generated an enormous amount of publicity. They all loved the banquet and spared no ink to compliment it. Initially I was planning to offer the banquet for just a couple of weekends. But the JP was doing virtually full house businesses in every one of the three seatings. So I was able to extend it to a five-week celebration.

Sparked by the reception I offered the banquet in successive years with equal successes. Jim Barniak of the *Bulletin* wrote in 1976:

> "My heart, not to mention stomach and overall waistline, goes out to the Chinese who at last report are still celebrating New Years (sic.) And, apparently, with no intention to let up until sometime later this month."

> "Even then, says Ben Lin, proprietor of the Jade Palace, renowned as one of Philadelphia's most consistent Chinese restaurants of quality, 'the culmination is negotiable.' The meal, while of excellent quality, does tend to linger like a medium size anchor. There is a bonus in it for you if Lin himself is on the premises.

He is an engaging chap with expertise in subjects as varied as his dishes.

"Four of us recently opted to usher in The Year of the Horse, an aptly named year."

But because there was too much food "we pleaded with owner Lin to call the whole thing off after the ninth course. He agreed, as we clumsily attempted to reward him with a standing ovation."

Bob Shryock of the *Courier-Post* gave a blow-by-blow account of the 10 courses which included phoenix tail shrimp ("large and cooked quickly in a light batter, are worth the price of the meal alone"), Sichuan diced chicken ("by consensus the best dish"), and a "delectable sweet and sour fish."

Going beyond reviewing, Shryock wrote about me in glowing terms which I am humbled to quote:

"Try ordering Ben Lin, the personification of the perfect host. He can mesmerize you detailing the origins of the food and explaining the preparation of each course. And at the same time he can dazzle you with stories of his own amazing life with a charm and wit that made the unbelievable believable. He teaches Chinese cooking and has lectured frequently on the culinary art. Lin has studied music and has a degree in chemistry. He currently is hung up on being an actor but has had to be content with doing commercials out of New York City including one for Chase Manhattan Bank. He is pursuing a master's degree in communications at Temple University and has been a restaurant reviewer for *Philadelphia* magazine. Reservations can be made by phoning 215-342-6800. And don't forget: ask for Ben."

Staging these events and dreaming up unusual PR ideas was not just great fun but also necessary to keep the JP in the mind of the public, which tended to be fickle and short on memory. That's why even famous movie stars required publicists to keep their names in the limelight. Aiding me in no small way was *Inquirer*'s Bill Curry. Though I had never entertained him at the JP or even met him, he was highly accessible and accommodating. Whenever I sent him some PR news he invariably reported it in his column "On the Go," including helpful details about our annual Chinese New Year banquets, and such quotations as:

- "Ben Lin, the multitalented owner of the Jade Palace, is keeping up with the political times in renaming one of his staples, chicken with peanuts (Kung Pao chicken) as the 'Jimmy Carter Special' (when the former peanut farmer was elected President). Says Ben: 'the Sichuan dish has the fiery character of a southern Baptist preacher and the tenderness of a Southern belle.' He'll demonstrate preparation of the dish on an upcoming segment of Jack Helsel's 'How-to Series' [on TV]."

- Add screen actor to the many talents of the Chinese restaurateur-writer-musician Ben Lin. Lin, owner of the excellent Jade Palace, received his Screen Actors Guild card after a gig in a NET production called *Jade Snow.*

- Ben Lin jokingly complained to friends that he has been demoted to a waiter. Lin, who also does television commercials, was cast as a Chinese waiter in a beer commercial featuring former Dallas Cowboy Ralph Neely. Lin's restaurant, by the way, won third prize in the appetizer category in a national menu contest sponsored by American Express.

While it's gratifying to achieve some fame and glory I especially enjoyed cultivating friendship with journalists because of my love for journalism, and by extension, its practitioners. Among them: John Bull, a 28-year veteran of the *Inquirer* whose numerous positions included assistant to the editor, ombudsman, suburban restaurant critic, and one of seven founders of First Amendment Coalition of Pennsylvania. We shared a passion not only for food but also music. I was grateful that on occasion he invited me along on his restaurant reviewing.

Once when he was one of my multi-course banquet guests an amusing thing happened. At one point after an elegant chicken dish was served, to my surprise—and embarrassment—another chicken dish immediately followed, which I had not planned. The plain-looking fowl was intended for my restaurant staff but got mixed up by the server. Despite its unassuming appearance Bull was astute enough to detect the virtues and quick to rave it as the best entrée of the evening. We had a good laugh when I revealed the faux pas.

Another writer I became quite fond of was Bill Collins. My connection with him began before I became a restaurateur. In reviewing the Fortune Cookie restaurant he expressed special appreciation for the "lobster taste" in the popular dish shrimp with lobster sauce. Correcting his error, I wrote him a letter pointing out that the sauce contained no lobster, only ground pork and egg. So named because it's the same sauce for "lobster Cantonese," just as "duck sauce," another seeming misnomer which contains no such fowl and is intended for the duck. I expected no reaction from him. But he surprised me in his next column by printing the gist of my letter and admitting he was "lobster red-faced."

After acquiring the JP I was delighted to meet him. He was a vivacious, voluble, warm man gifted with an exceptional voice whose rendition of "O Danny Boy" was heartfelt "and moving. An excellent rewrite man, he had a stint at New York's *Daily News*. After joining the *Inquirer* he was assigned as a food writer in the early 1970s. While he admitted to having little food background initially, he learned fast and soon became knowledgeable and elucidated authoritative articles on culinary matters. Indeed, he even wrote a book titled *Where to Eat in America,* in which he lauded the best restaurants in 30 most-traveled American cities. For Philadelphia he cited the JP as one of the most notables. (Later, when I was completing my graduate program in journalism he was my thesis advisor. Still later he left the *Inquirer* and became a restaurateur or manager himself.)

My friendship with him yielded some unexpected dividends. As I searched my mind for PR ideas I remembered a frequent question people asked me: "What drink goes well with Chinese food?" I came up with the inspiration of having a wine tasting session. So I consulted with Collins. He thought it was a great story angle and volunteered to lay the groundwork. The first man he approached was Herb Engelbert, one of the foremost wine scholars and consultants (Air France was one of his clients). Engelbert in turn suggested a panel of experts, and on an April night in 1976 we had a five-course banquet with 13 diners. There were 11 wines from various parts of the world including Wan Fu, an import from France, and two provided by me: Great Wall, a white wine from China, and Shao Hsing, a rice wine from Taiwan.

Giving the group a little background, I advised that the Chinese were quite fond of the bottle. Typically, beer would go with a meal. In formal banquets, Shao Hsing, and particularly, mao tai, a fiery sorghum, were served. In the British-influenced Hong Kong hard booze like Scotch and cognac were very much preferred. I also mentioned that history of drinking in China went way back and that Li Pao, one of the country's greatest poets, wrote about the joys of wine and spirits some 1,000 years ago.

As observed by Collins in the *Inquirer*, a 1973 Bernkasteler-Riesling, a firm, medium-dry German Moselle and two

California champagnes, both by Korbel (the brut and extra dry), worked extremely well. Less successful were two domestic whites, Gallo Colombard ("too fruity and flowery") and Paul Masson Chablis ("needed a little more edge"), as was a 1973 Niersteiner Riesling Auslese, a premium vintage from the Rhine ("too big and sweet"). The Shao Hsing wine, which was like the Japanese sake, was an acquired taste. Two reds, a 1974 Beaujolais from France and Paul Masson Zinfandel from California, both very light, might go well with certain beef dishes but not with such delicacies as boneless duck, scallops, shrimp, and lobster.

The number one winner turned out to be Wan Fu. "The French, it seems, have a wine and a word for everything. Wan Fu, a white Bordeaux with a Chinese name was the unanimous choice. It is a very light wine, with a slight bite to it."

As a restaurateur part of my job was dealing with the public. Generally, it was highly pleasant and rewarding. I enjoyed talking to them, helping them order, and being complimented on our cooking. But once in a while I had to cope with some problem cases.

A patron told me she broke her tooth from the bone of a chicken dish and demanded $10 to pay her dentist. Since we used chicken breast which was always completely deboned her complaint had no merit and seemed just a way to milk some money out of us. Though she could not provide any bone as evidence—and I thought $10 would not be enough to repair a broken tooth even in the 1970s—I yielded to her demand as a goodwill gesture.

Another time a party of six was unhappy about the food and/or the way they were being seated. Despite my effort to mollify them they walked out angrily. The following day health department officials came to investigate, saying some customers got sick from food poisoning. I asked the officials if there were similar complaints from other JP customers and the answer was no. So it was obviously a case of trumped-up charges. Nevertheless, the officials spent a good two days investigating but could find nothing wrong and spared me the agony of shutting down the JP. The incident did show how vulnerable a restaurateur could be and how easily customers could disrupt his business.

One evening a couple griped there wasn't enough meat in the chicken chow mein they had ordered. I should have simply treated them to it. Instead, I offered a discount. Unsatisfied, the man grew abusive and started to make a terrible scene. Instinctively I called the cops. They appeared almost instantly. Following a brief interrogation they concluded that the customers were in the wrong and proceeded to handcuff the man. I quickly asked them not to and that I would not press any charges. After the officers led them away I realized the way I had handled the situation was an egregious mistake and cursed myself for not trying to resolve our conflict peacefully. This mistake apparently came back to haunt me a few weeks later as the JP was vandalized with a broken kitchen glass door, various property was damaged, wires and cables cut—surely acts of revenge.

I handled yet another incident unwisely. One Saturday evening in addition to full house guests there was a long line of takeout customers, and we were overwhelmed. One customer by the name of Schwartz, who always ordered pork lo mein, became furious about the delay. Despite our apologies and offer of free shrimp toast, he stormed into the kitchen, where I was busy cooking (I had replaced Che as the head chef then) and raised hell with me.

"Ben Lin, Ben Lin, how could you let your regular customer wait for 45 minutes?"

"We got behind schedule. I am sorry."

That wasn't enough to pacify him; he kept badgering me. Now when a chef was working furiously under great pressure he could be easily provoked as had happened to me. I angrily shouted at him: "We don't run our cooking like clockwork. Now get the hell out of here. We don't want customers like you." These were terrible words and I regretted afterward. The funny thing was he came back a week later and ordered the same pork lo mein.

One complaint had to do with monosodium glutamate (MSG) a controversial flavor enhancer that Chinese restaurants used as did the JP. But whenever a customer asked us to skip it we always obliged. On this day such a request came, and I personally filled the order. But to my surprise the customer accused the kitchen of ignoring her request because she was suffering terrible ill effects. I confronted her and said in no uncertain terms that I did the cooking and there was not one iota of the additive. Not surprisingly, what were obviously her psychosomatic symptoms immediately disappeared.

Because the truth of MSG has never been revealed it remains a mystery that still raises some eyebrows. I believe I may shed some light and answer the unanswerable.

This was the background: in 1968 a Chinese medical doctor by the name of Ho Wan Kwok wrote a seemingly innocuous letter to the *New England Journal of Medicine* about certain culinary experience of his. Little did he realize it was to spark an extraordinary controversy that sent shock waves throughout the nation and whose effects are still being felt to this day. His letter: "For several years since I have been in this country I have experienced a strange syndrome whenever I have eaten in a Chinese restaurant. The syndrome, which usually begins 15 to 20 minutes after I have eaten the first dish, lasts two hours, without any hangover effect. The most prominent symptoms are numbness at the back of the neck, gradually radiating to both arms and the back, general weakness and palpitation."

Dr. Ho went on to say his Chinese friends had suffered the

same experience and suspected that MSG might be the culprit. He also called upon his medical colleagues to do research on it. Ho's observations instantly became national news as people everywhere echoed his experience. They complained also, with symptoms including nausea, abdominal pain, burning sensation, tightness in the chest and the face, and thirst. Soon these complaints gave rise to the term Chinese Restaurant Syndrome (CRS) which struck terror in the millions of Chinese food lovers.

Predictably Chinese restaurants found themselves in the doghouse. In panic New York's Chinese Restaurants Association, which boasted over 2,000 members, held emergency meetings. The upshot: Many decided to withhold MSG or skip it on request; others still found it indispensable and tried to ride out the storm and after an initial drop in business it eventually bounced back. But the damage was done. To much of the public and for a long time, CRS and MSG became one and the same and the latter became synonymous with something close to poison.

As a marketer of my widely distributed packaged won ton soup, I had relied heavily on MSG to replenish some of the lost flavor caused by the canning process. Alarmed by the public furor, I immediately withdrew the ingredient from my product. But the difference in the taste was quite palpable. Finally, when the controversy died down I reinstated the additive with no loss in business either way.

In earlier years MSG, which had been present in all baby food, was found to cause lesions in the brains of infant monkeys and banned for this particular use by the Federal Drug Administration (FDA). However, many questioned the wisdom of this decision because the amount of MSG administered to the monkeys was thought to be many times what an infant might consume.

Subsequent tests by the private sector proved inconclusive.

While numerous respondents experienced ill effects from MSG, others reported psychosomatic reactions from placebos. All in all none of the researchers were able to prove with statistical significance the correlation between MSG and CRS. Some of them like P. L. Morselli and S. Gartattini concluded that "there is no evidence that Chinese restaurant syndrome follows ingestion of MSG." Others were baffled by MSG, calling it a "mystique." Drs. H. Ghadimi and S. Kumar in the July issue, 1972, of the *American Journal of Clinical Nutrition* summarized the various findings and concluded with: "the value of monosodium glutamate as a 'flavor enhancer' remains in question. However, concerns about possible dire effects of such culinary use on the central nervous system is clearly unwarranted."

The FDA, after its own research, pronounced its official verdict, categorizing MSG as "GRAS," or generally regarded as safe, and allowed the continued sale and use of the product. This pronouncement, however, failed to clear the name of MSG, for a number of people would not touch it with a 10-foot pole. Their suspicion, in my mind, was not unfounded, and the mystery of MSG remained unsolved.

As a Chinese chef and having been a former analytical chemist I took special interest in the controversy. I proceeded to do my own empirical research and I believe I've successfully unveiled the mystery.

Monosodium glutamic is the sodium salt of glutamic acid, or the crystallization of the amino acid which is present in all living cells. So theoretically its ingestion should be totally harmless. First produced by Japan in 1909, it was used in the making of soup stock. The Chinese also began to mass produce and called it "wei jin," meaning the essence of taste. As the name implied it did have a remarkable ability to improve the taste and was an essential ingredient in many a home. And to my best knowledge there had been no reported incidents in China.

How much MSG one should use was a personal preference. In my own cooking if my ingredients were fresh I skipped it altogether. But when the ingredients were pre-frozen I would sometimes use very minute amounts to replenish the loss in flavor. True, some Chinese restaurants, in their eagerness to provide tasty food, tended to over-rely on it. However, they were not the only ones favoring MSG for it was—and is—found in a plethora of American food products from canned soups, packaged food, frozen entrees to snacks.

Traditionally, MSG was produced industrially by fermentation process and the most popular American brand was Accent. However, the process was relatively expensive and time consuming. To counter that, a Japanese company was able to devise an alternate chemical synthesis to mass produce faster and cheaper, the cost being about half that of Accent. I'll call the more affordable alternative brand X to minimize possible legal complications. Understandably, for reasons of economy Chinese restaurants all opted for this brand. I believe that's when problems with MSG arose, but it took Dr. Ho's letter in 1968 to cause the national uproar.

Since the chemically made MSG was never 100% pure, only about 99%, I concluded what caused the ill effects was not the MSG itself but the by-products, the impurities from this chemical synthesis. In contrast, MSG made by fermentation method was virtually 100% pure and therefore had no noticeable harmful effects—if any. The reason the scientists got inconclusive research results was their colossal mistake of choosing the sources indiscriminately, making no distinction between the kinds of MSG they used. If they chose the synthesized version there would invariably be adverse reactions, while its counterpart made by fermentation process would have none.

To back up my hypothesis let me cite some personal experiences. I, too, found CRS very real. My symptom was one of itchiness on my back. As I started to scratch, it would be increasingly itchier and in no time my back would break out like hives. Another symptom was that I would develop a funny taste in my mouth. Yet, when I used Accent judiciously at home I didn't experience such symptoms.

At that time I frequented China Boy restaurant in Philadelphia's Chinatown. Every time I dined there I would develop severe itchiness. Being very friendly with the owner-chef, I often went to the kitchen to watch him cook. I noticed the MSG he was using was brand X. I suggested that he switch to Accent to avoid CRS of which he had been keenly aware and wanted to eliminate. Though Accent was a lot more expensive he followed my advice. Sure enough, the next time I dined there I experienced no allergy. When my itchiness returned some weeks later I suspected he switched back to brand X and that was indeed the case.

In my cooking classes I told my students to use MSG judiciously and only the Accent brand. As a precaution I advised them never to use MSG as a crutch; it would not remedy or mask one's inadequacy as a cook and that it was better to strive for natural flavor and not artificial flavor. In my 14 years of teaching in New York and Philadelphia not one of my pupils reported CRS. Moreover, during my four plus years' tenure at the JP we used only Accent and no customers ever voiced any complaints.

To further support my hypothesis the company that manufactured brand X apparently discovered that its chemically synthesized MSG was indeed the culprit and stopped its production in the 1970s, and returned to its older, safer fermentation process. (My inquiry to the company received no response.) That's why complaints about CRS have been steadily diminishing or disappeared altogether. However, when subjected to excessive quantity of MSG—even if it's Accent or is equivalent—I still experience an unpleasant aftertaste.

The quest of using extraordinary means to achieve delictability reminds me of a true story. An 80-year-old lady in Beijing was a devout Buddhist and vegetarian who loved the pleasures of the table. Searching far and wide, she was ecstatic to find a talented chef who could prepare delicious food while complying with her dietary requirements. She especially enjoyed the soup he made. One day the chef was entering her kitchen from a grocery trip carrying some ingredients wrapped in newspapers. When he met the old lady he became unusually nervous and dropped his package onto the floor, with the contents spilled all over. To the horror of the octogenarian they were all chicken heads. Pressed why he brought them to her vegetarian kitchen, he confessed that they were the ingredients with which he made the scrumptious soup that she so enjoyed. Upon this news she was so shocked that she dropped dead from heart attack.

In the summer of 1976 my thoughts turned to the more mundane matter of travel as I contemplated taking a vacation in Europe where I had visited in the summer 1974. It was cut short by my skiing accident in Zermatt. Always eager to return, I bought a Eurail Pass which would allow me to visit a dozen Western European countries in air-conditioned, first class trains. Armed with *Harvard Student Travel Guide* in addition to travel guides by Arthur Frommer and Eugene Fodor, I planned to travel independently without any hotel reservations or definite itinerary. Instead of a carrying a burdensome 45-pound luggage as I did on the first trip, I traveled light with an 18-pound shoulder bag with things that were absolutely indispensable. Since it was in the dead of summer I had no trouble wearing clean clothes by washing daily.

I began my journey in Northern Europe where I landed in Bergen, the gateway to Norway.

After visiting Sweden, Finland (by an overnight Russian ship), and Denmark I traveled southward, ending in Spain, covering a host of countries in between. Some recollections:

• Struck by the omnipresence of Chinese restaurants I dined in two out of curiosity. In Munich one was located right across from the train station. Though my dish was not particularly memorable it was quite authentic. Surprisingly the portion was gargantuan and served inside an enclosed container with heating elements to keep hot—as in Switzerland. In Paris the one I went to (out of some 20) was disappointing because the cooking was far from authentic, tasting almost like a foreign cuisine. I discovered the kitchen was staffed with Vietnamese-Chinese who apparently adulterated the food to suit the Parisian palate but seemed sacrilegious to me. In Stockholm a fellow restaurateur told me startup costs were high because the Swedish government mandated shower facilities for his employees, as well as an air-conditioned kitchen and storage room for garbage.

• I enjoyed Copenhagen's open face sandwich with its infinite variety, especially those with seafood toppings. For those into the Atkins diet as I was once, using one piece of bread instead of two was a smart way to cut carbohydrates into half. In Helsinki I patronized a Russian restaurant and ordered a bear dish. In ancient China bears' paws were considered one of the greatest delicacies. Poaching bear is banned by the Chinese government today but it's still reportedly being done and served secretly. The Russian dish was not bad, tasting very much like beef stew.

• Elsewhere I found some specialties bearing kinship to their Chinese counterparts: Swiss-German geschnetzeltes, in which meat and mushrooms were sliced and sautéed separately and then blended together, was like a typical Chinese stir-fried dish;

Bavaria's schweinshaxe was similar to one of my Shanghainese favorites, red cooked pork shank; Spain's jambon, preserved ham from black hoofed hog, rivaled the famed Jinhua and Yunnan hams (air-cured and made from special breeds of pigs); paella from Valencia seemed to be a veritable cousin of the Chinese fried rice with meat and seafood.

• One of my most depressing experiences was visiting Dachau, the notorious concentration camp for Jews outside Munich. Like the Japanese's rape of Nanjing during WWII, the gassing of innocent men, women, and children was one of the worst examples of man's inhumanity to man. The sight of the gas chambers and crematoriums was incredibly sickening and disgusting. When I saw a picture of innumerable emaciated corpses packed together like sardines I was moved to tears.

• Using my guidebooks I found a hotel in Paris within minutes after my arrival and on the left bank, no less, for only $5.95 that included a continental breakfast. I was able to hit virtually every desirable attraction via its excellent subway and a rented moped. The motorized bike was a great way to get around: one gallon of gas could cover over 100 miles and parking was so easy. At one point I was riding around the river Seine. A gendarme grabbed me and shouted at me in French. Though I could not understand his words I knew instantly I had violated the law. Having studied the language for one year I blurted out the only thing I could think of: "je ne comprende pas," or "I don't understand." Instead of hauling me to the police station he said with great frustration "allez, allez," or "go, go," when he really meant "get the hell out, you bum."

• As I was taking a leisurely stroll on Barcelona's Las Ramblas, a colorful promenade, I suddenly heard my name called: "Ben! Ben!" To my upmost surprise it was a friend of mine, a Cuban lawyer whom I had met at Philadelphia's International House years ago. Like me he was a music lover and had a good voice, and I used to accompany his singing on the piano. To run into him so unexpectedly had special resonance with the phrase "it's a small world." He treated me to a nice lunch and we bade goodbye to each other wistfully. We were never to meet again.

During my glorious, lengthy vacation I never thought about the Jade Palace except toward the end. I had a grand time and knew I would return to Europe repeatedly, which I did. I also swore never to visit another church or museum; I had seen enough to last a lifetime.

To my relief nothing untoward happened at the JP. In subsequent months business progressed well and did not require any special attention. It allowed me comfortably to continue my graduate work at Temple University, manage my won ton soup business, and teach cooking. Once in a while I went to New York to audition for acting jobs, do a little extra work on TV and even landed a few jobs as a principal.

Not long after my return from Europe the JP attracted the attention of Confrerie de la Chaine des Rotisseurs, and I was honored to be inducted as its member. Founded 1950 in Paris, this exalted gastronomic society boasted international memberships in 75 countries and just founded a chapter in Philadelphia by Jack Rosenthal, former president of the Culinary Institute of America. The induction, which consisted of placing a sword on my shoulder—as if being knighted—and a Chaine des Rotisserie insignia around my neck, was a formal black-tie affair held at the Cobblestones restaurant featuring an all-game feast. The *Inquirer* did a big story with a photo of me digging into prized caviar.

As a follow-up Rosenthal asked me to prepare dinner for the society's inaugural Philadelphia chapter. Rosenthal—who was also a national officer-member of such French gourmet organizations as Confrerie des Chevaliers du Tastevin, Les Amis d'Escoffier and L'Academie des Vin de Bordeaux—endeared himself to me by his pronouncement that Chinese cuisine was superior to all others including French, a view shared by several of the other 44 guests as duly reported by Marilynn Marter in the *Inquirer*.

Commenting on the nine-course banquet she observed: "Some (of the guests) however, had never before experienced the delights of such dishes as Abalone Royale, with its textural contrast of sliced abalone, chicken and ham, Cantonese Steak, cuts of super tender beef marinated and sautéed with a sweet gravy; or Sweet and Sour Fish, sea bass in batter crisply fried and the classic Peking Duck." At her request I provided a recipe for the roast duck. It's a complicated process that would take hours to complete but well worth the effort. Indeed, in formal banquets Peking duck is often a "must" and the highlight.

Notwithstanding all the publicity and fame garnered by the JP, it was not immune from the vagaries of the market-place, the force of business cycle which did not always travel in a straight line but had its ups and downs, and in the summer of 1977, I started to notice a decline in our revenue. Soon, to my surprise the JP was in the red partially because of the gas crunch. Since the JP was located in Northeast Phila-delphia, far from downtown and other areas where most of my customers resided, to patronize us meant driving some distance and expending precious gas.

As a result we lost much patronage. To deal with this problem the obvious solution would be to downsize our operation. But when I asked chef Che to lay off some kitchen staff, he adamantly refused, threatening not only to quit but also take our second chef, Eddie Lau, with him if I should force the issue. That's a strange way of showing his fealty as a JP part owner and my partner. Eventually when our financial problem so deteriorated that bankruptcy seemed imminent I gave Che an ultimatum. He reluctantly gave in. The irony: While I voluntarily took a cut in salary he demanded and got a raise because "I have to do more work with the shortage of one cook." As a nice guy, I gave in to his demand.

Even in good times it was an economic fact that profit margins for Chinese restaurants had always been slim. It was one of the most competitive businesses and the fatality rate was exceptionally high. So were operating expenditures, including the fact that the owners had to pay income taxes for their cooking staff, and provide lodgings in cities other than New York and Los Angeles. In my case I had to do both for Che though he was a partner.

So I began to have second thoughts about being in the business. Besides, running the restaurant had always been a sideline for me. My real interest then continued to be journalism. By that time I had completed my master's program at Temple University and was looking forward to a career in the fourth estate. In fact, I had already begun my job as an intern at the *Courier-Post*, a South Jersey daily. So that seemed a good time to call it quits. Unfortunately, because of our declining business caused primarily by the gas shortage I knew I could not get a good price for the JP. So I decided to hang in there a little longer.

Then the unexpected happened.

Che had a stroke, his wife Susan said, sobbing on the phone. In fits and starts she told me she feared for the worst. I tried my best to console her to no avail. As it turned out the stroke was not life threatening but he had to be bedridden for a period of time. This threw the JP in turmoil. Sometime before, Che had a fight with second chef Eddie Lau who angrily walked out and quit for good. All of a sudden I was stuck with a restaurant devoid of a head chef and a second chef. How was I to open for business that night? The only way out was trying to get Eddie Lau back. Luckily, he had not yet found a job. Taking sympathy on my plight and to my profound gratitude he reluctantly returned right away on the condition that as soon as Che recovered he would still depart.

But Che could never fully recover, for his stroke had paralyzed his right hand rendering him permanently incapacitated as a chef. And so I was faced with three options:

1) Looking for a replacement; but I lacked connections. By contacting one of the employment agencies in New York's Chinatown I would get an experienced head chef relatively quickly. But how would he fit into my operations and how would I get along with him? Furthermore, since culinary staff was notorious for being transitory, quitting at the drop of a hat, quick turnover was the rule rather than the exception. I would likely end up with rapid successions of chefs going through a revolving door.

2) Sell the restaurant. But as mentioned, it was not an opportune time. Though there was never a shortage of potential buyers none would make a decent offer when our business was still anemic.

3) To be a head chef myself. The typical way to become one was to start at an early age doing menial work. Then, through slow progress of training and experience, a process that might take 15 years, to finally ascend to this position. I had none of that background.

But against all odds I decided on this option. It would give me a rare chance to operate the JP from the perspective of the kitchen. Also, watching my chefs wokking up a storm never failed to fascinate me; to see them turn out dish after dish of artistic creations with panache, fluidity, and speed was like watching concert artists making sweet music with dazzlingly virtuosity on their instruments, and many a time I secretly wished I was in my chefs' place, vicariously experiencing the joy of professional cooking. It helped that I had been an avid cook since my 20s and a cooking instructor since 1970. Plus, I had a strong culinary instinct, retentive taste memory, and a sensitive palate that should serve me well.

However, there was a world of difference between home cooking and restaurant cooking. Firstly, the latter utilized powerful gas stoves capable of generating the most intense heat. Consequently, the dishes had to be done at lightning speed or they were easily scorched. Secondly, stir-fried dishes often were not exactly stirred with a spatula but involved the tossing back and forth of the ingredients to blend everything evenly. (Many chefs preferred the use of a ladle to push the ingredients forward for faster tossing and cooking.) Initially I was very awkward and couldn't help spilling some of the contents. But with practice I soon mastered the technique.

Mentoring me was second chef Lau. In his 30s he could be temperamental and a little arrogant, often bragging he had been a chef since 15. But he was quite talented and could duplicate all the JP dishes (except for some elaborate banquet ones) that Che did with similar results. The standard Cantonese fare was easy to learn. Just by observing I was able to quickly master such favorites as beef lo mein, pepper steak, and almond chicken. I especially enjoyed doing fried rice with a gigantic 27-inch wok. Using a ladle in one hand and a spatula in the other I found the rigors of stir-firing highly athletic, exhilarating, and fun.

Mandarin and Szechuan selections were more complicated. Some of them utilized a technique virtually unknown to the public but favored by many Chinese restaurants: "passing through oil" or "guo you." It's an extraneous, optional step superimposed on a stir-fry dish. The ingredients are first par-fried in hot oil for the briefest of time—15 to 30 seconds. After being drained of oil they are then stir-fried. This process enables meats to be more tender and succulent, shrimp crispier, vegetables, and even scrambled eggs more flavorful.

One typical example at the JP was mou shu pork, one of our best dishes. Thus treated and stir-fried, the ingredients, comprising pork, golden needles, wood ears, cabbage and eggs, took on a wonderful transformation, redolent of enticing aromas and accentuated with an ingratiating taste not possible otherwise. When wrapped in a freshly steamed doily and graced with hoisin sauce the result was an incomparable tour de force.

The two more complex dishes were Peking duck and glazed banana. For the former, we used Long Island duck. It was first blanched in a hot broth containing ginger, scallion, and corn syrup. After air drying overnight it was roasted and just before serving, deep fried to a golden, crispy finish and carved. The latter was one of China's greater contributions to the world of deserts. The banana was freshly batter-fried and coated with caramelized sugar which had to be done carefully at just the right moment resulting in thin shreds of spun sugar. The banana was dipped in icy water just before serving and what emerged was a crusty, cold exterior but a hot interior like the reverse of baked Alaska.

As to the requisite condiments for each dish, Eddie Lau would tell me what they were but never the precise quantity. When I asked him "exactly how much?" his stock answer was "a little" but never a defined amount. To me, one of the most critical criteria for the success of a dish was its seasoning.

Unless done just right it could never be tasty. That's why I read that in France when a chef applied for a job he would be required to make soup, one sure way to test his sensitivity to taste and seasoning.

Fortuitously, I had an excellent taste memory, so I was able to figure out the right quantity of condiments and duplicate what Lau was using. While he didn't seem to care how my cooking turned out—and I never asked him—to my surprise he often sampled my dishes secretly, for at one point he told me approvingly "your seasoning is all right," adding "but your 'huo hou,' (literally fire and timing, or the precise control of cooking temperature and cooking duration) is still off."

Making my job as a head chef easier was the fact that much of the prep work was done by my assistants: deboning, slicing various ingredients into bite-sizes, wrapping of won tons, and other menial chores. Furthermore, it's the responsibility of the second chef to assemble all requisite ingredients for a given dish. So my job was to use whatever appropriate techniques to treat the ingredients, add the precise condiments, and then apply the proper "hou huo" to live up to the well-known culinary canon of "Se, xang, wei," or "aesthetic appeal, aroma and taste."

Right from my first day as a new chef I carried over a practice from my days as a lab chemist at Merck and DuPont: I was required to wear safety glasses to protect my eyes. Working now in the kitchen where I was constantly dealing with hot oil for stir-frying, deep-frying and par-frying, the danger to the eye was even greater. And so I never did any cooking without these strange-looking protective glasses. Later, when the sizzling and humid summer set in I would wear a large sweat band on my head in addition. With these accoutrements I no doubt became the weirdest looking chef this side of the Yangtze River.

Happily, my on-the-job training was much faster than I

had anticipated, for within two weeks I was able to learn all the dishes. On Saturdays and Sundays, our two busiest days, I'd be filling dozens of dishes practically nonstop—at the rate of about two or three minutes each, reluctant to take even a few seconds to quench my parched throat. At the end of the evening I would be drenched of energy and sore all over. But the feeling of accomplishment and creative joy was ineffable; I was absolutely turned on. Indeed, it was such a heady experience that I fell hopelessly in love with professional cooking and banished all thoughts of selling the JP—at least for the time being.

Until I wore a chef's hat I often wondered why many of my counterparts seemed to be so anger prone, so quick to bark with the slightest provocation. Now I realized the reason: working under intense kitchen pressure and heat did tend to make one irascible and shout fiercely. And when I started to be snappish and yell at my help I knew I had finally become a bona fide executive chef.

Growing in confidence, I began to put my personal stamp on some of the cooking. While Che invariably added excessive amounts of MSG to virtually every selection, I skipped it altogether in vegetable dishes. In meat and seafood dishes I used a fraction of what he did. Whenever possible I minimized the gravies, thereby cutting down the use of cornstarch. When passing through oil was required no matter how busy I was, I took the time and effort to drain the oil completely so that the final product was free of grease, more aesthetic and satisfactory. In some dishes, especially our General Tso chicken, Che tended to be too salty, prompting complaints from the customers. I avoided over- and under-seasoning by tasting all my cooking. In my eight-month tenure as a head chef I got a complaint only once: a customer thought my yue hsiang eggplant was not pungent and sweet enough.

Otherwise, I didn't tarnish the reputation of the JP. On the contrary, occasionally I got compliments from my guests. Some even told me my cooking was better. Appreciation was especially gratifying from my fellow Chinese, who were notorious for being the world's most fussy and harsh restaurant critics. One of them said he had enjoyed my Sichuan lobster. A few days later he came back with three other Chinese and said "your cooking is excellent."

Halfway into my tenure as a head chef our business, which was declining, started to turn around. This was helped by two developments:

> • *Philadelphia* magazine, the prestigious and influential publication, conferred annual "best" awards for various business establishments and the ones for food always aroused great interest. In the July, 1978, issue the Jade Palace won the "Best Chinese Restaurant Award" outside Chinatown. With effects similar to getting a highly favorable newspaper review, our business improved.

> • On July 12 the JP was featured as an outstanding restaurant on the *Evening News* on KYW TV, a CBS affiliate. Taped earlier in May at the JP with me presiding at the dining table and second chef Lau doing the cooking, hostess Marian Robinson and producer Sally Jewett recommended five selections including Cantonese steak, Kung Pao chicken, and mou shu pork. Robinson said: "Your cooking is particularly good; equal to the best of Chinatown." As expected the airing brought us numerous new customers.

Just as things were going well a series of incidents started to unravel. It began on a Wednesday when second chef Lau said he wanted to take Friday and Sunday off, two of our busiest days.

"I want to look at a restaurant I'm thinking of buying."

"With Friday only two days away do you think I can find someone on such short notice and for two days only?" As my right-hand man he was not only doing about 30% of the cooking but had the critical job of assembling the requisite ingredients for various dishes.

"That's your problem," he rudely retorted. "I'm interested in my future and you can't stop me." I was surprised by his belligerence; I had always treated him courteously.

"That's most unreasonable." I tried to reason with him. "Even if I could find a substitute in one day, he would not be familiar with our routine and do his job fast enough."

"I don't care about your problem."

He was obdurate and there was nothing I could do. Luckily, I remembered having met a Peter Hu who at one time considered buying the JP. Since he claimed to have 15 years' experience as a chef and expressed willingness to work for me if I should need him, I immediately phoned him. He agreed to pinch hit for two days and on that Friday afternoon he showed up. But having so little time to learn he was slow, disorganized, and unsure what his responsibilities were. As a result, I could not fill orders fast enough. With the on rush of customers that Friday night many were unhappy. On Sunday when we were busier we offended more guests.

A week or so later Lau made good on his promise to quit. I was devastated. In a business where employees seldom stayed long he had been with me for almost four years. He was a hard worker and acquitted himself well. Furthermore, he had the distinction of helping me become a head chef in just two weeks. It would be difficult to replace him. Since Peter Hu was available I offered him Lau's job.

In his first days he was utterly disappointing. Customer

after customer complained: egg roll stuffing that was tasteless, lumpy fried rice, chow mein either too salty or too bland, greasy pepper steak, beef with broccoli terrible in appearance and flavor. One couple found their hot and sour soup so watery that they swore they'd never come back. One day 16 customers walked out because the soup and fried rice were too cold.

It was disheartening to see the business that I tried so hard to build being ruined. I should have immediately fired Hu. But failing to find a suitable replacement quickly and with the thought of seeking a journalism job soon, I decided to keep him for the time being. I just had to try my best to make him cook more carefully and responsibly and keep an eye on him as often as possible. He improved substantially but was still a source of worry.

Meanwhile my third cook chose this inopportune time to quit, and I had to speedily fill the position which was not easy, either. The new employee didn't last long and I had to repeat the annoying hiring process five more times that summer. Once I was so desperate I hired a person who had no experience whatsoever. Another time for two days I had to pull double duty as a third cook as well, making egg roll stuffing, shelling and deveining shrimp, roasting spareribs, slicing beef, cooking rice, etc.

To add to my woes was the problem of equipment failure. The restaurant that I bought in 1974 was already very old. By the torrid summer of 1978 everything began to malfunction. First, the air-conditioner stopped working, turning the dining room into Dante's inferno. Next, the walk-in-box broke down, spoiling some of the food. And then, our steam table started leaking badly and I had to disassemble it and take it to a welder.

Beset by all these ills and scarred by the painful memories of my torturous relationship with the ill-tempered Che, whatever thrill I had enjoyed could no longer sustain me. I simply got burnt out and resolved to dispose of the restaurant. Toward this end I spread the word around and advertised in Chinese newspapers. Soon I got inquirers and offers, but none attractive enough.

Meanwhile, there was a final irony just before JP's denouement.

H. John Heinz III, the high profile and influential senator from Delaware and owner of the H. J. Heinz Company, apparently was so impressed with the encomiums lavished on the restaurant that he sent an emissary to check it out and met with me with the implicit intention of dining there. But the expected reservation did not materialize—at least not soon enough—for my restaurant changed hands not long afterward, or possibly because the JP was too unassuming, totally lacking in ambience and elegance. Whatever the reason I felt honored to be considered and regretted not having the opportunity to serve this senator and food tycoon. (Heinz died in a plane crash in 1991. Subsequently, his widow Teresa married John Kerry, former senator and Secretary of State.)

Finally, one potential buyer made an offer that topped all others: David Mark, whom by coincidence I used to patronize as he was the owner of a laundry near my home in West Philly. He was an astute businessman who drove a Cadillac and owned real estate properties in Canada. He and his wife were both avid cooks and wanted to go into the restaurant business in the worst way and were elated when we came to terms. And in November, 1978, they became the new owners.

To capitalize on the reputation of the JP, the Marks ran the restaurant as if it was still under my management; they kept not only the name and menu but for years also a newspaper clipping on display at the window with a picture of me and Craig Claiborne, the *New York Times* food critic, detailing JP's first anniversary celebration in 1975. To help Mark and his wife Linda get started I spent two weeks gratis to teach them our dishes as Mrs. Liang did with Che when I first bought the JP.

Certainly, my association with the JP had been an electrifying journey that expanded the dimensions of my life, challenged my culinary vision, and taxed my ingenuity and imagination. During my tenure, I succeeded in elevating a little-known restaurant into one of the most famous, with more publicity than any of my counterparts. I exulted in a version of Chinese haute cuisine with a number of specialties unknown to the public and was elated by the enthusiastic responses.

My culinary saga, however, did not end with the sale of the JP. To further my joy of cooking, I launched a catering business. I opted to start on a small scale as a one-man operation. As such it had some distinct advantages: I was completely independent with no need to rely on any kitchen personnel. Plus, I used my own kitchen for prep work and so there was little overhead.

For best results I preferred cooking right on my clients' premises. For large parties, I would bring my large wok and portable candy stove which had the same fire power as that of a restaurant. I discovered I had no trouble catering to parties numbering up to 150 guests unaided. They included such institutions as the University of Pennsylvania, the Curtis Institute of Music, and the County Medical Society. My biggest job was a six-course dinner for 235 guests for the Museum of Natural History, for which I did get one cook to help my preparation, and I did the cooking in advance.

The crux of my business was small parties for which I would use the owners' kitchens. In one such party, one of the guests was folk singer Peter Seeger, who extolled my cooking as "a work of art."

In another job, my client was a very rich man who owned several homes and a private jet. The catering took place in his huge mansion in a Philadelphia suburb. Among the guests was Ed Snider, one of the most successful businessmen best known as the owner of his hockey team, the Philadelphia Flyers. He was so taken with my cooking (and most likely also my JP success) that he wanted to go into business with me. He thought the city was in sore need of an upscale Chinese restaurant serving the most elegant food with an ambience and décor to match. He already owned a bar/restaurant downtown on Locust St., which could be converted.

I certainly agreed with him that such an opulent restaurant would fill a great need. Snider told me a few such restaurants had already existed in New York City and suggested that I check one out, and I did (the name escapes me). It was a very fancy place where the dishes were eclectic and extremely expensive and yet there was no lack of well-dressed patrons. With Snider's wealth, connections and celebrity and my JP background if I were to be his partner we could be a hit. The only problem was that my heart was no longer in the restaurant business and no inducement—no matter how attractive—could change my mind.

CHAPTER THREE (1945–1970)

English Education

Of all my academic studies my worst subject by far was English. Growing up in China I had a few years' schooling but never developed the interest in or aptitude for this inscrutable language. As a student at Columbia University in 1951, my second year in this country, I once wrote a history report that was so atrocious and inept that the professor chewed me out mercilessly. Worse, I suffered the ignominy of flunking a course in English for foreign students and had to repeat it.

And so, it was a long journey from being a horrible English student to a fledging writer in America, a span of several decades that were often painful, occasionally funny, but ultimately exhilarating.

My story begins in 1945 at the end of World War II when I relocated from Chongqing, China's wartime capital, to my beloved city of Shanghai. One of the city's more eminent citizens was my father, Peter W. Lin, a banker. He naturally wanted me to get the best education the city had to offer. And that meant St. Francis Xavier College, a Jesuit all-male middle and high school, because of its high scholastic standing and especially its unparalleled English program.

I was hoping to get into the ninth grade, which was not

easy. It required a tough entrance exam consisting of just one hurdle: proficiency in English. Now I had two years of elementary English in Chongqing but the level there was extremely low. So I had serious doubts about my prospects.

Accompanying me to the exam was Mrs. James Cheng, one of my mother's best friends who noticed I was struggling helplessly. A perfectly honest woman and wife of one of China's most prominent physicians (one of his patients was Generalissimo Chiang Kai-shek), on this occasion she was not above subjugating her rectitude to the exigency at hand. When the proctor stepped out for a short time, Mrs. Cheng quickly looked at my test questions and quietly whispered one answer after another. And I was all too glad to accept her offer, however shamelessly. But alas, that didn't last long and I flunked the entrance exam. The only way I could get into this prestigious school was at a lower grade.

I adamantly refused. Earlier with my eldest brother David's coaching one summer in Chongqing I had studied very diligently and was able to skip one year's schooling. I didn't want to give all that up. To her credit Mrs. Cheng was able to strike a bargain with the school. I could enter the ninth grade by studying with a St. Francis Xavier tutor daily and on the condition that my English made great improvements.

I improved enough to remain in ninth grade but barely eked out. I knew only a handful of vocabulary words, I could never parse a sentence properly, write a competent composition, or carry on simple conversations. In short my English was terrible. It didn't help that I had to struggle against other burdens. School hours were from 8:00 A.M. to 5:00 P.M. All courses were mandatory including physics, chemistry, and calculus with a ton of homework that kept me working till midnight daily.

While other schools had midterm and final exams, St. Francis Xavier imposed exams weekly. On Fridays Father

Alexus, our severe, goateed class master, would announce the names with their respective test scores, starting from the highest in descending order. It was embarrassing to keep waiting and hoping he would come to my name sooner. But all too often that happened only after he was way past the midpoint or sometimes toward the end of the list, making me nervous and ashamed.

The only two things I did well were non-academic: handball and soccer. We used tennis balls for the former on an outdoor court without gloves. In the winter when Shanghai could get extremely cold, it was not easy to hit a heavy tennis ball with our bare hands. I could slap it so low against the wall that the ball would bounce back just inches above the ground, making it difficult to return.

In soccer there was nothing more exhilarating than to dribble past the defense and score a well-placed goal. As captain of my team, my best position was center. Because we were playing junior soccer with a smaller ball, a seven-man team and a smaller playing field, I could lead the charge to attack and then run right back to defend without getting out of breath. The more I played the more I fell in love with this international sport. As a matter of fact, I looked forward to each game with an eagerness that bordered on insanity. I once rode my bicycle for 30 minutes in the rain to a weekend match. No one else was foolish enough to be there. Instead of going home I kept waiting for the rain to stop and my fellow players to show up but none did. I went home totally drenched and disappointed.

My life and studies at St. Francis Xavier were interrupted by the raging civil war, and in particular, the victory of the Communists led by Mao Zedong over Nationalist China under Chiang Kai-shek. My family and I were forced to flee to Hong Kong as refugees in 1949.

In Hong Kong I continued my education at St. Stephen's

College, a British style high school, located in Stanley, an outskirt of the island. A beautiful boarding school, it was graced with its own beach, regular size soccer field, and tennis courts where I learned to swing a racket for the first time. There the English standard was rather high, and I began to converse a little better and improved my comprehension but English remained a struggle. Moreover, the English that I learned was what my father called "Missionary English," marked by formal expressions, British terminologies, distinct, crisp pronunciations, and an absence of slang and idioms, which did not prepare me well to cope with my early life in America.

At St. Stephen's one of our favorite hobbies was telling ghost stories, the scarier the better. These stories, however, could not compare with the horror of real incidents allegedly happening there. Some students talked about having seen ghost shadows. Others swore they heard the sound of tennis playing in total darkness at night with no one at the courts.

My most frightening experience took place one evening when someone claimed he had just seen a ghost in the dorm, terrifying the whole student body. We were all biting our nails wondering whom the ghost would visit next. As I stepped into my room not only did my roommate, who had been there earlier, disappear but so did his bed. At this horrifying sight all my hairs stood up and I bolted out screaming "THE GHOST HAS COME! THE GHOST HAS COME! THE GHOST HAS COME!" further exacerbating the air of fright and doom. Everyone else became as terrified as I was.

What happened was my roommate, Eddie Young, who had been studying in our room, got scared of being alone. So he moved his bed to spend the night with other students, causing my absolute panic. Since I dared not return to my room alone I begged him to move back with me. Gingerly and nervously he did but we had a fearful night and did not calm down until the following morning.

As a senior I was hoping to attend college in the U.S. But except for Harvard, which rejected me, I didn't apply for any other, not knowing how soon our applications for a green card would come through. Until the 1960s quota for Chinese immigrants was a measly 105. Not surprisingly, normally an applicant had to wait for years to qualify. But because the new regime of Communist China had no diplomatic relations with the U.S., only those applicants lucky enough to get out of the country were able to wait their turn. With a much shorter waiting list we got our permanent residencies in less than two years, just as I finished high school.

Toward the end of August 1950, my parents left the crown jewel of England with me and my younger brother Henry boarding the *President Cleveland* liner for our long journey, our slow boat to San Francisco.

On the ship my father became friends with some American missionaries. When they found out I had not yet chosen a college, they suggested Wayland, a Southern Baptist school in West Texas. It was an idea that greatly appealed to me since I was highly religious. What's more, the missionaries knew Wayland's president, Dr. James Marshall, well. By wiring him from our ship they obtained me not only instant admission as a piano major but a full scholarship including room and board.

In mid-September 1950, we arrived at San Francisco and became downhearted immediately. My father, who had studied at Columbia University in the 1920s, didn't know the proper gratuities for the porter after so many years. Obviously not tipped enough, he reacted with a scowl, sneer, and three words that hurt me profoundly: "For heaven's sake!" It was not a good introduction to America for which I had such high hopes and anticipation. Instead I felt insulted, humiliated, and depressed for days.

As I set out to travel all by myself to Wayland Baptist

College in Plainview (near Amarillo), Texas, I faced the trip with much anxiety. I was two weeks shy of my 17th birthday, a stranger in a strange land, with poor communication skills. Nevertheless, I reached my Texas destination by train with no difficulty. At the depot I ordered a bottle of milk. As I took one sip I was revolted by the terrible sour taste. I thought the cafeteria was taking advantage of me as a foreigner and purposely sold me rotten milk. But I didn't know how to ask questions or complain. Actually, what I ordered was not regular milk but buttermilk.

I began my life at Wayland Baptist College with puzzlement. The English I heard sounded so bizarre with its southern twang and strange usage and slang. It was a totally alien tongue that I had to learn all over again. Consequently, I had trouble understanding Texans and vice versa.

Wayland was a small college with 500 students. It was known for its championship women's basketball team, a large percentage of foreign students including half a dozen Chinese, and a famous International Choir that performed all over the U.S. and abroad. A typical fundamentalist school, Wayland allowed no smoking, drinking, or dancing and discouraged going to the movies. On Sundays every recreational facility was shut down to make sure we observed Sabbath. We attended Sunday school and then church service in the morning. In the evening we had fellowship followed by another church service. I had no trouble observing these practices; as a born-again Christian I adored the religious atmosphere.

My first class was Bible. Before lecturing, our professor, Dr. Dobson, terrified me with a request: "Let's bow our heads and ask Ben Lin to say a prayer." Having never prayed in English I was racking my brains to think of something appropriate to say. But I was at a total loss for words. Meanwhile everyone was getting fidgety and kept waiting for me in vain to start. After what seemed like an eternity I apologized in a

heavy Chinese accent: "I don't know how to pray in English."
I could have saved the day by praying in Chinese but didn't
know any better.

"That's quite all right," the kind professor consoled me,
then asked someone else to do the job. After this embarrassing
experience I took the trouble to learn and memorize a prayer.
But Dr. Dobson never asked me again.

I continued to struggle with my English and had a few
comedic experiences.

When meeting me people often asked, "What do you
know?" I thought it was highly impolite of them to ask personal question about my knowledge. I bristled at this rudeness
until I discovered it was a common greeting like "How are you."
Similarly, in Shanghai when people meet each other they
would say "Have you eaten?" which was not meant literally
but a way of greeting.

My schoolmates loved to tell jokes. But my English was so
poor that I had trouble understanding, much less laughing at
the punch line. When I drew a blank naturally there was
disappointment in the jokers' faces. So I'd ask them to repeat.
The second time around I could comprehend no better.
Eventually I learned this trick: when the story came to a short
pause, I knew it was the end and I just pretended I caught the
drift and responded with a hearty laugh. My laugh was so real
and my appreciation so deep that I would be awarded with
more jokes. And I'd respond with more faked laughs.

The first time I wanted to dry clean some clothes I used a
literal translation from Chinese.

"Please dry wash them," I told the laundryman.

"What do you want?" He was confused.

"Clean my clothes. Dry wash them."

"I don't understand you."

"I want you to wash my clothes but don't use any water."

"How can I wash without using water?"

"That's why I ask you to *dry wash.*"

"You either want me to wash or dry clean."

"Doesn't dry wash mean dry clean?"

"No, no, no."

"Then I want dry clean."

Thereby I learned another bit of English.

During my spare time I followed the examples of my fellow students by passing out religious tracts on the streets, which was easy enough, but up to that time I had never tried something much harder: knocking on strangers' doors to spread the gospel.

In 1950 in the college town of Plainview prejudice against blacks was rampant. I was surprised to see segregation all over the place: housing, buses, public water fountains, and rest rooms. And the signs FOR COLORED PEOPLE were a common sight. Though I had never met an African American, I was familiar with their history of oppression and suffering and I had a world of sympathy for them.

One day I went to their ghetto to give my personal testimony. I randomly knocked on one door and a young woman answered.

"I want to talk to you about my savior Jesus," I said.

She was very polite, making no objection to this strange-looking intruder. Indeed, she was highly attentive as I launched into the story of my salvation. For 10 minutes or so I spoke from the core of my being, with all my heart, mind, and soul. I was hoping my passionate message would move her, or at least find a sympathetic ear. At the end of my testimony she said these very words, "Honey, I don't unnerstand a word you saaid."

Soon I added a new religious activity: daily prayer meeting. Getting up at 5:00 A.M. to emulate a prayer group in South Korea, about eight of us from my dorm gathered in our living room suite, kneeling and taking turns praying. By that time I had learned to pray in English haltingly. Afterward I studied the Bible before breakfast at six-thirty. It was a wonderful way to start the day; I would feel joyous, optimistic, and grateful for my blessings.

One weekend I had the happy memory of attending revival in a nearby town. I had gone to a few revivals in Chongqing and watched Billy Graham's *Crusade for Christ* on TV and they never failed to stir me. In this Texas revival I was also asked to accompany the hymn singing as a pianist. I certainly didn't ask for or expect any remuneration but the church insisted on using part of the donations to reimburse me. It was a nice little sum.

I wondered what I should do with this windfall. Remembering my musical and religious mentor Stephen Shao in Hong Kong was not well off, I sent him half of my earnings.

When he received the money he wrote me a heartfelt letter of gratitude; he had gotten married recently and was financially strapped. In the past when facing a similar situation he always eked out and would never ask the Lord for monetary help. But this time was different. With two mouths to feed and unable to put food on the table, he did the unthinkable by praying for money one night. And the following day my check arrived. He thanked me profusely and the Lord for answering his prayer. Actually it was no great magnanimity on my part. I had a full scholarship, my father gave me a small allowance with which I could buy some piano music as needed, and I had no unmet needs. What I did was an expression of my love for Shao and my small way of thanking him for leading me to the path of Christianity and music.

During Thanksgiving most students went home. Foreign students including the Chinese who had no place to go remained at school. It was during cotton picking season. I had never done any manual labor. But I heard in the U.S. it was not considered demeaning as in China; on the contrary it was respected. I was especially inspired to note that often children of highly affluent families did not think it was below them to do such menial things as delivering newspapers to earn a little pocket change.

Why not spend the Thanksgiving holidays picking cotton?

Accordingly, a few of us Chinese put on old clothes, wore gloves, shouldered a long collection sack, and began to pluck cotton from the brown bolls. It was pretty hard work. Sometimes my face got scratched by the branches. When the sack became fuller, it weighed heavier and heavier as I progressed from row to row on the cotton field, pulling the load like a mule. When the sack was completely full I weighed it and recorded the poundage before dumping the cotton into a large container. After three days' intensive work I was sore all over but proud of the experience and treasured the first U.S. dollars I earned from the sweat of my brow.

But I didn't earn enough money to travel to Philadelphia and enjoy a family reunion during the ensuing Christmas holidays. Making this possible was older brother Harry who generously bought me a round trip train ticket with stipend from his student aid. To be united with my three brothers and parents during this all-too-brief a period was so precious and joyous. Especially memorable was attending the Christmas Spectacular at Radio City in New York of which the famed Rockettes kicked up a storm with precision and flair, and the giant pipe organ astonished us with its sheer volume and dramatic impact. Among the musical offerings was the carol "O Holy Night" which turned out to be a swan song for Harry, because I never saw him again after that Christmas. He was soon to return to China under the delusion that his calling was to serve the people and help build the new Communist regime. But sadly, after suffering unbearable persecution, he committed suicide eight years later. And whenever I hear "O Holy Night" my heart sinks.

Returning to Texas, I began to appreciate the true meaning of southern hospitality. Just about everyone was so warm, gracious, and friendly, treating me as one of their own. And when people said "Howdy, pardner" I felt like a real buddy. Occasionally I was invited to private homes for dinner. Once I was surprised that a classmate, Claudia, invited me to spend a weekend home with her and her parents. I had never dated her—or anyone else for that matter—and she had never showed any romantic interest in me. I guess she was just being hospitable. But I was extremely shy and lacking in social grace. So I thoughtlessly turned her down, embarrassing her and hurting her feelings.

Strangely, in such a religious and friendly environment I experienced my first racism. Though I had no enemies and never provoked anyone, one person sliced my Hanon piano exercise book from the first page to the last. It was obviously a deliberate effort to mutilate my little property. I could think of no other reason than the fact I was an ethnic minority. It was impossible to find the culprit. Perhaps I should have shown this book to my piano teacher David Appleby, but I did not. I just taped up the book at best I could and chalked off this experience as an isolated ugly incident.

David Appleby was an established concert artist and a graduate of the Juilliard School of Music. In his concerts, he impressed me with his sensitivity, nuanced playing, and grasp of musical styles in such works as Beethoven's "Les Adieux" sonata, Chopin's "Nocturne. Op. 37 No. 2," and Rachmaninoff's "Concerto No. 2" with an orchestra. Regrettably, his teaching was not as illuminating as his performing. Hampered further by my technical limitations and despite my arduous effort, I was making so little progress that I got thoroughly discouraged. Toward the end of the spring semester he suggested that I try to get into Juilliard by first studying with Miss Lonny Epstein, one of his teachers.

In 1951 I moved to New York to enroll in the summer session of Juilliard. I was so glad that Epstein accepted me as her pupil and that the city was only two hours away from my Philadelphia home. What a dramatic change from the tiny town of Plainview to the gigantic metropolitan of New York! Having just become accustomed to the sweet southern dialect, now I had to adjust to a new, New York sound, so hard and alien to the ear, and a completely different environment. Here the pace of life was quick. People had a hard veneer and were often very rude and impatient. One of my great shocks was noticing signs in front of churches that said "Dance on Friday Night." I had trouble reconciling the disparity between the attitude of Wayland College, which considered dancing sinful, and that of New York churches that not only approved of dancing but sponsored it.

My studies with Lonny Epstein made advances but were far from ideal. Still unable to acquire some essential techniques, I had trouble mastering some assignments. By summer's end she and I both realized I was not ready to pass Juilliard's rigorous entrance exam. I remained in New York to study with Epstein while enrolling as a music major at Columbia University's School of General Studies.

There, my inadequacy in English surfaced again. One of the courses I took was history. To my utter humiliation and embarrassment, the professor rebuked me for writing a horrible report in front of the whole class. Without mentioning me by name he made it in no uncertain terms that he was talking about me, the only foreign student in the class: "It doesn't matter where you came from, write in simple English. Don't be so complicated and obtuse."

I had a worse experience in my English for Foreign Students class, better known in subsequent days as ESL, or English as a Second Language. We didn't have a good teacher. Facing a room full of aliens speaking broken English, Mr. Ross didn't seem to realize the difficulties confronting us, and in particular, our lack of composition skills. He gave no pointers such as the need for a good outline, how best to define and develop a theme, the importance of organization, and sticking to things that we could relate to. Once he asked us to write an essay based on words originated from our own native tongues that had become part of English vocabulary. It turned out to be an impossible assignment.

For the final exam we had to write a composition. Ross gave us four topics to choose from including 1) "Beyond the Horizon" of which I didn't know the meaning. 2) "The World's Greatest Poet." I didn't even know who China's greatest poet was, let alone the world's greatest. 3) "Night Life." I opted for that. But at this very moment my mind drew a blank. I attributed it in part to my crazy schedule.

My day began at 6:00 A.M. and lasted till midnight. I was taking five courses, working two hours daily as a dishwasher at Columbia's Faculty Club in exchange for two meals, practicing a few hours on the piano, and singing as a choir member at the St. Paul Chapel with daily and Sunday services. In this final exam I was nervous, worried, and totally incapacitated. It was the worst case of writer's block. During the 50-minute period I produced just a single paragraph and could add nothing to it. Ross flunked me. Since I had a passing grade going into the final, I begged him to give me another chance to write a composition. But he insisted I repeat the course.

I resolved to master English.

It's no easy task. There were so many obstacles. A 1,700,000-word vocabulary; innumerable irregular verbs; difficult conjugations; six tenses; words that have opposite meanings; and over 5,700 idioms, some of which don't make sense, e.g. "happy as a clam," "dead as a doornail." (Chinese in contrast, notwithstanding its pronunciation difficulty and cumbersome written words, has the simplest grammar, with no irregular verbs, no conjugations, and just three tenses: present, past, and future.)

I decided the best course of action was self-help, and my best teacher was the venerable *New York Times*. I took special interest in editorials and speeches. The former were so well written and thought provoking. The latter were models of exemplary and enlightening compositions, eloquent and rousing, and sometimes graced with well-turned phrases and colorful words. At that time the *Times* was still faithful to its motto "All the news that's fit to print" and important speeches were invariably printed in their entirety. Despite my insane schedule I tried to squeeze a little time daily to read the paper.

It was a grueling undertaking. I had so little vocabulary that I needed to resort to an English-Chinese dictionary repeatedly. As soon as I deciphered the meaning of one word I would promptly forget it and had to repeat the process. Soon I learned to write down all the translated words. There were so many that they resembled little ants crawling all over the page.

Before the approach of June 1952, I decided to help pay my college expenses by getting a summer job. But I had very few opportunities, lacking appropriate skills and experience. I thought being a waiter could be a possibility. Never having been one, I was confident I could learn the craft fast. But when I applied for such a position at a New York Chinese restaurant the Cantonese owner not only didn't hire me but treated me with such contempt and abuse as if I was the lowest creature on earth. I was just a stranger seeking a summer job that might not rank very high professionally but I should merit a little respect and kindness. Obviously he thought table-waiting was a lowly, despicable occupation and anyone considering it had to be a lowlife that deserved to be derided, though the restaurateur couldn't operate his business without such help. This may be an atypical case but I swore I'd never again seek jobs in a Chinese restaurant.

Instead, I sent out some 50 letters to various hotels for any job available. Two came through: one in Lake George and one in Lake Placid, and I chose the latter. Part of the Adirondacks in northern New York, Lake Placid was an incomparable scenic wonder whose beauty surpassed that of Lake George, Saranac Lake, and others in the state. It was the site of the 1932 winter Olympics, and its nearby White Face Mountain was a great ski resort with the highest vertical drop in the East.

My employer, the Whiteface Inn, was one of the most beautiful luxury hotels whose celebrity guests included King Peter of Yugoslavia, Perry Como, and Spencer Tracy. Located on the shore of Lake Placid, it boasted numerous amenities including individual log cabins on its large, sprawling ground, a gorgeous golf course, indoor and outdoor swimming pools, a huge convention hall, marina and boathouse, and barbecue facilities for daily cookout by the water's edge.

It was also blessed with an amiable organist at the bar, Harry Blonde. He had spent some time in the Far East and learned the popular Chinese love song "When Will You Return?" and whenever I entered the bar, no matter what he was playing, he would immediately segue into that song to honor my presence. He also played the piano in a Lake Placid Village bar and would honor me the same way whenever I stopped by to say hello. Once in a while he would ask me to take over and entertain the guests with my piano playing.

Whiteface hired a large working staff during the summer, including college students. My job was primarily bussing and secondarily, breakfast room service. Working seven days weekly, I received free room and board but no pay. My income came strictly from the waitresses for whom I bussed and room service tipping. It was a novel experience to work full time and a welcome change from the hustle and bustle of my life at Columbia University. I had a little more time to myself with which I read the *New York Times* ever more diligently, practiced the piano at the convention hall, learned to ice skate in the village's indoor rink and water ski on the lake.

For my busboy job I was assigned to four waitresses. Since kitchen doors of all restaurants swung to the right I quickly learned to carry a heavy tray on the left hand, balancing it on the palm. Being considerate, my waitresses obviated this need by entering the dining room first while holding the door open for me so that I could hold the tray with my right hand. Once I was assigned to a new waitress. For dinner her guests had ordered 15 steaks. But not knowing the proper protocol she didn't hold the door for me as I followed closely behind her. When it was slamming shut on me I was caught helplessly and struggled hard to keep it open with the heavy tray resting on my right palm. I ended up losing balance of the tray and all 15 steaks flew into the dining room. They landed all over the carpet, made a loud crashing sound, and caught the attention of all the diners. My boss, the maître d', instantly rushed to the scene of the crime and I expected to be balled out severely. On the contrary, Leonard Morris, whom I had always admired as a no-nonsense and kind gentleman, and who in turn liked me because I was a college student and pianist, consoled me sympathetically, saying "It's okay. Don't worry about it."

My room service duty was never marked by such dramatics. It was a nice change of pace, giving me a chance to interact a little with the guests and earn tips directly. One middle-aged guest always smiled warmly at me whenever I passed by in the dining room. One morning I happened to pick up his room service order. When I entered his room he was very friendly and tried to be sociable. But I couldn't spend more than a minute or two with him, being extremely pressed for time in the morning when I was pulling double duty bussing for my waitresses. As I was about to leave he said: "Do you want to make a little extra tip?"

"Of course."

"I have some dirty ashtrays. Will you clean them up for me?"

"Glad to."

I proceeded to dump the ashes in the bathroom and was about to wipe the trays clean. To my surprise he followed me. The next thing I knew he was groping for my privates.

"I'm not your type," I said and bolted out of his room.

Now in the early 1950s, when homosexuality was condemned as sinful, I never looked down on it. I accepted gays as being a little different, just as people having different colors. They were still part of humanity and God's creatures. When I was working as a dishwasher at Columbia University's Faculty Club, an African American kitchen worker often looked at me affectionately and made amorous remarks. But when he tried to rub his body against mine I learned to avoid him civilly and smilingly. And we remained on friendly terms.

At Whiteface I had a very different encounter with another guest, a European nobility, a countess of some sort. She seldom had breakfast in the dining room, preferring her room instead. Sharing the room service duty with me were a few other busboys. It was pretty much on a voluntary basis. Usually whoever was not busy bussing would fill the order. But we soon discovered that this countess never tipped, even though when we had to climb four long flights to her room (management discouraged us from using the elevators). So she ended up waiting longer and longer for her breakfast.

One morning when her order arrived, as usual nobody was eager to accommodate. Having also been stiffed by her I, nevertheless, chose to give her a break this time. When I quickly brought her the food she was shocked.

"Why did I get my breakfast so fast today?" she said in accented English. "Normally I had to wait for a long, long time."

To discuss tipping with a customer was never easy; it was

too embarrassing, and I had never complained to any offender. But I decided to speak my mind this morning, albeit politely. "You probably don't realize it, but we room service boys depend on tips as income and some of us are college students who pay for part of our tuition with tips." She seemed bewildered. Later when I picked up the dirty tray outside her room I found a precious quarter.

In contrast I had the biggest tip from someone I had never even met: a CEO of a department store chain (I believe it was Sears & Roebuck). When he checked out he took the trouble to find out how many employees Whiteface had and left an incredible $25 for everyone. I was touched deeply. For a captain of industry to care for us with such kindness could happen only in America. It embodied the generosity, spirit, compassion, and goodness that made the U.S. great and affirmed my love for this adopted country of mine.

Hampered by my English deficiency and lacking social skills, I was shy among Caucasians. And so I had difficulty making friends. But somehow, I was able to bond with two waitresses, Mikey, a high school student, and Shorty White, an art major from Pittsburgh. United by karma, we three enjoyed a pure, beautiful friendship that was extremely endearing and precious.

On rare occasions when I was not studying the *Times* or practicing the piano, we three would spend time together relishing each other's company. One day we wandered to a secluded spot. While both of them had boyfriends back home, Shorty and I suddenly found ourselves drawn to each other on impulse, embracing and kissing as two sex-starved lovers. It was a long, lingering kiss that sealed our lips passionately, spontaneously and neither of us wanted to let go. When we finally broke loose, inexplicably Mikey and I followed suit by locking our arms and lips with the same intensity, urgency, and longing. None of us really thought of going a step beyond.

Indeed, having sex, cheapened so much by today's permissive society and promiscuity, was the remotest thing on our minds. Yet the kiss was a most intimate sexual revelation, awakening, and fulfillment that turned our bodies into tingling masses on the verge of collapse. Puzzled by the magical moment, we three wondered how kindred spirits could rise to such heavenly, poetic heights with a simple smooch. In subsequent days we never thought of reliving that experience, as if we did not want to violate the sanctity of a treasured memory seared indelibly into our brains.

The following summer when the three of us returned to Whiteface Inn, Shorty astonished me with three words that reflected the most profound of all human emotions: "I love you."

"What about Serge?" I asked. "You told me you were deeply in love with him."

"I really love you."

I was stunned by her confession. My incredulity and lack of responsiveness made her sob. Dogged by a deeply ingrained inferiority complexity since childhood, a result of alienation from Mother's love, I never entertained the possibility that any woman could care for me so much. Intensely moved, I nevertheless didn't know how to handle the situation, which was compounded by the fact I was dating another waitress. Thoughtlessly spurning her, I didn't even have the decency and sensitivity to console and hug her at this emotional moment. It could have been an unforgettable romance between two soul mates but to my upmost regret I let a rare opportunity slip by and broke the tender heart of this poor teenager.

At the end of each of the two summers at Whiteface, I returned to Columbia University refreshed, some $1,000 richer and progressed further in my English education.

When it was time to broaden my horizon to go beyond

newspaper reading I got the guidance I needed from my closest friend at Columbia, William S. Y. Wang. He and I shared some common traits: Chinese roots, Shanghai up-bringing, identical age, remarkable facial resemblance, and a penchant for wrestling with each other—usually to a draw on bare floors. Multitalented, he was a voracious reader, budding writer, and a scholarship student with broad interests, one of which led him to be a foremost linguistic scholar, researcher, and professor. He impressed me especially with his literary erudition and taste, which steered me to:

- Bernard Shaw's *Caesar and Cleopatra*, in which Caesar's monologue to the Sphinx struck him as the most vainglorious he had ever encountered: "I have wandered in many lands, seeking the lost regions from which my birth into this world exiled me, and the company of creatures such as I myself. I have found flocks and pastures, men and cities, but no other Caesar, no air native to me, no man kindred to me, none who can do my day's deed and think my night's thought. In the little world yonder, Sphinx, my place is as high as yours in this desert . . ."

- Edmond Rostand's *Cyrano de Bergerac* from which he could recite salient lines, e.g. in the balcony scene: "Your name is like a bell that swings and rings in my heart, and when I think of you, I tremble, Roxane . . ." He also loved this passage in act one: "I carry my adornments on my soul. I do not dress up like a popinjay. But inwardly I keep my daintiness . . . I go caparisoned in gems unseen, trailing white plumes of freedom, garlanded with my good name—no figure of a man but a soul clothed in shining armor, hung with deeds for decorations, twirling—thus—a bristling wit, and swinging at my side courage, and on the stones of this old town making the sharp truth ring like golden spurs!"

- Dostoevsky's *Crime and Punishment* and *The Brothers Karamazov*. Although my perusal of these classics was difficult and painfully slow (for a long time I could not do better than one page per hour) they gradually lifted my English education to a new level and direction. Eventually I was to relish Dostoevsky's *The Idiot, The Double, The Gambler*, and *Notes from the Underground*.

But I was engaging in too many activities. It was stupid of me to bite off more than I could chew; something had to give. That happened to be my astronomy class which I was close to flunking. To cram for the final exam during the Christmas holidays, I bought four books on the subject and slaved over them during every waking moment. My effort paid off. For the final exam I believe I answered every question perfectly. When the professor's assistant next saw me, he bubbled with enthusiasm and compliments and gave me a hearty congratulations. This experience proved that "If there is a will, there is a way." By working tirelessly I could overcome overwhelming odds and turn weakness into strength.

In the next semester, my last one at Columbia, again I was a sucker for work by adding one more course to my curriculum so that I was enrolled in six. To my horror, my French was suffering and destined for a failing grade. Just before final exam our teacher, a very considerate French woman, told the class: "If you have any difficulty I'd be happy to help out." I was the only one to accept her offer. Generous with her time, she came to the lobby of my Fernald Hall dorm and spent several hours coaching me. I repaid my gratitude by exerting every ounce of my energy into my final preparation. To her utter surprise and elation I passed with flying colors. (That semester I achieved the highest scholastic average of my student days by getting three As and three Bs.)

My piano studies with Miss Epstein did not fare as well. In 1953 I reluctantly gave up my career goal and returned home to Philadelphia to live with my parents. Opting to be a surgeon like my oldest brother, David, I transferred to Penn as a pre-med student. An unexpected non-academic honor was an invitation by the soccer coach to join its varsity team. As a former soccer fanatic in Shanghai, I was still crazy about this sport. But it required practice every afternoon which would impede my studies. So I gave up this opportunity and played for the junior varsity team, which required no practice.

One of the courses I took was History of the English Language. By this time my proficiency in the language progressed so much that I was among the top students. An American-born Italian classmate, however, was having great difficulty and thought she would flunk the course for sure. Knowing I was doing well, she was in desperate need for my coaching.

"Please help me prepare for the final," she implored.

"I'd be happy to." It struck me as strange that an American native would seek assistance from me, who was foreign-born and had flunked his English course just two years before.

"If I get a passing grade I'll pay you thirty dollars."

"Please don't offer any money. I'm your classmate and your friend. I'll help you to the best of my ability. But I'd do it only if I do it for free."

"We'll see about that."

We worked together for hours and days. She was making good progress and elated to pass the course. True to her promise she insisted on paying me $30, and I strenuously resisted. After shuffling back and forth, finally she just stuffed the money in my shirt pocket and quickly walked away.

I next took up public speaking. The latent actor in me made me enjoy the sensation of addressing an audience. It's like being a director, a playwright, and an actor all rolled into one. In return I could see the power of verbal communication at work with the undivided attention and riveting eyes of my captive audience. Our professor, Dr. Charles Lee, made us do two types of speeches: a prepared one and an un-prepared one. The latter was, of course, a lot harder. Dr. Lee would give us a topic at the last minute, and we had to come up with a cohesive, organized, short speech. It was a wonderful training that forced me to think fast and be articulate.

I graduated from Penn in 1957 with a BA in chemistry. Accepted at the Jefferson Medical School, I flip-flopped about my career choice and once again aspired to be a concert artist. Working as a chemist at Merck in Philadelphia while taking weekly lessons with a pedagogue in New York, I ended up with a disabled finger and was drafted into the army.

My religious beliefs at this time underwent some dramatic changes. I was no longer a die-hard Christian endowed with a missionary zeal. I lost my unquestioning blind faith and became more rational. While still retaining many of the Protestant tenets, I stopped interpreting the Bible literally. Furthermore, like the song "Que Sera, Sera" I believed we were all predisposed by the force of nature, our genes, and God's will to fulfill a specific destiny. To be sure there was a little freedom, a little room for free will to do what we pleased, but I could no more be an Einstein than he could be a Chinese acrobat. The Chinese have a saying that's almost identical to its English counterpart "man proposes. God deposes": "mou shi zai ren, cheng shi zai tian" meaning "man initiates. God consummates." If it's God will that I could not become a world class piano virtuoso, no amount of practice or prayer could make any difference.

After my two-year army tour in 1959 I returned to my chemist's position at Merck in Philadelphia, the job I had held before I was drafted. It was in the quality control department, assaying various drugs and raw materials to ascertain their purity and contents. Because I had good hands—possibly the result of my piano training—in time I was promoted to senior analytical chemist. But I wasn't sure what I wanted to do with my life; I certainly had no great love for chemistry. Eventually my future would lead me to such diverse career paths as an entrepreneur, journalist, and actor.

Working the second shift from 4:30 P.M. to 1:00 A.M., I was one of a six-man team including George DeFoney, Walter Hall, John Doulis, Joe Holochuck, and Earl Oberholzer. We had a very good boss, Walter Eberbach, a soft spoken, highly knowledgeable chemist who treated us with respect and benevolence. Daily he gave us a specific amount of work, which was challenging but never overly heavy. And as long as we could finish our assignments Eberbach didn't mind whatever else we wanted to do. I would read a novel or newspaper, which continued to improve my English, while playing classical music on my radio. My colleague Joe Holochuck gainfully crammed for his LSAT to get into Temple University's law school (later he became a hot shot attorney in Minersville, PA). On occasion he would disappear mysteriously from the lab. Soon it became apparent he was going to our dispensary, not to seek medical help but on a romantic mission to court JoAnn, a very personable nurse whom he eventually married.

The six-man team was a close-knit group; we were not just professional colleagues but good friends who immensely enjoyed one another's company. Frequently, after work on Fridays we would repair to South China, our favorite restaurant in Chinatown. Once in a while we went to a bar. Normally our drink was beer. On this night somehow our conversation turned to booze. Holochuck, a former Marine and the most vivacious and fun loving of the six of us, made a bold challenge to me:

"How much hard liquor can you handle?"

"I don't know."

"I bet you can't have 10 drinks without getting drunk."

I had very little capacity for alcoholic beverages; after one beer or a shot of bourbon I would feel blood rushing to my head. With two drinks my head would start to spin. But I wasn't going to let Holochuck get the better of me.

"I bet I can do it."

"Okay. I bet you twenty dollars. Pick whatever drink you want. If you can walk out of this bar and stay sober you win the bet."

"How much time do I have to finish the ten drinks?"

"How about one hour."

Very foolishly, I accepted the dare without thinking of the possible dire consequences. Indeed, I knew of individuals who died after having too many drinks too quickly.

"Can I eat some food to make the bet easier?"

"Sure."

So the bet was set. Side bets were placed by my other Merck colleagues, all against me.

I opted for Manhattans and ordered several hamburgers. To finish that quantity meant I should average six minutes per drink. Looking at my watch carefully, I proceeded to down the booze according to this schedule and ate as much hamburger as possible in between drinks. But with each additional Manhattan my face looked redder and redder, like a monkey's ass, and my head was feeling heavier and heavier.

But I pushed on, dictated not so much by the possibility of losing $20 as by my stubborn pride. To the surprise of everyone I was able to collect the bets by walking out of the bar unassisted. Furthermore, I drove home without killing anyone or hitting any obstacles, although I feared my alcohol content was way above the legal limit. That was a stupid and dangerous bet!

Early the following morning my telephone rang. It was Holochuck.

"How are you feeling?"

"I'm all right."

"How is your head?"

"Not too bad." Actually it was top-heavy.

"I wanted to make sure you are okay."

"Thanks for calling. I think I'll live. See you at work."

I made it to the lab with no incidents, to the relief of all my colleagues. Despite the lingering effects of my hangover, I was able to do my assays without mistakes or miscalculations. But I became allergic to Manhattans for the rest of my life.

I had a far scarier experience that almost ended my life.

Merck was located at the intersection of Broad and Wallace Streets, Philadelphia, in a very bad neighborhood surrounded by ghettoes, although it was only about 10 blocks north of city hall. I usually found a parking spot on Wallace St. just before starting my job at 4:30 P.M. When I finished work at 1:00 A.M. the streets were always so deserted that I never gave a thought about any danger lurking in the dark.

Such was the case one cold wintry night. After starting my car I waited for the engine to warm up. Suddenly someone knocked on my side of the window and it was an African American. A nearby streetlight allowed me to notice that this man was wearing shabby clothes. Strangely and foolishly, I thought he needed help and was about to roll down the window. But out of the corner of my eye I noticed he was hiding something in his right hand. A closer look revealed that it was a long knife just like the killing knife in the movie *Psycho*. Instantly I was horror-stricken. At this point my door was not even locked. The man could have easily opened it and plunged his knife into me. Perhaps he thought otherwise. In any case, I wasted no time stepping on my accelerator and taking off like a bullet, shaking uncontrollably.

Another incident was not life threatening but nonetheless scary and took place on the same street. After parking, I absent-mindedly forgot to lock my car. When I opened the door at quitting time I found a black man lying there. My first reaction was that it was a corpse and I was again scared stiff. As it turned out, it was a live person who found my car a restful place to spend the night. I woke him up and wasted no time kicking him out. He didn't fight back, and fortunately he had no weapon on him.

Sometime afterward, Merck's management decided to do away with the second shift, and I was thankful to be transferred to the day shift working from 8:00 A.M. to 4:30 P.M.

Around that time in the 1960s I became interested in the theater and telling jokes. Three of the latter:

> • An Asian diplomat and his wife are invited by President John Kennedy to a state dinner. Afterward, the diplomat feels obligated to say a few words: "I want to thank the president from the bottom of my heart and my wife's bottom, too."

> • In a Chinese restaurant an American customer tells the waiter: "I want to order some fried rice."
> "Okay, one order of flied lice."
> "It's not flied lice; it's fried rice. You stupid China-man. Can't you say it right? It's FRIED RICE. FRIED RICE."
> "Okay, one order of fried rice, you lotten plick."

> • A 90-year-old man is about to get married. Pleased by the news, a friend of his asks: "Who is the lucky bride?"
> "A 22-year-old beauty."

"Congratulations! I hope you two will be very happy together."

"Thank you."

"But may I offer a suggestion? Since she is so much younger, if you have problem keeping her occupied and happy, how about taking in a young boarder. Nobody needs to know about it."

"Excellent idea."

Five months later this friend runs into the old man.

"How are you doing?"

"Great. My wife is pregnant."

"That's wonderful news. And how is the boarder doing?"

"She is pregnant, too."

Having become proficient in my English, I found special joy in writing skits and comedies in the 1960s. As president and program director of Philadelphia's Chinese community, I had an easy outlet for my comedies—producing, directing, and starring in productions that were featured as part of the Chinese New Year celebration annually. One of my favorites, written during the rise of the feminist movement in the 1960s and spearheaded by such leaders as Betty Friedan and Gloria Steinem, was *The Cause of Dr. Mead.* Edited excerpts:

Mead is a world-famous sociologist and also president of the NAAFX, National Association for the Advancement of the Fair Sex. She calls on Dr. Stein, a beautiful and prominent psychiatrist of 29, to solicit support by discoursing vital feminist issues and the plight of women in a male-dominant world.

"I applaud and fully support your crusade," said Stein.

"There is, however, one area seldom explored: our lack of equal rights to woo the opposite sex." Mead continues.

"I never thought much about this."

"It has always been a one-sided proposition whereby men

initiate the move, call the shot, and lead the way while women play the subservient role."

"You are absolutely correct."

"Now suppose you find yourself attracted to some man, wouldn't you like to take the initiative to ask him out, perhaps to wine him, dine him, entertain him—or even go further?"

"Yes—to be totally honest," replies Stein. "But realistically, no. It's not the proper accepted etiquette; indeed, society considers such behavior anathema and looks askance at it."

"It's precisely the inequity we are subjected to. While we have the same emotions, instincts, and impulses as men, and the same craving for love and affection, we are chained to an antiquated social norm. It relegates us to play the second fiddle, to be the pursued and not the pursuer. It's time we fight for our just cause and strike a blow for independence, equality, and freedom."

Mead's eloquence moves Dr. Stein to eagerly join the NAAFX and make a generous donation.

Our scene next shifts to a plush office where Miss Kramer, also a stunning beauty in her late 20s and a conglomerate CEO, is busy with paperwork in the morning, while her office boy, Larry, a handsome, introverted young man, prepares coffee for her.

Kramer is beset with one problem after another: shrinking profits, production failures, and a rapidly declining stock market in which she has invested heavily. Things have become so hectic, frustrating, and overwhelming that she is near the breaking point. Canceling all her appointments, she storms out.

She finds herself seeking counseling from Dr. Stein, with whom she just had her first session. Our perceptive psychiatrist says: "You are a workaholic. You have been so obsessed by business that you are neglecting your duties as a woman. Consequently, your emotions are suppressed and there are no outlets for them. This leads to the frustration and unhappiness you have been experiencing, culminating in your terrible upset today. What you need to do is to learn to relax, have fun, develop an active social life, perhaps find pleasure in the company of men."

"I don't have time for this sort of thing. Besides, I find most men such a bore, or else intimidated by my looks and high position."

"Isn't there anyone who strikes your fancy?"

"These is actually one man I'm quite fond of. He is a wonderful guy, very masculine, with beautiful shoulders and yet so gentle and shy."

"Who is he?

"My office boy, Larry."

"Why don't you invite him out some time?

"I can't; I am a woman. He has to date me first but he is so shy that he'll never have the courage."

Advising Kramer to ignore the traditional passive role played by women, Stein, who by this time has become vice president of the NAAFX, eloquently replicates the thesis espoused by Mead, the sociologist, and suggests Kramer invite Larry for dinner, possibly on the pretext of discussing his future in the company.

Convinced and elated, the businesswoman makes a contribution to the NAAFX and walks out of the office as if dancing on air. Next evening in an elegant, romantic French restaurant Kramer entertains Larry allegedly to discuss his possible advancement. She orders oysters and beef bourguignon. Although he is a teetotaler, Kramer manages to loosen him up with a double scotch. Trying to get a little intimate with him, she holds his left hand and ad-libs about his fortune: "Your career line is weak but you'll be very rich and your love line is excellent."

After getting him a little inebriated she invites him to her apartment for a nightcap. They are soon married. On this morning Larry is making breakfast while Kramer is reading the *Wall Street Journal*. Larry is unhappy because Kramer forgets this is their one-year wedding anniversary. After being reminded of this, Kramer further disappoints him because she is entertaining a Hong Kong businessman that night and in fact won't be back till very late. As if cautioning about her negligence, he says: "When I went shopping yesterday a very striking woman followed me home, smiled at me, chatted with me, and asked for my telephone."

"Probably a lady wolf. Just ignore her." She leaves for work.

A few hours later a basket of flowers arrives with the note "Compliments from an admirer." Shortly afterward the admirer appears. It turns out to be none other than Dr. Stein. "I find you very desirable," she says.

Though she knows Larry is a married man she doesn't mind and invites him to paint the town with her. The story ends with Stein taking Larry's hand and the two leave the house to some unknown destination.

Another comedy was *Mr. Wong: or How I learned to Love the White House*. It was inspired by the news that Lyndon Baines Johnson, who assumed presidency after the tragic assassination of President Kennedy, was looking for a new chef to replace the French chef he had inherited. Edited excerpts:

Mr. Wong, a most talented Chinese chef, decides to apply for the job. To scrutinize the candidate Johnson personally conducts the interview. He is impressed at once by Wong's astute observations.

Wong: With me as the White House chef no one will have any weight problem. Chinese food, you see, is low in calories.

Johnson: Come to think of it, I have never seen a fat Chinese.

Wong: Chinese food is not only tasty it also has infinite variety.

Johnson: I'm afraid my knowledge of Chinese food is limited to chop suey and chow mein.

Wong: It may surprise you but chop suey and chow mein were unknown in China and invented in this country.

Johnson: I learn something new every day. What then is Chinese food?

Wong: Spaghetti.

Johnson: Spaghetti! *I'd be a registered Republican!* Now that you mentioned it, I remember reading something about Marco Polo bringing it back to Italy around the 13th century.

Wong: That's right. He also brought back other pasta. Won ton is identical to tortellini and "da bien" or big pie, is shaped, sized, and baked just like pizza. There is a host of other similarities. In short, Chinese cuisine and Italian cuisine are brothers under the skin, the twain of East and West that do meet.

Johnson: Well spoken, well spoken, Mr. Wong.

Wong: Not only Italians love Chinese food but Jews do, too. As a matter of fact they are largely responsible for the booming Chinese restaurant business. And that has great political implications.

Johnson: Are you implying that if I have a Chinese chef I will get the Jewish votes?

Wong: Precisely.

For a sample of his cooking Wong brings one of his masterpieces: an inimitable soup the likes of which Johnson has never tasted. He created it especially in honor of Mrs. Johnson and named it "Lady Bird Nest Soup." When Johnson professes his love for cakes and cookies Wong lets him sample his specially made fortune cookies. "Excellent taste," says our president. He is happy to read the message: "You are ordained for four more years." But he is more than a little piqued to read the message of another: "Nixon's the one." It happens to be the hottest campaign slogan in 1968 when Richard Nixon was running for presidency against Johnson. But Johnson quickly realizes that the message is a jest, a satire, reverse psychology that taunts his unworthy rival. Appreciating Wong's sense of humor, cooking prowess, and keen analytical mind, Johnson hires him on the spot.

In one scene Johnson sets up a summit meeting with his Russian counterpart, hoping to cement a peace treaty. But the stern-faced President Brezhnev keeps saying "nyet, nyet, nyet," because he wants to achieve parity in nuclear weaponry first, even if it means an endless spiral of arms race. It's around noon and Johnson invites the Russian to break bread over Chinese food.

Summoning Wong, Johnson tells him to prepare lunch, preferably something that "will put our Russian friend in a good mood so that he may reconsider signing the peace treaty." Mr. Wong nods knowingly, steps into the kitchen, and returns with kung pao chicken comprising dark meat stir-fried with vegetables, peanuts, and a plethora of the hottest Sichuan peppers. A few bites into it and the Russian shows a wounded look as his palate becomes a towering inferno, a hotbed of excruciating pain. With tears streaming down his cheeks, he asks for water. But Wong seems hard of hearing. Brezhnev becomes increasingly desperate, shouting and pleading for water. Waving the treaty in front of him, Wong promises help if Brezhnev pays the ransom with his signature. A happy ending ensues. Johnson is ever so pleased that his Chinese chef helps achieve detente with U.S.S.R and make the world a safer place.

The climax takes place when Johnson plays host to a dozen heads of state to celebrate United Nation Day. He asks Wong to prepare a banquet that will invoke the spirit of the United Nations and reflect Confucius' dictum that "Within the corners of the four seas all men are brothers."

Rising to the challenge, Wong creates a dinner worthy of

three Michelin stars.

But the distinguished guests are totally puzzled by the chopsticks. They are inordinately long, measuring some three feet long and making eating impossible. Just before Johnson flies into his well-known monumental rage, Wong smilingly points out that while the guests cannot feed themselves, they can use the unwieldy utensils to put food into their neighbors' mouths across the dining table. The guests quickly learn the trick and happily dig into the delicious feast, thus achieving the ideal of peaceful cooperation among nations and the universal brotherhood of men.

This comedy was so well received by the Chinese community that it was also presented at the University of Pennsylvania where the largely Caucasian audience seemed to like it, too.

My other comedies include *The Battle of the Sexes, Chinese Style; The Return of Marco Polo*; and *An American Education,* the only one in Chinese. After penning and staging *Jimmy Chang*, a three-act comedy in 1970, I stopped all such efforts because of my changing priorities and time constraints (although I did take a playwriting course with Tony Award-winning playwright David Henry Hwang years later for kicks).

Writing comedies might be a pleasant diversion but it also became an informal part of my English education that paved the way for me to become a journalist.

CHAPTER FOUR (1933–1950)

Growing Up

I was born in Shanghai on September 28, 1933, the same day as the venerable Confucius. I also happened to be the godson of a direct descendant of his, S. W. Kung, who bore the same surname. My official birth year, however, was 1934; a mistake inadvertently made on my government ID that stuck. My father, Peter Wei Lin, gave his four sons English first names: David, Harry, Henry and Benjamin. As a little joke I tell people my middle name is Frank which, sandwiched between my first name Benjamin and last name Lin, becomes my namesake, the historical Benjamin Franklin. My Chinese middle names are phonetically spelled, Bing-Heng, the first word meaning *polite* and the second *permanent*.

Happily, I was born to one of China's most prominent bankers. So I grew up in relative affluence, attending the best schools and never lacking in material things. But what I craved the most was elusive: parental affection. Having lost his mother when he was just four years old and having lived with a very reserved father and an uncaring stepmother, my father Peter did not know how to express his paternal love. I don't remember his ever cuddling me when I was growing up. What's more, as a banker he wasn't around very much, constantly busy entertaining or traveling. Generally, I saw him only once a week on Sundays when we had breakfast together, mostly in silence. He almost never talked to me or asked me how I was doing. I was partially to blame; I didn't know how to be affectionate, being shy and a little afraid of him, respecting him as an authoritarian figure and not someone to get close to.

In reality he was a caring and affectionate father. Behind his impassive façade and reluctance to display emotions he had a soft heart. I didn't realize this until many years later when Mother revealed to me that he on occasions shed tears over me. As an example, in 1948 when Shanghai was facing possible invasion by the Communists, Father sent me and younger brother Henry to stay with relatives in Hong Kong (my two older brothers had already gone to the States to study). When I complained about my unhappiness of living under some else's roof, he wept and immediately and brought us back. And upon our 1950 arrival in San Francisco from China, just after sending me off to attend college, he became distraught because I was a naïve youngster not yet 17, a stranger facing a world of uncertainties and carrying very little money on a lone journey to Texas. He was so grief-stricken that he broke down and cried. I wished I had known about these incidents earlier so that I could have been a more affectionate son.

With my mother, Priscilla, I had a different relationship. She was a loving woman and as devout a Christian as Father. Gifted with a special ability to resonate with children, she taught kindergarten and elementary school for 18 years with great distinction. Above all she loved her sons. But I was the one who gave her the greatest agony at birth. Because I had wide shoulders they caused her to bleed excessively and suffer unbearable pain. And suturing was required. What she gave me in return was pure joy—at least initially. As a newborn I had her all to myself, luxuriating totally in her love. But sadly it lasted only one short year until the birth of Henry. I immediately sensed a shifting of affection as he replaced me as Mother's new favorite. Born after only seven and one-half months, and weighing a mere five and one-half pounds, he certainly deserved special attention. Furthermore, he was the baby of the family, the cutest, most adorable tot whom we nicknamed Pon Pon, an endearing term for an obese boy. But being self-centered, all I could notice was Mother's unmitigated devotion to Pon Pon and seeming neglect of me. It was sheer torture. I kept hoping things would change and that I finally would win what was the most important thing in my life: maternal love. Failing that I felt I was an ugly reject that nobody cared for and suffered the worst inferiority complex imaginable. It cut a deep gash on my psyche, became my albatross, and influenced my later life in a most profound way. I never told her—or anyone else—about my plight. But in many of my childhood photos I exhibited a long, unhappy, troubled face and nobody noticed or bothered to find out why.

Meanwhile China was undergoing civil war. The year 1937 turned out to be a telling one for the country, which was under the Nationalist administration. Just then it was relentlessly pursuing the Communists and on the verge of annihilating them. But that year marked the beginning of the Sino-Japanese war when the Nipponese empire launched an attack and bragged it would conquer China in 30 days, a boast that proved hollow. In the interest of fighting a common enemy the two Chinese factions joined hands and displayed a surprising resilience and unity, which made the war last eight long years, ending with Japan as the loser. But initially the Nationalists did fight poorly, exhausted from the civil strife, and within months Shanghai and Nanking, the capital city, fell.

However, the Japanese refrained from occupying a section of Shanghai known as the International Settlement where my family was living because it was under British rule.

In November 1941 Father and Mother decided to vacation in Hong Kong. Things worsened for me emotionally for it was Mother's decision to take Henry—and not both of us. To me it was concrete evidence and further affirmation of Mother's partiality toward Henry and indifference toward me. As a result I was consumed with rejection and self-loathing.

It was lucky for Father to cut short his vacation by business which required him to go to Chongqing, China's wartime capital, where his bank had already moved. Some two weeks later on December 7, 1941, "The Day of Infamy," Japan attacked Pearl Harbor. Since Great Britain joined forces with the U.S. to fight the Axis nations of Nazi Germany, Fascist Italy, and Imperialist Japan, the last wasted no time to invade Shanghai's International Settlement and Hong Kong. Poor Mom and Henry became refugees unable to return to Shanghai. Our family was split three ways. Worse, David, Harry, and I were totally devastated upon the rumor that she had died.

As a result of the Opium War, Hong Kong was ceded to England as a colony, and part of Shanghai was partitioned into three concessions controlled by the British, French, and Americans, known collectively as the International Settlement. Later it became primarily a British concession.

With no income, David, who was 12 years Harry's senior and 15 years mine, became head of the household, our surrogate father, trying to eke out a living while taking pre-med courses. He resorted to the dangerous trade of selling rice on the black market. If caught by the Japanese he would face dire consequences and possible death. Once when carrying rice in a bag he didn't realize there was a slow leak. Fortunately a stranger alerted him.

David had also done other daredevil things. One morning he found a beggar who had just died on the street in the frigid winter. Mindful of the shortage of cadavers in his anatomy class, he hailed a rickshaw. While he was placing the corpse on the vehicle a cop came and asked what he was doing. A born actor, Dave replied, "I'm a doctor. This man is dying and he needs immediate medical attention. I have to take him to a hospital to save his life." The cop believed him and let him go.

Another time he was disheartened to discover the husband of our servant, Xiao Ju Ma, was a hopeless drug addict. With great audacity and fortitude David chained him to our bathroom radiator to forcibly detoxify and rid him of his horrible habit. It worked. Days later he lost so much weight that he broke loose from the shackle and walked out of the bathroom, completely cured and never touched the white powder again. But I shudder to think of the possible consequences of going cold turkey.

Despite his busy schedule David became an active community leader as the head of a youth organization. He was especially well liked among the neighborhood kids. Through his encouragement they would not hesitate to ask him to treat their bruises and wounds, or even have their ears safely cleaned. His love for his brothers was boundless. If we showed potential in anything he would do his level best to help develop it. When I exhibited a little aptitude in the piano he made me take lessons. Hoping to develop Harry's musical appreciation, he also made him take lessons. When he discovered Harry was averse to piano practice he sat by Harry for one-half hour daily to make sure he would follow the regimen.

He also helped me do daring things. One day he and some friends went swimming and brought me along. To make me conquer my fear and learn the meaning of bravery, he urged me to jump from the high diving platform although I didn't know how to swim. He assured me that he and his friends would be waiting down below, and the minute I landed they would pull me out of the water. I was persuaded to climb up the steps. But the pool looked so far away and forbidding. I was just a little boy, terrified and hesitant. To take the plunge would be like making a bungee jump without the cord, a one-way street to an aquatic tomb—if things went wrong. But with enthusiastic cheering from my would-be saviors I found the courage to plunge. Before I swallowed a mouthful of water they brought me to safety. I was happy about the feat and grateful for David's encouragement.

In the meantime, of more pressing concern to my brothers and me was the paucity of news from Hong Kong, which kept us terribly worried about Mother's fate. It wasn't until a few months after Japan's occupation that we discovered to our utter ecstasy and gratitude the rumor about her demise was groundless. Indeed, she was alive and unharmed—and so was Henry. But she did endure extreme danger, moving from place to place to stay with different friends to be safe. At one point to her horror she found herself occupying the same building, the Philip House, as the Japanese. Being a pretty woman, she had to disguise as a servant hiding in the base-ment to avoid being noticed by the lecherous soldiers. They were notorious as the world's worst sex criminals for their rampant raping in Nanking (spelled Nanjing today) and elsewhere for kid-napping and forcing countless Chinese—and Korean—women to serve as sex slaves. Mom was spared such a horrible fate and survived her refugee days with the help of her religious faith, steady prayers, and vigilance.

Five months later when she finally returned to Shanghai with Henry, it was like a miracle. We three brothers were jubilant beyond words and kept asking her incredulously: "How are you able to come home?"

She noted our reunion in her journal with the following words: "After hugging and shouts of elation we turned our laughter into tears. I led the boys to kneel down to pray, thanking the Lord for His blessings and guiding hand to return home safely for the reunion.

"Ben told me he missed me so much that he always cried himself to sleep. He would then dream about my return. But when he awoke and realized it was just a dream he would become sad and cry again. He also showed me his diary titled 'I Saw Mommy Coming Home in a Dream.'

"Harry said he cried several times when he saw my clothes in the closet. But David never cried because he had the abiding faith that 'Mommy would escape all misfortunes and return safely. So, what need is there for crying?'"

I was also happy to reunite with Henry. Despite our sibling rivalry I never resented him. After all, it was not his fault for being such an adorable child. On the contrary, I loved him as my kid brother and never more so than after a painful separation and I delighted in taking him sightseeing with me on my bicycle.

However, our days in Shanghai were numbered. With Father in Chongqing urging us to speedily join him we had to decide how best to escape from Japanese-occupied Shanghai. There were just two ways: by sea or land. Both were highly dangerous and often fatal. Mother chose the former. Our plan was to travel to a border town first where we would escape to Fujian in free China. On November 24, 1942, we left our beloved Shanghai carrying an amazing 27 pieces of luggage; Mother wanted to make sure we brought along every household need imaginable, fearing Chongqing in interior China might not have sufficient consumer goods. Our party included a cousin and a teenage servant girl, La Ying, whom we regarded as our sister and whose mother Xiao Ju Ma had served us for many years and was like part of the family. David was not one of the fleeing members. He came along only to help guide us to the border town. He would then return to Shanghai to complete his pre-med program at St. John's University.

The border town was called Sun Gia Men. Two days away from Fujian on high seas, it was heavily guarded by Japanese navy. When we were arriving by steam ship from Shanghai, Japanese soldiers lined up all the passengers for some kind of vaccination, using the same syringe for everyone. There were two lines: one for those to be vaccinated and another for those just vaccinated. A keen observer with a very quick mind, David made us stealthily sneak to the latter line while rubbing our upper arms as if the deed was done. And we succeeded in eluding the forced vaccinations.

To get from Sun Gia Men to Free China of Fujian, we had to meet two conditions: a favorable wind and when the Japanese navy was loosening its guard. It happened one day when the navy was celebrating some holiday and its fleet was seen sailing away and wind was blowing toward our destination. So we made a quick getaway on board a Chinese junk. However, if we were caught by the Japanese we would suffer certain death. And on the high seas Chinese pirates abounded. They were notorious for being merciless; after looting they usually sank the ship and drowned everyone.

We were able to leave the seaport without incident. At one point while staying in the bowel of the junk, I climbed up to go to the restroom. No sooner had I reached the upper deck than our captain frantically shouted to me to get back down. Later I discovered at that very moment there were five pirate ships hot after us, and the captain was afraid they might be shooting at us. The captain immediately took evasive action and returned to the bay. After waiting till dark, we sailed again. Thanks to his bravery, vigilance, and resourcefulness, the skipper, who stayed up two days and nights, maneuvered us safely to the shores of Fujian.

From there we took a river route to go to Fuzhou, the capital of the Fujian province, and home of my uncle, my father's younger brother. To prevent Japanese from traveling to Fuzhou the river was heavily mined, and we depended on a guide to carefully steer us. Fortunately the mines didn't get drifted from the anchors and our guide had a good memory or good map, and so we reached Fuzhou in one piece.

During our two and one-half month stay in my uncle's house, I never learned to speak the Fujian dialect, which was so different from all other dialects that it was like Greek to me. I did, however, develop a lifelong weakness: the pleasures of the table, initiated by the inimitable Fujianese cuisine, one of China's major schools of cooking. Particularly noteworthy were stir-fried hair thin rice noodles, garnished with vegetables, meat and/or seafood; a delightful red condiment made from fermented rice which enhanced the flavor of fish and chicken; fish balls that contained smaller meat balls inside; and won ton soup called "yien pee tong" of which the wrapper was made from fusing flour and pork together, resulting in an unusual texture and captivating taste.

To continue our journey to Chongqing, we boarded a bus and had a narrow escape. Climbing uphill on a high mountain during heavy rain, the bus stalled. It began to roll backward and was headed for a precipice with no protective railings. The driver quickly ordered everyone out while he bravely stayed on. Luckily the rain stopped suddenly. Meanwhile the driver managed to stop the slide, restart the engine, and resume our journey. After successive bus rides we arrived at Guilin, our last stop before Chongqing.

Guilin and its environs were known for their scenic beauty, particularly the wondrous, strange-shaped mountains and the striking river, Lijiang. It was said that in ancient China an aspiring painter had to live there for three full years to have any chance of becoming a true artist. Today it is one of China's top tourist destinations.

From Guilin to Chongqing we could travel by land or air. The former required a perilous bus ride going through some

70 hairpin turns on a steep mountain, and accidents occasionally happened. So we opted for flying, but flights were few and far between and we had to wait for weeks.

In the interim we had a chance to explore the fascinating Seven Star Caves in which stalactites dating back millions of years created colorful formations, some of which bore remarkable resemblance to animals and humans. Some had inscriptions like "Old Man Watching Opera" and "Old Buddhist Beating Young Buddhist." The latter looked so realistic that it seemed more like a human sculpture than an accident of nature. I was also captivated by aqua-farming in ponds where juvenile fish, typically carp, had been stocked earlier, water was drained, forcing large fish to jump frantically for survival while fishermen easily harvested them with a net. Another discovery was a most unusual amphibian called "wa wa yue," literally baby fish. It resembled a human baby, could leave its water habitat to climb trees, and had powerful jaws with very sharp teeth. If one was unfortunate enough to be caught with a finger in its mouth, the fish would twist with all its might and possibly break one's finger. But I heard it was a great delicacy and very tasty.

At long last we caught a flight to Chongqing. Because we had so much luggage the pilot had to dump a few dozen gallons of fuel to compensate for the heavy weight. Upon landing, according to Mom's journal: "All three sons were overjoyed and shouted at the sight of Father. 'WE SAW HIM. DADDY, DADDY, DADDY.' At this outburst, all the passengers marveled at our innocence and enthusiasm with amusement and rejoiced with us for uniting with our beloved father."

After so many trials and tribulations and near-death experiences, our happiness could only be topped by the day when David, who was still studying in Shanghai, could join us for a reunion.

Chongqing is located in Sichuan in southwest China, the

country's largest province. Home of pandas and birthplace of the great poet Li Bai, Sichuan boasted some unique customs. In certain areas when two persons had a dispute, they did not resolve it by legal means. Instead, they would go to a tea house to settle their differences called "chiang cha," literally "talk tea." Each would present his case to the patrons. They would deliberate and pass judgment that the loser would accept civilly, with no questions asked.

Another custom, still true in many parts of China, is to bury the dead in their birthplaces, requiring transporting if they died elsewhere. In Sichuan years ago the transporting was accomplished by eerie and seemingly impossible means, according to folklore. Certain Taoist monks were seen at times to lead a group of corpses literally jumping, yes jumping, two feet together step by step on the streets, with their faces covered with a sheet of paper. This tradition of "walking the dead" lasted a long time until the discovery that the "corpses" were live people who were cleverly being used to transport drugs, capitalizing on people's superstition and ignorance.

Upon our arrival Father's top priority was to hire a tutor for us three sons to make up for almost one semester's lost time. I successfully entered the fifth grade. Initially my only difficulty was leaning to speak the Sichuan dialect, which turned out to be fairly easy as it was not too different from Mandarin, China's official dialect.

Thankfully, my inferiority complex by this time had largely dissipated, because Mother did not show any favoritism during our long journey. Better still, in Chongqing my self-esteem got a tremendous boost from my fifth-grade teacher. She was a sensitive, caring woman endowed with a strong maternal instinct as we bonded easily. Complimenting me for being a top student, a "lovable boy," and her protégé, she lavished me with so much attention and affection that she became my surrogate mother, who subjected me to a redemption, euphoria, and sense of being whole never experienced before. Noticing I had a pigeon-toed gait, i.e. my toes pointed inwardly when walking, she took pains to correct me; again and again she gently and patiently made me pace forward until I learned to walk properly.

To reciprocate her love and as a token of my gratitude I gave her a portrait of mine, one of the few in which I didn't have an unhappy face. She proudly showed it to everyone, saying "That's my favorite pupil. He was even better looking when he was younger." Once and for all I was convinced I might not have such a repulsive face and despicable personality. The world was no longer a desolate and despairing place, but one filled with sunshine, hope, and possibilities.

But one incident changed everything.

Taking a bath one winter, Mother was using coal to heat the water and it generated a lot of carbon monoxide. With the windows all closed the deadly gas so poisoned her that she was close to dying. Though she was half delirious she managed to cry out for help. The whole family ran to her and immediately opened all the windows. Prompt medical help was required, but we were living in the countryside and the closest clinic had closed for the day. There was nothing we could do except to pray while looking at her helplessly. It was terrifying to see her fight desperately for life. I was heartbroken to think that I might lose forever the one person I loved so profoundly.

What happened next dealt me a fatal blow. Seemingly oblivious to the people surrounding her, she had just one thought on her mind. "Where is my Pon Pon? I want my Pon Pon. I want my Pon Pon," she cried out weakly. Her preference for Henry at this critical moment pained me as never before and destroyed whatever shreds of self-esteem that had remained with me. Once again I was brought to the lowest depths.

Fortunately Mother survived. But my emotional health did not. Filled with self-pity, I often climbed a little leafless tree and just sat there sulking for long hours, unnoticed by my family members and possibly making pedestrians wonder what that sad little boy was doing up on the tree.

The psychological wounds soon emerged in an unexpected way. A pretty girl living next door one day told me—to my utter surprise—that she liked me. She was about seven years old, and I was ten. As a lonesome soul craving for affection, I should have felt elated and gratified. On the contrary, my instant reaction was loathing for her. If I thought I was so worthless, any girl who adored me had to be even a lower creature. And so I brushed her rudely aside.

Meanwhile life in Chongqing was not easy. One constant fear was the perennial bombings. Deliberately targeting residential areas, schools, businesses, and hospitals, the Japanese army and navy air forces had conducted some 5,000 sorties, dropping an estimated 11,500 bombs. They killed over 5,000 civilians in 1939 and in 1941; 6,000 were asphyxiated hiding in a tunnel. Thankfully no additional bombings had materialized since our arrival. However, I had a grim reminder swimming in a lake because part of it felt particularly cold, the result of an errant bomb and marked by the statue of a Buddha on the shore.

To instill students' patriotic fervor, our schools taught us nationalistic songs. They were deeply moving including such famous ones as "The March of the Volunteers" (it has become Communist China's national anthem since coming into power in 1949), "On Songhua River," "Guerilla Song," and "Fighting the Enemy." I learned a good many and to this day I remember some of the melodies and lyrics well. Two examples:

Threesome, five some
One horde, two hordes
On flat land
On high hill

We are the guerrilla brothers
Turn zero into whole
Turn whole into zero
We fear not the enemy's ferocious fire
Seize their provisions for our use
Plundering their arms we'll end their being
We plain civilians, threesome, five some and tens of
    thousands strong
Striving for a year or two
We'll vanquish our enemies for good
We plain civilians, threesome, five some and tens of
    thousands strong
Striving for a year or two
We'll vanquish our enemies for good

Another song chronicles the story of a young woman tending sheep at a foothill by some willow trees. While the sheep are grazing she is busy sewing clothes for her husband who is leaving to fight the Japanese. Wearing these clothes, he will stay warm and bolster his courage a hundred-fold. He may risk his life for the sake of liberation, but he will render the enemies defenseless and be victorious. When returning home singing songs of triumph he will happily tend to the sheep with his beloved by the foothill.

The music was ardent and moving and the lyrics resonated with my love of China and hatred of the Japanese, who wantonly invaded China and committed appalling atrocities especially in the capital city of Nanking, so tellingly depicted in Iris Chang's *The Rape of Nanking*. It detailed the massacre of some 300,000 civilians and soldiers (half the population) including women and children, mass raping, and such barbaric acts as tortures, mutilations, slashings of the uteri of pregnant women for amusement, a contest to see who could chop off more heads, etc.

At one point, Chongqing had a very close call. Guilin, the last line of defense, fell into enemy hands and invasion of the wartime capital was imminent. Wondering where to retreat to and worrying about being refugees once again, or worse, becoming captives of the murderous Japanese, my family was relieved the Chinese army won a major victory.

Less worrisome but life threatening, nonetheless, I experienced an intense pain in my right abdomen one day. A nearby American clinic diagnosed it as acute appendicitis and immediate surgery was required. In the interest of time Mother took me to the nearest hospital not knowing it was one of the worst. Shortly after my arrival the operation began. I didn't think it would be much of an ordeal. About four years prior I had five teeth extracted at one sitting without Novocain. I survived with a minimum of groaning and the dentist called me a "brave boy." For my appendectomy I thought my seda-tion would spare me of any agony. But as soon as the surgeon made his incision I felt a sharp cutting sensation and cried out in pain. Apparently I didn't get enough anesthesia. Instead of administering more, the doctor behaved as if there was nothing wrong and continued his surgery. The pain worsened and was so excruciating I tried to jump off of the operating table. To restrain me, two nurses on each side of me held me by my shoulders. The more I struggled, the harder they immobilized me. But my screaming continued to resound.

At this time Mom was waiting in the hallway and heard the piercing cries but she thought they came from someone else. A few years before when she accompanied older brother Harry for his tonsillectomy in Shanghai, she heard similar screams and thought they emanated from Harry. They turned out to be from another patient in an adjoining operating room. And so she became exceedingly worried unnecessarily. This time she didn't want to make the same mistake and was not concerned in the least.

I didn't realize humans could endure so much pain without losing consciousness for I was awake during the entire operation and fully felt the surgeon's every move. It was a most tortuous experience. I shrieked and shrieked until I was spent.

After the operation I was wheeled into a room that had 11 other patients. One was a young horse attendant whose animal had kicked him blind in one eye. The hospital was so inept that maggots were found inside the eye socket during my stay. When I returned home a few days later my surgical opening would not heal. A doctor at the American clinic thought it was due to insufficient sterilization and repeatedly treated it as such to no avail. Finally he found the cause by probing deeply into the opening: something was left inside, most likely a piece of the suture. After its removal my wound healed.

I should be grateful I did not suffer anything worse at the hospital. A family friend was once a patient there, too. When asked to take certain medications, fortunately she knew something about medicine and suspected they were intended for someone else. Insisting on consulting with a physician, she found out that the medications would have killed her had she taken them.

A short time after my operation and return to school, oldest brother David arrived in Chongqing. Successfully escaping to free China from Shanghai, he came by land, a combination of train and bus rides, which, like escape by sea, were no less dangerous. En route he had to bribe his way by giving his valuable watch to a Japanese soldier. Finally my family had a reunion, with all four sons and parents celebrating together. It was, however, a short reunion for David, who soon departed to begin his medical studies in Chengdu.

He returned the following summer for a short one-month vacation. Noticing I was doing well at school, Dave spent hours daily coaching me to bypass one year's study. Thoughtful, meticulous, and methodical he proved to be a great teacher, making me progress by leaps and bounds. While mostly gentle and patient, he could be a little intimidating. One day he said with a severe look, "I want you to memorize China's 28 provinces by this evening. If you don't I'll whip you." Whether it was an empty threat, I took it seriously as he had subjected me to corporal punishment once or twice in Shanghai. And by dusk I could recite the provinces backward.

Thanks to Dave's coaching I skipped the sixth grade by passing the entrance exam to a junior high school. But I was profoundly saddened by the thought of leaving my beloved fifth-grade teacher. She was equally dejected. As a farewell gift I gave her an expensive Chinese calligraphy inkstand with these carved words: "To my favorite teacher from your devoted pupil." We were never to see each other again. I am forever indebted to her for giving me a much-needed sanctuary and warmth during one of the darkest periods of my life.

After one semester at the junior high I transferred to the Holy Light Middle School, which was discovered accidentally by my parents. Visiting a navy academy in a Chongqing suburb, they heard hymns from a building next door and went there to investigate. To their delight it was a Protestant school and a very good one where the sons and daughters of very prominent families attended. The upshot was that both my brother Harry and I became boarding students there.

If my parents' motivations were to give us excellent education while molding our spiritual life, they succeeded brilliantly. Staffed with topnotch teachers, Holy Light also provided a strong religious atmosphere, aided in no small measure by its headmaster and his wife, both dedicated Christians, and two British missionaries whose love for the Chinese and zeal for teaching were extraordinary. Especially popular was Gordon Addis, whom we called Yao Mou Sze, or

Reverend Yao. He was a loving teacher, friend, counselor, and spiritual guru all rolled into one. Small wonder we students loved to spend time with him in his one-room living quarters every chance we had.

It was at Holy Light that I was converted to Christianity. I was just 12 years old, believed literally in every word of the Bible, and too young to be concerned with the theology and the more complex issues such as "Why does God seem so cruel at times?" and "Are all non-believers doomed to hell?" Nonetheless, it was comforting to have a source of spiritual nourishment, a sense of belonging, a faith that there was something bigger than us.

On a few occasions when there were revival meetings, I eagerly attended. Especially memorable were two hosted by a Reverend Gee. Each time his impassioned, eloquent, and powerful preaching moved me to tears. It also effected a catharsis that was redemptive, liberating, and joyous. Another thing I enjoyed was hymn singing including some of Mother's favorites such as "What a Friend We Have in Jesus" and "Sowing in the Morning." I also fondly remember an early Easter morning when a small group of us went from door to door to proclaim the good news of Resurrection with songs of rejoicing.

Holy Light also had some strange social conventions: boys and girls had no interactions whatsoever. Segregated on two sides of the classroom, there seemed to be an invisible wall between the two sexes. They never talked to one another, not even a simple word of greeting. If one was caught violating this unwritten rule he or she would suffer horrible jeers from fellow students. This resulted in some wrenching stories. Lena Jung, née Liu Kwon Chin, a classmate of mine, was a 13-year-old raving beauty who attracted the intense adoration of several upperclassmen. Unable to express their feelings openly, one wrote about it in a diary. When word got out about the secret writing he set it on fire and almost burnt down the school. A year or so later when Lena relocated to Shanghai, another admirer repeatedly went to her house, just standing outside to be near her but afraid to ring.

While my inferiority complex abated considerably in this new, boarding school environs, it resurfaced from a different source: my eyes. They were not elliptical as most people's, but three-cornered like triangles. I never noticed that until several classmates started to taunt me, calling me "san joy yen," or "triangular eyes." They were relentless in their ridiculing and hurt me deeply.

If anything good came out of my screwed-up psychology it might be my determination throughout my life to try harder to overcome difficulties and win approbation. While I'm not particularly gifted—certainly having no great talent in any specified field—I do have an abundance of curiosity and joie de vivre. With widely diversified interests I try to invest my full passion and every ounce of my energy into whatever I put my mind to. It's only through my stubbornness, perseverance, and herculean effort that I was able to achieve a measure of success in my endeavors. But I have also been painfully aware of my tendency to minimize my shortcomings and—to compensate for my inadequacies—exaggerate my small accomplishments.

One thing that did not need exaggeration was the notorious, monster Sichuan rats that I had seen but could hardly believe. They were as big as a small cat and known to have devoured babies. They were to cross my path in a different way. On occasions when a few daring students like me sneaked out of Holy Light, which was strictly forbidden during weekdays, we would order a nearby vendor's "yang chuan mien," noodles with soup. It was highlighted by pieces of very delicious non-descript reddish meat which we relished until the discovery that it was most likely the monster rats.

More reassuring was my fondness for Sichuanese cuisine, known, of course, for its hot spiciness. Many of the specialties are defined by three other characteristics: sweetness, pungency, and numbness. They temper the burning spiciness in a marvelous, multidimensional way. The numbness, induced by Sichuan peppercorn, is definitely an acquired taste. But to the initiated it's a delightful sensation that adds to the enjoyment. Among my favorite dishes: kung Pao chicken, named after a Sichuan governor whose title "kung pao" means palatial guardian, and its inclusion of peanuts as a counterpoint is a stroke of genius; "hot oil won tons," a wonderful appetizer, of which the taste is enhanced by chili oil and Sichuan peppercorn powder; "yu hsiang pork," literally fish fragrant pork, in which slivers of meat are blended with wood ear fungi and bamboo shoots or water chestnuts; "ma pu tofu," literally pock-marked tofu, comprising tiny cubed bean curd and ground pork and accentuated with an enticing piquant sauce. Allegedly it was invented by an old woman from Chengdu whose face was scarred by smallpox and whose tiny eatery attracted patrons from far and wide.

I also enjoyed non-spicy Sichuanese dishes. To name just two: the poetically named "ants on tree" in which cellophane noodles, signifying tree, are graced with antlike pulverized pork. Part of its pleasure comes from the contrasting textures of the two main components. And "camphor tea duck," which is made by smoking the fowl with black tea and camphor twigs and leaves, resulting in an idiosyncratic, unforgettable flavor.

My appreciation for the cuisine and education at Holy Light came to an unexpected end. The Sino-Japanese war concluded in 1945 with the unconditional surrender of Japan, materialized only after the deployment of two atomic bombs by the U.S. To this day Japan never apologized for its wanton invasion and war crimes, made reparations to China, or compensated the sex slaves. Moreover, it repeatedly whitewashed its barbaric misdeeds in its textbooks or denied them totally.

Peace and prosperity, however, did not come to China in 1945 as it again embroiled in civil war. The Mo Zedong-led Communists, which came within a hair of being entirely annihilated in 1937, not only survived but thrived during the eight-year Sino-Japanese War. Consequently, they were in a much better position to fight the Chiang Kai-shek regime, which was significantly weakened by bearing the brunt of the fighting against the Japanese.

For my family the war's end meant saying goodbye to Chongqing and returning to Shanghai for which I had such yearning. But the memory of my Holy Light days remains strong. Some of my schoolmates—including those females whom I had never talked to—became my very, very dear friends since. We keep close contact with one another and frequently have reunions. Among them: Lena Jung, the stunning beauty, became a chemical engineer, fellow music lover, and an accomplished pianist; George Wong, art connoisseur and my soul brother; Lin San, an education book author and a woman about town; and Stella Hu and He Yen-Sen, both research scientists. After Holy Light relocated to Soochow, many of its Chongqing students—including my brother Harry—rejoined the school. I chose to stay in Shanghai, following Father's recommendation to transfer to St. Francis Xavier, an all-male Catholic middle school.

When not busy with my studies, I developed a host of hobbies. A pet lover, I had some typical companions: goldfish, hamsters, turtles, rabbits, birds, ducks, chickens, and an aristocratic Persian cat that was endowed with beautiful, luxurious fur and eyes of two different colors. Mostly playful, it once became moody and violent and clawed my breast so fiercely that I suffered a long scar. It was, however, a small price to pay for such a gorgeous animal. But, alas, basking on the windowsill of our eighth-floor apartment, it rolled out accidentally and fell to its death. When I sadly tried to retrieve it, my prized cat was already gone, most likely swiped by someone because of its rich furs.

I had two other diversions: raising crickets and silkworms. Male crickets are great gladiators. When two are prodded to face each other with a straw stick, sometimes they start by chirping to intimidate each other (they can hear with their legs). Other times they engage immediately by locking each other's wide-open mandibles, forcefully twisting and turning while pushing forward with their powerful hind legs. The contest is so ferocious that both may go belly up with their mandibles still intertwined. But instantly they will right themselves and continue. If the two are evenly matched, they will fight till the bitter end, lasting a minute or so.

When the victor emerges, it struts and chirps to proclaim and celebrate the victory, and sometimes accompanied by chasing the loser for a split second—and not longer—not so much to further humiliate as to affirm its success. Once a cricket loses, unlike a human pugilist, it will never regain its fighting spirit and the owner simply sets it free.

Cricket fighting is a popular sport dating back over 1,000 years in China and enjoyed by both owners and spectators of all ages. Gamblers place big bets and connoisseurs pay large sums for prized fighters. Unlike cockfighting and dog fighting which are very cruel, cricket fighting is far more humane and no deaths ever occur.

At the beginning of every cricket fighting season I would buy about 40 from street vendors. Keeping them in round clay containers, I looked forward to challenging my neighbors who shared my hobby. At night I kept these crickets in my bedroom. Their chirpings (produced by rubbing their forewings together) were so loud that they sometimes woke me up but hardly annoyed me because of my love for them. At the end of the season as cold weather set in before our apartment heat was turned on, it hurt me to see my crickets die off one by one.

Raising silkworms was more than just a hobby but a study in biology, an epiphany that celebrates the miracle of life, an evolution unfolding in mere weeks.

To witness a microscopic egg being hatched into a tiny larva is fascinating enough. The fascination grows as it goes through four stages of molting. In each stage the larva raises its head high, totally motionless for a day or so as if praying before shedding its skin to grow bigger. In the final stage the caterpillar grows to be about three inches long and undergoes a phenomenal change in its salivary gland: the manufacturing of a secretion with which the larva spins a fine, delicate silk cocoon, enclosing itself inside where it is transformed into a pupa.

The cocoon is the source of commercial silk. Originated from China a few thousand years ago, it could be woven into excellent, lustrous, durable textiles, worn at one time only by kings and royalty. The cocoon is usually white but on rare occasions when mine took on the color of orange or blue I'd be absolutely thrilled. Inside the cocoon the pupa undergoes one more metamorphosis by changing into a non-flying moth. It will chew its way out and instinctively mate with the opposite sex. The female will then spawn eggs to complete the cycle, which takes about 45 days.

The caterpillars feed only on mulberry leaves and their appetite is enormous. Indeed, when not molting it gorges nearly nonstop. So it became my regular chore to procure the leaves. Most times I would buy from street vendors. But when my weekly allowances ran low I would scout for mulberry trees in my neighborhood. And many a time I had to climb a high wall to steal mulberry leaves from someone's backyard.

I resorted to another form of stealing out of greed and addiction.

When Father entertained at home there would be cases of

a beverage that I fell in love with at first sip: Coca-Cola. It is phonetically written in Chinese as "Ke Ko Ke Lo" which aptly means tasty and pleasurable. I became so addicted that I would stealthily help myself to some 30 bottles and hide them in my bedroom bureau. To prolong my enjoyment I rationed myself to just one bottle per day, slowly savoring and hoping my father would host another dinner party before my precious supply ran out.

My father's post-war days in Shanghai as a banker lasted just three years. During this period the Chinese government in power, the Nationalists, no longer had the leverage it once did against the Communists. Fighting resourcefully, relentlessly, and brilliantly the latter won not only battles but also, with its new ideology and promise of a better life, the hearts and minds of the people, 80% of them impecunious farmers.

In early 1949 the Nationalists retreated to the island of Taiwan. Despite president Chiang Kai-shek's oft repeated vows of retaking the mainland, he could only hope to stay in power and defend Taiwan against any possible invasion with the help of Washington, and in particular the Seventh Fleet, as bound by their mutual treaties.

In April 1949, one month before the People's Liberation Army took control of Shanghai, the Bank of China chartered a seaplane that flew its top officers and families, including ours and that of my godfather, S. W. Kung, to Hong Kong. After graduating from St. Stephen's, a British system high school, I began my new life in the States filled with hopes, dreams, and anticipation.

CHAPTER FIVE (1941–PRESENT)

Music

Of all the things I cared deeply about one stood out above all others: music. My particular passion was the piano. It gave me the greatest joy, a direction and purpose in life. It also proved to be the greatest challenge—and a tormentor at times. If I had no affinity for it I would never have spent so much time and effort. The problem was I had an abundance of musical feeling, and could identify so intimately with some composers, but for a long time lacked the means to express, being limited by my technical inadequacy. So playing the piano was all too often a struggle, trying to tame the beast, sometimes coming very close but almost never quite succeeding. Yet, so inspired by the beauty of music and the ingratiating ecstasy of playing, I never lost hope completely and gave up. I just had to reconcile to the fact that life was not perfect and playing the piano would at times leave a gap between what I heard in my head and what my fingers could deliver. The bottom line was as long as I could derive some pleasure from it I was willing to pay the price, no matter how dear.

Fortunately, my persistence paid off. I eventually was able to overcome enough adversities—including the trauma of nearly severing one finger in an accident and the agony of a disabled finger due to over-practicing—to rise to a higher level of proficiency, culminating in soloing with an orchestra.

I came from a family that was not entirely musical. Father never displayed the slightest interest in music but rented a piano for Mother. She had enough inclination to study with a German teacher and learned to play a few tunes but lost interest after a while. Intrigued by her playing, I started to tinkle with the instrument and was able to pluck out the Chinese national anthem with one finger. Upon this discovery my eldest brother David, who was a music lover, found a Mr. Chang to be my teacher.

When it was time for my first lesson, I was nowhere to be found, for I was hiding under my bed trying to avoid the dreadful ordeal. I had to be forcibly dragged out fighting with all my might, kicking, bawling, and screaming "wu bu yao, wu bu yao," or "I don't want! I don't want!" But at the age of seven I was no match against the powerful arms of my 22-year-old brother. I had no choice but to face my teacher with rebellion and tears. Subsequent lessons became a little less painful. I didn't mind spending a little time practicing daily but I was indifferent to music and didn't care if I learned anything. During the Sino-Japanese war when we moved to Chongqing, we had no piano for a couple of years, and I didn't miss it at all.

At the Holy Light Middle School the chapel had an upright piano that allowed me to reconnect with this instrument. One of my assignments was Bach's "Two-Part Invention #5" in F major. It was my introduction to the bard of baroque music and made a deep impression on me. Years later I became one of his greatest devotees, exulting especially in his seminal *Well-Tempered Clavier*, my veritable bible, which I tried to play daily. I also attended my first concert at Holy Light. I was struck particularly by the rendition of Chopin's "Polonaise in A flat, Op. 53" (nicknamed "Heroic Polonaise") by Paul Hu. I have been in love with this composer since.

Upon the end of the war I returned to Shanghai, my birthplace. Nicknamed "Pearl of the East," Shanghai even then was China's most vibrant, sophisticated, and cosmopolitan city. As such it attracted the best talent in every field of endeavor, from the arts, science, commerce, industry to education. Shanghai had another distinction: an open-door policy providing a sanctuary for numerous Jews from Russia and some 20,000 from Europe who had escaped from Nazi Germany, and built a thriving community with synagogues, schools, newspapers, hospitals, theaters, and sports leagues.

The city boasted five symphony orchestras, numerous musicians from Europe and Russia, and a great piano pedagogue, Mario Paci. Also a conductor of the Shanghai Municipal Orchestra, he trained a number of top students including Fou Ts'ong, who won third prize in the International Chopin piano competition; Yin Chengzong, who shared second prize in the Tchaikovsky competition with American pianist Susan Starr; and my sister-in-law, Susan Hsueh, David's wife, who clinched the first prize in a Texas competition playing Beethoven's first concerto with the Dallas Symphony.

Spurred by Shanghai's musical environment, I began to attend piano recitals. One featured a very famous pianist, Louise Woo, whose playing so impressed me that I became her pupil, but more out of curiosity and idol-worshiping than a sincere desire to learn. My interest in piano had not yet taken root; I was not well motivated and spent very little time practicing, to the disappointment of my teacher who told Mother "He is not on the right track," a polite way of saying I was a bad student, lacking diligence and talent.

At that time in the late 1940s, the Kuomintang regime failed miserably not only in the civil war but also financially. Inflation reached an unsustainable level and the administration kept printing money without collateral. When my teachers at St. Francis Xavier high school received their weekly wages in cash, they had to carry a large suitcase to stash the money. And unless they exchanged it into silver dollars promptly, the money would be depreciating drastically by the hour.

During these difficult economic times, Father made some prudent investments and earned enough money to exchange for one single gold bar which was even more stable than silver dollars. He generously purchased a new piano primarily for me. Having a better action and beautiful tone, it turned me into a more studious student as I found myself playing with greater frequency and appreciation. On the eve of April 26, 1949, before we left Shanghai for Hong Kong due to the imminent invasion by the Communists, I played way past midnight, unwilling to take leave of this magnificent piano.

On the British crown jewel, Father's employer, Bank of China, provided us with an apartment on a secluded, bucolic mountain in western Hong Kong with a spectacular panoramic view of the ocean. To see sunlight bouncing off the waters while a few ships sailed by now and then, against the backdrop of mountainous islands far and near, was a feast for the eyes. To add to the delight, Father rented a piano especially for me. Making music amid such a beautiful setting, I couldn't help but feel inspired. I began to bond with the piano as never before. Despite my limited technique, I mastered Chopin's "Fantaisie-Impromptu," a virtuoso piece with rhythmic complexity in which the right hand's four notes are pitted against left hand's triplets. The middle section is exceptionally beautiful. I bought a recording of this that I would play simultaneously virtually every day.

To continue my piano study, I became the student of Lau Chuan Wah. Trained in the U.S., she admitted she did not have a great technique. Like my other teachers, she never stressed the importance of fundamentals. She gave me no finger exercises, not even scales and arpeggios to work on. "You can develop technique from the pieces," she said. That advice was so ingrained in me that I adamantly refused to play anything other than pieces which were, of course, a lot more pleasant than the drudgery of finger-breaking, monotonous exercises. That turned out to be a terrible mistake.

Virtually all concert artists were child prodigies who took their first lessons at an early age and had acquired the requisite skills of a professional in their early teens. There were no late bloomers. It's my belief that only those young enough with supple muscles could develop a first-class virtuosity. But past certain age stiffness set in and no matter how one toiled, digital excellence could never be achieved. I heard in Russia that instrumental students started at the earliest possible age and spent their first seven years on pure technique. Having built a solid foundation, they would have the facility to play the most demanding compositions. I started at seven and a half, perhaps not yet too late but a handicap nevertheless. With the interruption by war years in China and being ignorant of such indispensable exercises as Czerny's "Op. 299" and "Op. 740" and other advanced etudes, I had never built a solid groundwork.

In 1950 as a high school senior I had no firm idea what my career goal was. My grades were not outstanding. At one time I toyed with the idea of studying electrical engineering only because one of my closest classmates, Larry Ho, had that aspiration. After being rejected by Harvard, I did not apply for any other school. During that time my family was applying for green cards and thought it might take a long time, possible years, before we could get them.

At a piano recital I came across the advertisement of a Sacred Music School and decided to enroll there. I was to meet a man who changed my life.

Stephen Shao was the school's director, a dedicated Christian, a noted composer of secular and sacred music, and a teacher of consummate talent. Fond of quoting the saying "Music is nourishment for the soul," he had a bellyful of inspiring stories about music and religion. One had to do with the genesis of a composition, an assignment from his conservatory. The theme was God's love. To gain practical experience, he wanted to know what it felt like to be beaten up or slapped by someone and then try to emulate God's grace by loving this person. So he purposely bumped into people on the streets to provoke anger and retaliation. But he failed utterly as nobody attacked him.

Disappointed, he noticed a decrepit old beggar with a thick beard foraging for food by going through garbage cans. Shao had just received a tiny stipend from his conservatory with which he bought a handful of much needed buns, for he had been starving for lack of funds. But deciding the poor old man had a greater need, he stealthily hid his buns next to one of the garbage cans and walked away to watch in secret, preferring to be an anonymous donor. When the pauper found the buns, Shao could observe that he was beaming through his thick beard. Shao in turn became elated for being able to express God's love by giving. That night he was inspired to write a composition that was truly beautiful and compelling.

I also began to compose. After our evening classes at Sacred Music School, Shao, who was always penurious, would take me to his squalid living quarters to correct my compositions and talk about music late into the night. Soon he also became my spiritual guru and best friend. Until then, away from the religious atmosphere of Holy Light Middle School, my Christian belief was no longer fervid. But Shao awoke my zeal to a feverish pitch and gave me a different outlook on music. I finally found my destiny: to be a professional musician, possibly a concert pianist, or a musical missionary back in Communist China to continue the mission of my grandfather, the minister.

In the summer of 1950, Father succeeded in getting green cards for the family. Everyone was jubilant at the golden opportunity to go to the New World—except me. I was stubbornly opposed to leaving Hong Kong because I wanted to continue my composition studies and association with Stephen Shao. Only after my parents' monumental effort and finally with the blessing of Shao, I reluctantly changed my mind. And in the September of 1950, we boarded the *President Cleveland* ship to begin our journey to America.

Among the passengers was a small group of college-bound Chinese and Japanese students. One would think the two could not mix well. After all, Japan in its insane plot to conquer all of Asia had invaded China and during the eight-year war had committed untold murders and atrocities. Not surprisingly, dozens of years later many Chinese still abhorred the Japanese and refused to buy their goods. But on board this ship only five years after the war, the two nationals were not only fellow passengers but kindred spirits, who shared the same goal of pursuing education in a great country with hope and excitement. Furthermore, thanks to the forgiving spirit of the Chinese and the Japanese willingness to accommodate, there was actually surprising rapprochement and even amity between the two factions; we overlooked our national backgrounds and differences and spent pleasurable hours conversing in a foreign tongue that plagued everyone equally: the obscure English language.

I was almost 17. With my inferiority complex temporarily in recess I had my first romantic fling with a Japanese girl with pretty eyes named Maria Suzuki. We never got physical, not even a little hugging, but achieved a mutual intimacy and warmth I never knew before. A music lover, she listened to my piano playing and hung on my every note. One day we got up at four in the morning to watch the sun rise. Sitting shoulder to shoulder, we did not need any words to express our deeply felt emotion. It was my first love—with a former enemy, no less—so unlikely and yet so memorable, like Romeo and Juliet. Chinese men had always felt that Japanese women made the best wives because of their absolute devotion, tender care, and selflessness toward their husbands. And I was blessed with a Japanese girlfriend! Upon our arrival in the U.S., Suzuki headed for a college in the Midwest and I for a college in West Texas, not knowing when we would meet again.

My family landed in San Francisco in mid-September 1950. After a short interval it was time for me to bid farewell to my parents. While they and my younger brother Henry left for Philadelphia to join my two older brothers, David and Harry, who had come to the U.S. earlier and were both students at Penn, I headed for Wayland College in Plainview, a tiny West Texas town near Lubbock.

I didn't start off very well. During the first week I attended my first wrestling match. It was an exciting experience and all night long I was dreaming about this sport. At one point I dreamed that someone had picked me up and violently thrown me down. At that very moment I tumbled down from my upper bunk bed and landed on my neck. It made a loud noise that woke up my roommates. Noticing I was moaning in great pain, they alerted the authorities, who sent me by ambulance to a hospital. An X-ray showed that I had cracked the sixth vertebrae. I ended up staying in the hospital for several days with a 20-pound weight around my neck to help heal the crack. Although I fully recovered I refused ever to sleep on an upper bunk bed unless it had a guard rail.

While the faculty members at Wayland were mostly southerners, my piano teacher David Appleby was a Brazilian-born American. He was the son of a missionary and a graduate of the Juilliard School of Music where he had studied with two famous pianists, Carl Friedberg and Lonny Epstein. I was particularly struck by his fingers. Their tips were so flattened that they were almost twice the size of the other finger joints. This was obviously the result of his extraordinarily strenuous piano practice from an early age.

Unfortunately, he was misled by my playing of Chopin's "Fantaisie-Impromptu," thinking I was a highly advanced student, and asked me to tackle the monstrously difficult Beethoven's fourth piano concerto when I had never even learned a simple sonata.

I was doing a little better in Chopin's "Etude in F major," "Op. 10 No. 8" and occasionally performed Schubert's "Impromptu in A Flat" that has a soulful, lyrical middle section. But I made almost no headway with Beethoven. It didn't help that I still thought I could learn technique from playing pieces and not exercises, being ignorant that one had to learn to crawl before walking. So I just doggedly practiced, practiced, and practiced. I always remembered Father's oft repeated adage in German, "Ubung macht den meister," or "practice makes perfect." But it was not totally true. A more appropriate axiom should be "CORRECT practice makes perfect." Consequently, despite my hard work my progress was painfully slow.

In contrast, I did well as a choir member. My big job was learning Handel's "Messiah." Though I enjoyed singing, I had never taken a lesson and the tenor part was quite difficult. However, my piano background helped me read the score and master the thorny passages. To think that Handel composed this lengthy oratorio in 24 short days is truly mind-boggling. Especially awe-inspiring is the famous Hallelujah chorus with its architectural grandeur, sheer exuberance, and rousing spirit. No wonder when Queen Victoria first heard it in a concert she was moved so profoundly that she stood up, thereby establishing a tradition for the audience ever since. With several talented Wayland voice majors handling the arias, we performed this masterpiece in a number of venues including the riveting experience of singing with a full orchestra.

As much as I loved Wayland, I, however, stayed there for only one year. I knew I desperately needed a change in direction but didn't know how to achieve it. In discussing my musical future, Appleby suggested that I might do better by studying with one of his former teachers: Lonny Epstein at Juilliard, located then at 122nd St. and Claremont Avenue in Manhattan (before moving to Lincoln Center). And in the summer of 1951, I enrolled at that school's extension department, and Epstein accepted me as her pupil.

Born in Germany, she was an illustrious Mozart specialist, owned a duplicate of his piano (with the black keys white and white keys black), and performed worldwide and annually at the Salzburg Festival. She did notice my technical deficiency and immediately started me on Clementi's "Gradus ad Parnassum," along with Bach's "Three-Part Inventions" and "Well-Tempered Clavier" (WTC). Our goal was to try to enroll at Juilliard in September. To comply with the audition requirements, Epstein picked the "C Minor Prelude and Fugue" from Book One of the WTC, Beethoven's "Opus 10 No. 1 in C Minor," Mendelssohn's "Songs without Words" in E major and a selection from Bartok's "Mikrokosmos." It was not a very difficult program. But given my lack of proficiency, would I be able to master it in three short summer months?

I had dabbled in the famed "Moonlight Sonata" and felt I could relate well to Beethoven. Still, I always had doubts about my ability to express my deep feelings, and no teacher had ever complimented me. Hence, I was pleasantly surprised by Epstein's comment when I played the C minor sonata: "You have talent." Having always suffered from a lack of self-assurance, I never thought I was gifted in any way, but Epstein's words gave me a ray of hope for the first time. Unfortunately, she added: "But you don't know how to treat the piano."

Shortly after the summer session began at Juilliard I met a

tall, lanky man with bushy red hair in the hallway. A very friendly person, he stretched his hand to me and said with a heavy southern accent: "Howdy! My name is Van Cliburn. What's yours?" He said he was from Texas and was delighted that I had just attended college there. And like me, he was enrolling at Juilliard for the first time in the summer of 1951. While we never socialized with each other, he always greeted me warmly and exchanged a few words of pleasantries whenever we met. I was to see a lot of him in the master piano classes taught by the marvelous German pianist Carl Friedberg, who had studied with Clara Schumann, Robert's wife, and taught such pupils as Malcolm Frager and William Masselos.

I was the least gifted student in that class and never played, but many were eager to perform and get pointers from Friedberg. One was a frail young woman. After playing Mozart's "Sonata K. 332 in F Major," she elicited very severe criticisms from Friedberg. She instantly broke into unstoppable crying. Friedberg was totally stunned and visibly embarrassed. With great contrition he tried to console her unsuccessfully. And for about 10 minutes the class stood deadly quiet except for the sobbing. She eventually recovered but never played again.

Other students fared better and one in particular excelled with great confidence, brilliance, and romantic flair and was clearly the most outstanding talent: Van Cliburn. He performed often and invariably got high praises (except for his playing of Bach which Friedberg loathed). In 1958 when he made front page news as the first prize winner of the Tchaikovsky competition in Moscow during the height of the Cold War, members of this master piano class were overjoyed to have known him and been exposed to his genius before the world discovered him.

One fellow student who did become my very close friend was Georg Sementovsky. Already a concert pianist, he was studying with the same teacher as Van Cliburn: Rosina Levine. I had never met anyone quite like him. He was the most gregarious, garrulous, and warmest person one could come across. We hit it off instantly. Having an amazing breadth of musical knowledge, he introduced me to such eminent pianists as Friederich Gulda, who was equally at home playing classical music and jazz; Dinu Lipatti, who sadly died at the age of 33 and whose recital recording shortly before his death became one of my treasured collections; Benedetti Michelangeli, acclaimed as the "new Liszt"; and Solomon (last name was Cutner which he never used professionally), especially renowned for his Beethoven. Another well-regarded pianist was known more for his comic talent than his music making: Victor Borge. He possessed an unparalleled sense of humor and some of his antics including the famed "phonetic punctuation" were absolutely hilarious.

Knowing Sementovsky loved to have a good laugh, I told him a number of jokes. Two that he enjoyed the most were factual and concerned the Chinese statesman Wellington Koo:

- While a student at Columbia, his English was so outstanding that he became editor of the *Spectator*, the university's daily. When he visited a friend at Princeton, a Caucasian student out of curiosity with a little haughtiness asked him: "Are you Chinese, Japanese, or Siamese?" Koo retorted: "Are you monkey, Yankee, or donkey?"

- As a participant representing China in the formation of the League of Nation, he was invited to a big banquet in London. Sitting next to him was an Englishman who thought Koo could speak only Pidgin English. When the first course was served, he asked Koo "likee soupie?" A perfect gentleman, Koo smiled back politely but did not say a word. Upon the arrival of the entree the Englishman asked: "Likee you fishee?" Again, a courteous smile from Woo without talking back. At the end of the banquet the host told the guests they were honored to have Koo as the speaker. Koo, who had earned a Ph.D. in international law and diplomacy from Columbia and served as ambassador to France and Great Britain, gave a brilliant talk. As he was sitting down he asked the Englishman: "Likee speechie?"

No laughing matter, however, were my studies with Epstein. They were not progressing well. My technique remained underdeveloped, making it impossible to master my audition pieces in three short months. Deciding to remain in New York in the fall of 1952, I enrolled at Columbia as a music major while continuing my lessons with Epstein.

I had much less time to practice. Indeed, it was among my busiest times. My piano playing was further complicated by having little access to a good instrument. Once in a while I would go to Barnard College to play its grand piano or sneak into Juilliard to play a Steinway in one of its practice rooms.

Against all odds, I still aspired to be a concert pianist. But I came very close to cutting my aspiration short. In my part-time job I was washing a tall glass at Columbia University's Faculty Club kitchen with an automatic brushing machine. When I lost my grip of the glass, instead of stopping the machine I stupidly reached deep inside with my right hand to retrieve it and felt a sharp, lacerating pain. I pulled my hand out instantly and found my right small finger not only bleeding but cut open with the white bone exposed. Realizing this finger was almost severed, I was horror stricken and rushed to the nearest hospital where a doctor sewed up the opening. To my great relief, he assured me that I could still play the piano.

Trying very hard to change my career choice was my pragmatic father who knew while I had a little talent it wasn't enough to make a career and that only the most gifted could succeed in the highly competitive profession. Again and again he gently tried in vain to talk me out of it. In desperation, he once took the trouble to write a two-page letter to dissuade me—to avoid face-to-face confrontation. Yet no matter how often he failed, he never forced the issue by withdrawing financial support.

One day he was helpful enough to take me to Yale University in New Haven, CT, to explore the possibilities of being a piano performance major (Columbia did not have such a program). In my audition for the chairman of the music department I played the Beethoven "C Minor Sonata." He liked it and accepted me. It was a tempting offer. Though Yale was no Juilliard, it might be a good alternative and had some top teachers. But after careful deliberation, I decided I would be better off remaining at Columbia while continuing my studies with Epstein in the hope of having another shot at Juilliard in the near future.

Around that time I was delighted to be adopted by a warm and lovely couple, Dr. and Mrs. S. W. Kung, whom I first met in Shanghai, as their godson. (When a Chinese couple develop intense fondness for a youngster, it's customary to adopt the person as their godson or goddaughter as an affirmation of their affection, a testament to the bond. It has no religious connotations and involves no specific ceremony but is celebrated with a dinner sometimes.) Dr. Kung was Father's intimate friend and colleague at the Bank of China. We were neighbors in Hong Kong, where I spent many pleasant hours playing bridge with his son Eddy and daughter Lee.

To get away from my hectic life at Columbia, I always looked forward to calling on the family in Little Neck, NY, which also included two other offspring, Robert and Nancy.

However, lacking social grace and maturity, I invariably began my visits with horrible behavior. As soon as I entered the door, I would utter a quick word of greeting and immediately head for their piano to start practicing without even a moment's socializing. It was gracious of the Kungs not to take offense at my rudeness. They obviously realized I was an incurable piano nut and that I must be desperately starving for the instrument. In time they actually grew increasingly fond of me—and vice versa—culminating in adopting me as their godson. As a lone soul who still suffered the aftereffects of sibling rivalry while craving for parental love and approval, I could not be more grateful and was elated to be so embraced and be part of the surrogate family whose children became my fond godbrothers and godsisters.

Another person who cared for me a great deal was Maria Suzuki, whom I had met on board the *President Cleveland* and was the first girlfriend I ever had. We never exchanged correspondence during our one and three-quarter years' separation, and so I didn't know how she stood with me. Then out of the blue she came to visit me all the way from her college in the Midwest one summer day, apparently still carrying a torch for me. I could not help but being touched. We spent half a day together during which I took her to Juilliard to play the piano for her. She listened attentively as before with her pretty eyes betraying a deeper emotion. But alas, my passion toward her diminished considerably; I just could not revive the way I had felt about her once. My inferiority complex might also have been a factor in rejecting any woman who tried to get too close to me. We politely bade "sayonara" to each other, and I regretted the pain I must have caused her.

While I dated a couple of women from Barnard College, they were of passing interest. To broaden my social circle, I did something unthinkable two years before at Wayland:

dancing, which was considered sinful and forbidden. I discovered it actually was not only a wonderful social form but also a good way to relax. Enrolled in a dance class in an auditorium at Columbia's Teacher's College, I was disappointed there were no coeds. So my introduction to foxtrot and the like was to dance with someone of my own gender. It was, of course, quite awkward holding a Caucasian male as my partner who was as stiff, graceless, and inept as I. Nevertheless, that did not detract my interest from learning. Indeed, a few years later I became a most avid dancer delighting in everything from samba, rumba, cha cha, tango to disco, and even won a prize for dancing in a talent contest on a Bermuda cruise.

Meanwhile my piano studies with Lonny Epstein advanced so little that I was convinced I should set my goal on another profession. There was no reason for me to stay in New York and so I moved to Philadelphia to live with my parents. My oldest brother David, who was a surgeon at that city's Methodist Hospital, inspired me to follow his footsteps.

As a pre-med at Penn, my favorite course was cat anatomy. The animal assigned to me had triple color-injected arteries. Unfortunately, a few weeks into my dissection I discovered there were some ruptured arteries which would render any further dissection impractical. With a new cat I had to catch up. I went to the lab one evening, working so absorbingly and enjoyably that I became unmindful as to the time. When I finished it was around six in the morning. I had been working some 10 hours straight. I did not feel tired. Instead, I went home refreshed and joyful. Possibly my ambidextrous, long pianist's hands helped my dissection. At the end of the semester my professor, knowing my aspiration, told me "You'll make a fine surgeon." His remark gratified not only me but my brother David, for we were contemplating a Lin Bothers' clinic specializing in surgery someday.

Despite my heavy pre-med schedule, I was still inseparable from music; I was taking orchestration at Penn and looking for a piano teacher. Philadelphia had always been a great music city with its incomparable orchestra, the Curtis Institute of Music, Academy of Vocal Arts, and other good schools and there was no lack of wonderful piano teachers. I found one at the Philadelphia Conservatory: Claire Brown.

At the end of every semester I was required to perform for and be graded by the conservatory directors, Mr. and Mrs. Drake. Invariably, they gave me A's. However, I was never too excited by the grades, thinking that I didn't fully deserve them, or that they were overly exaggerated or a fluke. Such was my screwed-up psychology. Having low self-esteem, I craved approbation in the worst way. But when I did get it, I tended to downplay it.

Usually well prepared for my lessons with Brown, once I played a piece badly for lack of practice. Having a sense of humor, instead of chiding me she commended my playing with feigned enthusiasm: "You played so well today. You could sight-read so beautifully!"

Brown was a close friend of William Kapell and Eugene List. The three had studied with Olga Samaroff (married once to conductor Leopold Stokowski) at the Philadelphia Conservatory. A good raconteur, she told me a bizarre anecdote about her two colleagues: They went to a fortune-teller whose predictions turned out to be eerily true. The gypsy told Kapell that he would not live to be 32 and List would never rise above a certain level of high achievement. Indeed, the latter, a brilliant pianist who had soloed with the Los Angeles Orchestra at the age of 12 and Philadelphia Orchestra at 16, went on to achieve a distinguished career. But he never reached super stardom, soaring to the heights of some of his peers like Kapell.

In 1953 Kapell, who was proclaimed by Leon Fleisher as "the greatest pianist talent that this country has produced," after playing concerts in Australia was planning to join his wife in the States. Arriving at the airport before the scheduled flight, he decided to take an earlier one. That ended in a collision with a mountain near San Francisco and everyone on board died. Kapell was 31.

Pursuing my latest goal of being a physician, I began to apply for medical schools in my senior year at Penn. The few that interviewed me did not think my grades were good enough, which admittedly were just slightly above average. But through the help of my brother David and more importantly, his boss and chief of surgery at Methodist Hospital, Dr. Willauer, who was closely connected to Jefferson Medical College, I was admitted. I graduated from Penn in January 1957 with a BA in chemistry. With some eight months to go before starting at Jefferson in September, I got a job as a chemist at the Atlantic Refinery. I had a rough schedule alternating the three shifts: 8:00 A.M. to 4:00 P.M., 4:00 P.M. to midnight, and from midnight to 8:00 A.M. But I had a lot more free time. So I began to spend hours on the piano. I had been working on Beethoven's "Piano Sonata in C Major Op. 1 No. 3," and one day heard that piece played by Wilhelm Kemp on my car radio. I was so inspired that not only my passion for the piano returned in full force but my once abandoned dream of becoming a concert pianist became alive again, against the advice of everyone, including my teacher Claire Brown. Consequently, some lucky applicant to Jefferson on the waiting list took my place as freshman of the class of 1957, and I forfeited my $178 deposit.

Needing a better job and source of income, I accepted an offer from Merck as an analytical chemist in its Philadelphia plant. My shift was from 4:30 P.M. to 1:00 A.M., a huge improvement over the three alternating shifts I had with Atlantic Refinery.

Walking on the campus of Penn, I was happy to run into

my friend from Juilliard: George Sementovsky. Instead of discouraging me from pursuing a pianist career, he recommended one of his teachers, Madam Olga Stroumillo, a Russian émigré living in New York. After playing one of Bach's WTC preludes and fugues I became her latest pupil and began my weekly trip for my lessons.

Unlike most of my piano teachers, Stroumillo was not a concert artist but was one of the most revered teachers who was assistant to the well-known teacher Isabelle Vengerova. Both studied with Theodor Leschetizky, who had taught Paderewski and Schnabel. Leschetizky in turn studied with Carl Czerny, who was Beethoven's pupil. A large woman, she also had large hands, which she said were not the most conducive for a concert pianist. She liked the size and shape of my fingers and said they were wonderful pianist's hands. Her teaching followed the typical Russian school by stressing fundamentals.

Contradicting my theory that technique could be learned only at a very tender age, she assured me otherwise. In addition to the daily regimen of scales and arpeggios, she told me to spend one hour each on Pischna and Schmitt, the two most boring and tortuous exercises. When muscles and independence of the fingers were sufficiently developed, I would work with more melodious exercises, and then progress to Chopin Etudes and other advanced studies. "In time you'd develop the facility to play anything." These words were so reassuring that I redoubled my effort. Perhaps I found a sure way to success, a formula to acquire what had seemed impossible.

She also assigned some pieces like Schubert's "Impromptu in E Flat," Schumann's "Romance in G Sharp Major" and "Novellette in D Minor"—all of which were a nice respite from the monotonous exercises. The one thing she emphasized repeatedly: playing piano was a matter of pressing the keyboard. And volume should be achieved by the speed with which one pressed the keys. In other words, to get a louder sound, press faster and a softer one, slower. For lyrical passages "play them as if the whole world's survival depended on how beautifully you played."

Another thing she stressed was to play from the gut, the seat of deep emotions. Indeed, the Chinese have a similar observation and a well-known expression describing the nadir of sadness as "duan chuan" or broken gut. I have always felt when instrumentalists put all their feelings into their fingers from deep inside there is no need for any extraneous gestures. That was why I cringed every time I saw a pianist or violinist displaying an array of tortured facial expressions. In contrast, I better enjoyed artists exemplified by the absolute impassiveness of Jascha Heifetz.

Stroumillo was notorious as a taskmaster who often treated her pupils roughly. I heard that some of them would leave the lessons in tears never to come back. I had more than a little taste of her tyranny and severity. If I didn't press the piano as instructed, she would be very angry. Once I played something not to her liking and she screamed: "THIS IS NOT A CIRCUS!" making me feel like the scum of the earth. But for the sake of learning I swallowed my pride and never gave up. At home before going to Merck to work at 4:30 P.M., I spent six hours a day practicing. I was determined to succeed.

My studies with Stroumillo at one point actuated a change of emphasis. She became concerned that my thumbs were too rigid when playing the scale. The rigidity would impede the playing and even cause pain. Repeatedly she told me to relax them.

Following her method to change, I must have overdone it and to my horror I developed a disabled right index finger. It had no strength as if totally paralyzed. At first I was hoping I could solve the problem with self-designed exercises including the addition of weight to the finger. Nothing came of it. Next I sought the help of a hand specialist. He could detect nothing wrong organically but gave me diathermia treatments with no positive results. Was I doomed to the fate of two venerable pianists, Gary Graffman and Leon Fleisher? Both ruined their right hands from over practice. They sought help from the same specialist. After many years' therapy Fleischer regained the use of his injured hand with Botox injections but Graffman never did.

Whatever the reason for my disability, it was obvious I had reached a dead end. In utter despair, I abandoned my piano studies and stopped playing. I had already given up the possibility of becoming a surgeon. Now with no future in music I was a broken man with no known destiny. Worse, it was at this lowest depth that I got drafted by the army.

During my tour of duty my finger injury made a miraculous recovery, and I was so happy to return to my beloved piano. Discharged on December 1, 1959, I returned to Philadelphia and resumed my chemist's job at Merck. Meanwhile I decided to continue my musical studies for self-amusement. At the Settlement Music School I had the good fortune of being assigned to a terrific teacher, the Polish concert artist Marian Filar. Unlike Stroumillo he was gentle, kind, supportive and inspirational.

During one lesson he told me about a sensational Chinese teenage pianist by the name of Fou Ts'ong, a Shanghai native. In Poland he had studied with one of the most celebrated teachers, Zbigniew Drzewiecki, who had also taught Filar. Fou played Chopin with an understanding and flair that won the absolute adoration of the Poles. In 1955 he garnered third prize in the International Chopin competition and a special prize in Chopin's Mazurkas. Later he made London his permanent home, where by coincidence he became a good friend of my Holy Light classmate George Wong, who had also told me about him. So I eagerly awaited a chance to hear him in person.

That opportunity came in 1961 when he made his American debut at Carnegie Hall playing Chopin's "F Minor Piano Concerto." A total revelation to me, the performance reflected a keen grasp of style, rhythmic elasticity, temperament, and poetic beauty.

When I went backstage to greet him and asked him if he would like my company during his short stay in New York, happily he agreed. For the next 10 days or so we were together every waking moment. I took him to some of the best Chinese restaurants and entertained him with my raunchy jokes, and he invited me to his subsequent concerts including a recital in which he blew me over with the rendition of Schubert's "Ninth Sonata."

Our conversations frequently touched on Mozart with whom he also closely identified. He was especially fond of the Austrian's late piano concertos, ranking them among the pantheon of the greatest masterpieces. To him an essential quality to do justice to Mozart's music was "charm," which he found sorely missing as we attended a recital by a well-known piano duo. I had a special treat accompanying him to Steinway Hall to select a piano for an upcoming concert. In the cavernous basement there were numerous concert grands cluttered together. Also trying one out was the distinguished English pianist Clifford Curzon, whom I had long admired and was thrilled to meet. After the two exchanged warm greetings, Fou began to play snippets of music from piano to piano, listening to the tone quality and checking the keyboard action. It was like a mini recital.

However, we were utterly repulsed by Harold Schonberg's incredibly racist review of his debut concert in the *New York Times*. Known in the music circle as an erratic and biased critic, Schonberg had earned nothing but scorn from many of my musician friends. Moreover, he was a mean-spirited man.

In reviewing a Glenn Gould recital, he observed that the Canadian had carried a glass of water to the piano. Instead of sympathizing with the plight of a performing artist who sometimes might get dehydrated, Schoenberg wrote: "What next, a ham sandwich?" His impairment in judgment was also evidenced by his panning of Leonard Bernstein's conducting and doubts about Gould's technical prowess.

Concerning Fou's concert, he scathingly attacked the Chinese for "his accident of birth in which he was not exposed during his formative years to the ambience that nourishes a great Western musician," and hence he could not "hurdle the cultural barriers" and would "seem to be alien to the essentially Franco-Polish idiom of a Chopin." He went on to say Fou's musical conception was "heavy and sometimes awkward with little of the grace, charm, or sophistication that the 'Chopin F Minor' contains." And his playing was "almost elephantine." Had Schonberg done some research, he would have discovered that during Fou's childhood in Shanghai it was a great international metropolis where Western music was prevalent, and that it was graced with five symphony orchestras and top-notch Western musicians including the renowned Mario Paci, Fou's teacher. Furthermore, Schonberg was blind to the fact that Fou had gone to study in Poland in his teens, won prizes in the Chopin competition, and had given some 200 concerts in Europe to rave reviews.

I wrote a letter of protest to the *Times* saying that Mr. Schonberg had a prejudiced mind and his criticisms were without merit. We ended up having a pen duel. In a rebuttal he bragged about his association with legendary pianist Joseph Hoffman who had given him special insight into the "F Minor Concerto." He also averred that no Chinese pianist had achieved international fame. I informed him that in the year Van Cliburn won first prize in the International Tchaikovsky Competition, an 18-year-old Chinese, Liu Shikun, won second prize, not to mention the fact that Fou had already achieved international fame before he made his New York debut.

At a repeat performance of the "F Minor Concerto" a few days later, I ran into Eugene List who later served as a juror in the Tchaikovsky Piano Competition. Commenting on the Schonberg review, he said he disagreed with it 100%, that it was unfair, inaccurate, and demeaning. Indeed, he thought Fou was enormously gifted. Later, in a program note pianists Martha Argerich, Leon Fleischer, and Radu Lupu jointly lauded Fou's musicianship and Chopin interpretation and that he was "one of the greatest pianists of our time." But permanent damage was done by Schonberg. In a subsequent concert playing Mozart's last concerto, Fou told me the critic had so rattled him that he felt self-conscious and a little nervous, although he "knew the piece backwards." Unfortunately, the *Times* was such an influential paper and carried so much weight that it wounded Fou severely. Furthermore, after making some uncomplimentary remarks about the 1967 Six-Day Arab-Israeli War, he alienated some powerful people in Jewish circles. Consequently, he seldom performed again in New York.

I met him a few years later when he sadly relayed a family tragedy. Under the persecution of the Red Guards during the Cultural Revolution, his father Fou Lei, a man of letters and China's greatest translator of French literature, committed suicide. Shortly afterward his mother followed suit. I fully empathized with him and shared his grief as I recalled my brother Harry, who also took his own life under the persecution of Communist China.

Like Fou, my Jewish teacher Marian Filar also suffered a horrible family tragedy. Sent to Majdanek and other concentration camps during World War II, he and a brother survived, but his parents and a sister were murdered as chronicled in his riveting memoir *From Buchenwald to Carnegie Hall*. He later studied with Walter Gieseking, the greatest interpreter of Debussy and Ravel, and established a concert career internationally, having soloed with the Philadelphia, Chicago, and National Orchestras, and performed in Europe, South America, Israel, and Mexico. Luckily his New York debut concert was reviewed by a more perceptive critic from the *Times*, Anthony Tommasini: "Filar's incomparable technical facility is in the service of his utterly elegant musicianship. The performances are fleet, supple, and beautifully nuanced. He plays with flair and rhapsodic freedom, but never at the expense of musical structure and textual lucidity . . . truly impressive performances."

I studied with him for five years during which I learned a lot and progressed fast. A Chopin specialist, he taught me some of the nuances of interpreting this, the greatest of all piano composers. Commenting on rubato, he said it was a wonderful expressive tool, but one had to be careful in using it. He recalled how Chopin elucidated its subtlety to a pupil by lighting a candle. He then blew softly at it so that the flame flickered a little but came back to life. That's the proper way to play rubato, Chopin said. He next blew hard on the candle and the flame died. "That's how you played rubato." Filar also quoted an adage attributed to Chopin: "An aristocrat never rushes."

In addition Filar offered valuable tips on playing Bach. In his polyphonic writing, sometimes two voices at times may seem to merge into a single continuous line. One must not make the mistake of executing them as such. Instead, each voice should always remain a separate, distinct entity as intended by the composer, and never to comingle with any other voices. Yet I repeatedly came across pianists—including Bach specialists—who ignored this contrapuntal dictum which certainly detracted from the listening pleasure.

He broadened my repertoire with Bartok's Rumanian

Dances as well as impressionistic music and said I had "affinity" for Debussy when I played his "Suite Bergamasque" and Preludes. He also praised me for playing trills easily with the thumb and index finger, a challenging feat for many amateur pianists. Noticing my rapid improvement in technical facility, he assigned me Mozart's "Piano Concerto #21 in C Major, K. 467." It boasts a regal, Beethovenian first movement, an ingratiating second movement, and a playful rondo. It's a credit to Filar's guidance and encouragement that I thrillingly mastered this concerto and performed it in different venues a few years later.

Knowing his penchant for Chinese food, I occasionally invited him to the banquets I organized for my close friends. A talented raconteur, he invariably dominated the conversation and held everyone spellbound by his fascinating anecdotes. One concerned his long association with Walter Gieseking, whom he had idolized as the world's greatest pianist. Initially Gieseking was loathe to meet this total stranger who came to seek career counseling without a referral or even an appointment. But moved by Filar's pianism, especially his Chopin and his plight as a recent Holocaust survivor, the German volunteered to teach him gratis, took him under his wing, and made extraordinary efforts to help advance his career.

When I last met him in 2006 he was 89, still lucid and energetic. He said I was one of his best pupils, which came as a total surprise, and that it was his great regret *From Buchenwald to Carnegie Hall* was not made into a movie as was Wladyslaw Szpilman's memoir, which inspired Roman Polanski to direct the Oscar winner *The Pianist*.

Filar's life certainly had the makings of a compelling movie. Indeed, he enjoyed a more prominent career, having performed more extensively, gained greater recognition, soloed with more leading orchestras of the world with eminent conductors like Eugene Ormandy, Erich Leinsdorf, and Rafael Kubelik, and achieved fame as a Chopin specialist with few equals. In addition, he had participated in the Warsaw Ghetto Uprising and his concentration camp ordeal—including closer brushes with death, extreme starvation, and a severely mutilated finger (inflicted on him by a German guard for falling asleep on the job)—was more harrowing and dramatic. Unfortunately, his timing was off as his memoir was not published until 2002, the same year *The Pianist* was released. He died in 2011 at the age of 94.

The mid-1960s were among my busiest years, holding on to my chemist's job, marketing my Chinese food, and serving as president of Philadelphia's Chinese community. Hence, I suspended my piano lessons. When I resumed I decided to gain a different perspective by studying with Natalie Hinderas, a pretty, gracious young African American whose credits included soloing with the Philadelphia, Chicago, Los Angeles, Cleveland, and San Francisco orchestras.

It was during my five-year studies that she gave birth to a lovely daughter. Because Michelle looked surprisingly Chinese, I might have aroused suspicion of being a Lothario who had played footsie with my teacher—between an ode to "Salut d'Amour" and a tune of "Liebestraume." In truth, Hinderas' husband Lionel Monagas was from Trinidad where some natives had mixed blood, the result of interracial marriages with Chinese immigrants.

A marvelous teacher was Filar; she made every lesson a high mark and commended my playing of the Mozart "C Major Concerto." Going beyond the call of duty, she rented the Art Alliance to showcase her students. She accompanied me on that concerto which went well and paved the way for greater things to come: my soloing with a chamber orchestra.

This couldn't have happened had I not changed jobs.

In 1964 I transferred from Merck to DuPont, first as an

analytical chemist in Gibbstown, NJ, and then to its headquarters in Wilmington, DE, as a marketing executive, spurred by my experience as a won ton entrepreneur. I was happy to discover that a giant chemical company had enough interest in the arts to sponsor a chamber orchestra. I arranged to audition for its conductor, Fred, a Princeton, NJ, resident. I played the first and last movements of the Mozart concerto on an upright piano which, of course, was not quite the same as a grand piano. Articulation was more difficult and trying to effect a beautiful singing tone was well-nigh impossible. But I played with confidence. In one rapid passage, Fred even uttered "Bravo!" and I thankfully earned a spot as a soloist in the next concert.

In the coming weeks, I rehearsed with the same upright piano without being able to realize my full potential. I was reminded of a well-known Confucius axiom in his Analects: "Doing a job well requires appropriate tools." How I longed for a concert grand.

Shortly before our scheduled concert I was allowed to select such a piano from Steinway's nearest franchise in Philadelphia. Recalling the time when I accompanied Fou Ts'ong to select his piano in New York's Steinway Hall, I was excited now by the opportunity and felt vicariously like a famed pianist, going from piano to piano to select the optimal one. Steinway grand pianos might all be great instruments but they did differ in the action, tone, nuance, and persona. That's why a few concert artists like Horowitz habitually brought their own pianos around the world to perform. And Filar had his 80-year-old but elegant Steinway shipped from Germany to his American residence.

Finally, I was able to rehearse with a Steinway of my choice and what a difference it made! No more requests of "more tone" from Fred, and I had no more worry about the lack of articulation. I felt totally at ease and eagerly awaited my debut.

That took place at the DuPont Country Club in Wilmington. DE, on a wet Sunday afternoon in June 1968. After the orchestra opened with Schubert's "Rosamunde Overture," I plunged into the concerto—not without a little trepidation. But it disappeared as soon as my fingers struck the keyboard. I went on to tackle the first movement with aplomb, glorying in the virtuoso intricacies, dramatic sweep, majestic music, and stirring thematic development. When I concluded with a cadenza by Solima Stravinsky, son of Igor (Mozart did not write one for this concerto), Fred gave me a two-fingered "A-okay" gesture with a smile. The slow movement (adapted as the theme song of the movie *Elvira Madigan*) seemed deceptively simple but required great artistry to fully capture and illuminate its poetry and charm. Mindful of my teacher Stroumillo's exhortation on lyric passages, I tried to play "as if the whole world's survival depended on how beautifully I played." In the last movement I aspired to be bouncy, jaunty, and fast—yet well-articulated and not rushed—while savoring the brief but delightful dialogue between the orchestra and piano. Enhancing my performance was Fred's astute musicianship and incomparable collaboration that synchronized with my every move.

Otto Dekom of the *Wilmington News* reviewed the concert and praised generously. Not knowing my years of hard work and dedication, he said it must be very difficult for a DuPont ex-chemist and marketing man to rise to the challenge and lauded me as an "excellent pianist." I reprised the concerto with Fred several times elsewhere against my will because no grand piano was available, and I had to cope with a loathsome upright piano. Otherwise, soloing with an orchestra was singularly my most satisfying and happiest experience.

During the years before and after 1968, I got acquainted with two Taiwanese violin students successively: Michael Ma and Huei-Sheng Kao.

I met Ma, a child prodigy, in a circuitous way. As president of Philadelphia's Chinese community, I had the official duty to welcome his sister, Dolly Ma, as Miss China (Republic of China, known later as Republic of Taiwan), a striking beauty who went on to place eighth in the Miss Universe contest. Discovering I was a music lover, she asked me if her brother, who was to study with Ivan Galamian at Curtis, could stay with my family. I was more than happy to accommodate. To have a talented musician with what appeared to be a great future at my house would give me infinite joy. Despite our age disparity (I was 27), from the very outset we became bosom friends and hung out together as much as possible. I asked him to perform for the Chinese community, took him to New York to meet with Fou Ts'ong and his then wife, Zamira (Yehudi Menuhin's daughter), invited him to parties, cast him in a skit I wrote, and treated him to my cooking. In return, he gave me the thrill of playing duos together, and introduced me to two Curtis violin classmates with whom I also had fun making music: Yung Uck Kim, who was to become an internationally acclaimed artist; and Eliot Chapo, the future concertmaster of the New York Philharmonic and Dallas Symphony. In addition, Michael got me a paying job accompanying a violin friend of his in Mendelssohn's "E Minor Concerto."

Ma was a great charmer, a pretty boy with long eyelashes, who had an uncanny way of reaching women's hearts. Even at his young age, he started to have liaisons. Like Chapo, he loved having a good time and going to parties and both started to neglect their violin practice and schoolwork. While Chapo was able to get by and eventually graduated from Curtis, Ma did not. After finishing his studies at New School of Music, he, nonetheless, achieved a notable career, soloing frequently and serving as the concertmaster of such orchestras as the Oklahoma Symphony, Hong Kong Philharmonic, and Santa Fe Opera.

My other 13-year-old friend was Huei-Sheng Kao, nick-named Cowboy. He gave his first concert at eight and per-formed the Mendelssohn "Violin Concerto" at 11. Two years later, he entered Curtis and also stayed in my house, having heard about me from Ma. Unlike Ma, he was a very diligent student under the tutelage of Ivan Galamian and Jaime Laredo. Upon graduation, he immediately got a job with the Pittsburgh Symphony Orchestra where he later became the assistant concertmaster.

If his musical talent was obvious, his investment acumen was totally unknown until his move to Pittsburgh. There he taught himself all the intricacies, complex instruments, so-phisticated maneuvering of making money in the uncertain investment world. Doing original research, he had a perfect pitch for stocks that had extraordinary potential. With no exceptions, I made out like a bandit after the few times I acted on his recommendations. Furthermore, his winning strategy did not depend on bull markets. "It doesn't matter if the market is up or down," he said. "As long as there is movement I can make money." Once I asked him "How did you do last year?" "Oh, I made about one and a half million dollars," he said casually.

Not surprisingly, he was constantly bombarded by people seeking his advice. When Pittsburgh Orchestra's management learned about his extra-musical genius, it asked him to manage the players' pension and he succeeded in making double digit returns. With all the wealth he was amassing, he could have long retired. But his love for music made him stay with the ensemble while soloing with various orchestras from time to time.

Way before meeting Kao, I got interested in the stock market in 1957 when I began my job as a chemist at Merck. I belonged to a small group of novice investors who met with a stockbroker regularly. As my fascination grew I began to invest on my own, sometimes unwisely. Indeed, I made some colossal mistakes, due to acting on tips without research (e.g. Bomax, a mining company that I invested in heavily but went bankrupt) or my stubbornness and blind faith in holding on to some hopeless stocks (e.g. Countrywide Credit and Summit Technology, which both went under).

But after subscribing to a host of financial publications, I began to do better and enjoyed some gratifying successes. They included General Electric, the country's largest company under the leadership of Jack Welch with wonderful stock splits, ever-increasing dividends, and a 4,600% price appreciation; Fidelity's Magellan managed by Peter Lynch whose annual return was a whopping 28% during his tenure; Legg Mason's Value Trust fund managed by William Miller who for 15 consecutive years beat the S&P 500 Index; and Berkshire Hathaway, the holding company of Warren Buffet, this century's greatest investor.

Although at one time I owned some 20 stocks, I've learned to appreciate mutual funds much better because they are diversified and therefore less volatile. To improve my odds, I follow such common practices as dollar averaging (a set amount invested at regular intervals); studying the short- and long-term returns, expense ratios, and other relevant information; and making graphic comparisons on the Internet. To facilitate fast trading and access to the proceeds, I've established an ACH (automatic clearing house) with all my mutual fund companies so that I can move money into or out of my bank electronically. Today my portfolio comprises a few stocks, a handful of bonds, and mostly mutual funds—including index funds—that may not have phenomenal returns but are relatively safe with respectable records. Thankfully, in my 57 plus years of investing, aided by the incredible booming markets of the 1990s and 2000s, I have built a good nest egg that should allow me and my wife to enjoy our golden years relatively free of financial worries.

In 1989 I made a prudent investment—not so much for its potential appreciation as for my personal enrichment: a Steinway grand piano, model B. While its resale value has gone up appreciably over the years, what attracted me was the elegant sound, exceptional responsiveness, rich bass, and expressive dynamic range unmatched by its competition. Small wonder the overwhelming majority of the world's concert pianists are Steinway artists.

I wasn't always able to keep company with my prized possession. In pursuing an acting career, I had been increasingly busy auditioning and working in New York and elsewhere at the expense of music making. But since 2001 after I relocated to the Los Angeles area, my acting has been local, and I have gained precious time to revel in my Steinway. And when the mood is right and the music appropriate, I can rewardingly transport myself to a world of magic, a state of nirvana without parallel.

CHAPTER 6

Parents, Teaching, Community Service

MOTHER (1895–1972)

I had a complicated relationship with Mother. Long suffering from her seeming bias toward my younger brother Henry, I had been encumbered with an insurmountable feeling of worthlessness lasting well into my mid-50s. But notwithstanding my disappointment and sense of loss, I never stopped caring about her. As years went by my appreciation actually grew. Eventually I came to realize Mother had a boundless love for all her four sons equally. At different times she might be partial to one as dictated by the circumstances and exigencies. But there was no question she loved us all and considered each and every one of us unique.

It was a given that David occupied a special place in her heart as the first born, who commanded her full attention during the nine years when Dad was studying abroad and three more years prior to the birth of David's younger brother Harry.

As her new favorite, Harry was sentimental like her and the most emotional of the four brothers. Among his admirable attributes were kindheartedness, a passionate disposition, an artistic temperament, sympathy and concern toward the downtrodden, and a literary talent (as exemplified by his moving letters to Mother and an essay so well written that his Chinese literature teacher accused him of plagiarism). He and Mother also shared a remarkable rapport and intimacy. She was especially touched—and astonished—by his endearing gestures of kissing her on the lips, a social convention virtually no Chinese families ever observed. (Display of physical and verbal affection among Chinese families is rare. Other than hugging there is little else. My parents, for instance, never said "I love you" to me, or kissed me, and vice versa. This doesn't mean any lack of affection; just a reflection of our impassive nature, of keeping our emotions inside.)

In 1951 the Lins enjoyed a rare family reunion in Philadelphia. Regrettably, it didn't last too long. Harry had already been radicalized by Chinese Communists and decided it was his patriotic duty to return to the homeland within months. Completely distraught and fearing for the worse, Mother had many a sobbing scene with him and frantically tried to dissuade him in vain—although he was no less sad and wept frequently at the thought of leaving her on an uncertain journey.

After earning a medical degree in China, initially Harry was enthusiastic about the new regime and repeatedly urged us to return. Indeed, it was making significant progress that improved the lot of the people, including many indigent farmers, and began to transform the society from an agrarian one to an industrial one. A few years later, however, things changed drastically for him when the administration encouraged its citizens to speak their minds with the following slogan: "Let a hundred schools of thoughts contend; let a hundred flowers bloom." After making some honest criticisms, he was accused of wrongfully and insidiously attacking the government. It labeled him a "rightist," mercilessly persecuted him, and forbade him to practice medicine, worsened by the cruel policy of stationing his wife Doreen, also an MD, in Beijing, and him in Shanghai. Totally disillusioned, Harry desperately tried to exit the country without success. In one of his last two letters to Mother he wrote: "I would be contented to die and rest in peace if I could just see your face once again." And the last letter: "If I'm unable to leave the country, let my corpse float out on the water." Tragically, he took his own life at the age of 29 in 1959. Upon this news Mother became the epitome of sadness, with rainy eyes, utter despair, and unspeakable pain. Years later when talking about him, she would still be teary, mourning his loss as if he were the only son.

With younger brother Henry, I shouldn't have begrudged Mother's devotion during his formative years; he was the baby of the family, born prematurely but grew to be a most lovable child. He also had a personality that appealed to Mother in a special way, with frequent long, heart-to-heart conversations that I tried to emulate but never succeeded.

As an oversensitive and fragile soul, I was hurt too easily and blind to the real truth. In my more mature years, from observing her words and deeds, reading her letters to me and her posthumous journal, I was convinced she did not love me any less. After my brothers got married and moved out I made up for lost time by having her all to myself, and what a joy it was! Once in her 70s she was greatly concerned I might become a confirmed bachelor and asked when I was going to settle down. I replied: "If I did that I would not be able to enjoy "tian lun zhi le'" (the heavenly joy for aging parents and offspring to live together.) She was touched so deeply that she never broached that subject again.

Born in Shanghai but growing up mostly in Nanjing, she was the victim at an early age of one of the most barbaric social customs known to men: foot binding. In China starting in the seventh century it was thought women with tiny feet (admiringly referred to as "three-inch golden lily") who walked in dainty, small steps were highly aesthetic and desirable. To accomplish this, it had been the common practice to coerce young girls to have their feet bound to stop the growth for several years. This resulted in the most horrible pain and deformed feet that literally crippled them. Yet for hundreds of years and successive generations this cruel custom prevailed. Mother had no choice but to obey her parents to have her feet bound tightly by bandages. It's hard to imagine the atrocious torture she endured. Fortunately, before her feet were completely ruined and thanks to the compassion of her mother who took pity on her and broke tradition by removing the bandages, her feet were only partly stunted and deformed and she was able to walk almost normally but slowly.

Mother's father, Wang Run Qi, was a government employee prior to working for various business firms. But hobbled by frequent unemployment, he periodically made his children quit school for lack of tuition. On one occasion, he was so poverty stricken that he could not afford to get medical help for his sick mother or feed his family of six who had been starving for some time. It was then that Mother just reached her one-month birthday when Chinese families traditionally celebrated this milestone with parties, dinners, and gifts. So, her parents were overjoyed to receive $2 (Chinese currency) as a gift from a relative. Mother's mother couldn't wait to buy some rice, vegetables, and cooking oil to end their hunger pangs. But she had to delay this urgent mission as Mother started to bawl and kick violently which bruised her two tiny feet. Tending to the injury and petting her to sleep, Grandma placed the $2 on a table near the window facing an alley. Later when she tried to fetch the money it was gone; obviously someone had stolen it. Consequently, the whole family had to endure more hunger.

Somehow the family survived this and subsequent periods of food deprivation. And despite other hardships and adversity, Mother and her three brothers all grew up to lead exemplary lives. She became a noted educator; her youngest brother, Wang Xi Peng, was a bright star in the literary scene by being an award-winning novelist; her younger brother, Xi-Ling, became the dean of Amoy University; and the eldest brother, Xi-Bing, a top army general, president of the Air Force Youth Academy, and personal friend of Generalissimo and Madam Chiang Kai-shek.

In 1917 Xi-Bing introduced Mother to a bosom friend, Peter Wei Lin, an ex-army officer and YMCA employee. He impressed her as "an honest, kind, sincere, studious man" as noted in her journal and as committed a Christian as she was. One year later they were married. And in a strange way I owe my existence to Uncle Xi-Bing.

A ladies' man, he boasted numerous affairs and even fathered an illegitimate son while he was married. As a bachelor, just before his return from America he merrily seduced his Caucasian landlady. Endowed with rare verbal skills, he told my parents the tale of his latest conquest in such a compelling, graphic, and infectious way that they became amorous that night. And nine months later I was born. Mother confided in me that that was the reason I was named after him by having part of my middle name Bing (as in Bing-Heng) identical to his: Bing (as in Xi-Bing).

The birth of David in Nanjing also occurred under unusual circumstances: Mother didn't have the benefit of a sympathetic, concerned husband by her bedside for he was in France prior to going to study in the U.S. I can well imagine Mother's feeling of isolation, uncertainty, and anxiety, especially when she had no idea how long Dad would be away. Lacking in financial resources, he had to work his way through graduate school at Columbia University, and it wasn't until nine years later that he finally re-joined Mother and saw David for the first time. While shouldering the onus of raising David as a single parent during this long separation, Mother pursued her own studies and earned a degree in special education. She then embarked on her teaching career, first substituting, next part time, and eventually full time, earning a monthly salary of $34. In 1927 China was embroiled in civil war. She noted in her journal that the revolutionary army (Chinese Nationalist) was fighting to take control of Nanjing. Amid loud noises from artillery and gunfire, her two colleagues and she kept teaching. After the revolutionary army won the war and made Nanjing the nation's capital her school principal awarded her $30 "for her bravery, dedication, and selflessness."

After Dad's return from America, Mother continued to teach and at one time was the head of a kindergarten. Sharing her love for teaching, Dad became a professor of statistics for a few years before he began his long tenure with the Bank of China.

As he achieved prominence Mom never forgot her humble beginnings or her struggling relatives, even after many years of being an U.S. émigré as noted in her frequent conversations, journal, and letters, and especially during her birthdays. For example, for her 71st birthday her eldest son David, a surgeon then, sent her some money. She was stirred to write this Chinese letter to him, excerpted below:

"Today is my happiest birthday. I'm infinitely grateful for your two checks but my extreme jubilation turned to sorrow with tears streaking down uncontrollably because I thought of my relatives in China who are perennially poor, suffering frequent hunger and sickness and lack of freedom (under the Communist regime). I wonder why the Lord singles us out with so much blessings, replete with the happiness of bountiful food and good health. I hope America and China will establish diplomatic relations (it happened seven years later in 1979 after she passed away) so that I can send money to my impoverished relatives struggling so hard to subsist.

"Eighteen years ago in 1948 Harry (second son) gave me $10 for my birthday. I immediately sent it to my nephew in Chongqing who had no way of making a living and was lonesome with neither friends nor relatives. He used the money to buy a few pigs from which he gained a livelihood by raising and selling them.

"I also recall another birthday of mine. At that time my father had been unemployed for several years, and so the whole family was famished while lying in bed. Around noon my brother-in-law, who was also unemployed, appeared and handed me a red envelope containing 46 cents in copper coins as my birthday gift. It was hard-earned money which my sister (mother of the aforementioned nephew) made from drawing silk (from silk cocoons). I immediately got off my bed, bought some rice, cooking oil, and five pieces of "stinking" tofu [fermented bean curd appreciated for its reeking odor] and cooked a meal. That's how I celebrated my 20th birthday.

"On my birthday every year I always recall the stories of my poverty. I tell them only to you, my beloved son, and not to Ben and Henry for fear they would not want to listen."

How she misplaced her fear! These reminiscences only endeared her so much more to me.

Among her other engaging qualities was her extraordinary ability for storytelling. Like her brother Xi-Bing, she was a talented raconteur who told me excerpts from myriad novels she had read. Her favorite was *Dream of the Red Chambers*, likely the greatest masterpiece in all of Chinese literature, and she delighted in regaling me with some of the details, plots, and characters which she could bring vividly alive and made me absolutely entranced. She was especially captivated by the tortuous romance between the protagonists Jia Bo Yue and his cousin Lin Dai Yu, which was thwarted by Jia's forced marriage to another cousin, Xue Bao Chai, whom he did not love.

A nonfiction favorite she often told me about was *Queen of the Dark Chamber* by Christiana Tsai (Cai Sujuan in Chinese). Translated into 30 languages, it was the autobiography of a woman who grew up in a family of great wealth highlighted by her triumph over adversity and conversion to Christianity. The book title refers to her years of confinement to a dark room due to a rare malaria which made her eyes sensitive to light and kept her bedridden. But these difficulties did not deter her from tending to her ministry and becoming a beacon of bright light that reflected her exemplary life as a Christian.

Mother was also fond of telling jokes. One was a true story she learned from her ESL (English as Second Language) teacher: An 80-year-old Japanese lady was hoping to become an America citizen and her knowledge of our Constitution was required. When asked "Who takes over when the president dies?" she said without batting an eye, "The undertaker." She got her citizenship.

Another joke of hers concerns a physician. A patient of his dies as a result of his inept treatment. The authorities sentence him to carrying the victim's body and parading around the neighborhood as punishment. Being too weak, he is allowed to let his nurse carry out the sentence. Sometime later an obese patient calls on this doctor. But the nurse refuses to register him.

"Why?" the man asks.

"Because you are too heavy."

Since fleeing from Communist China and settling in Philadelphia, Mother was able to revive one of her great passions: caring for the very young. When a neighbor asked her to babysit she jumped at the chance. Because no one else could provide the kind of loving care, patience, and skill that she did, word got around and in time she became a famous babysitter and was in great demand far and near. Time after time I was amazed to witness this scene: a baby was crying unstoppably in her mother's arms no matter how she tried to quiet it. But the minute Mother took over and cradled it in her soothing arms, the infant immediately calmed down and stopped crying. Her service was so valued that our next-door neighbors, a physician and his MBA candidate wife, consulted with her regarding possible parenthood. Lacking the time, they asked Mother if she would be interested and available to shoulder much of the parenting. Only after she gave them an enthusiastic "yes" did the couple decide to conceive.

Aside from her love for children was her passion for gastronomy. It was enhanced by the fact that as a banker's wife she was constantly being entertained. Among her favorites were sea cucumber (prized for its unique texture and taste) with shrimp roes, steamed crabs served with a ginger dipping sauce (she had the skill and patience to devour every shred of the edible), Shanghai pork dishes, especially those with lots of fat such as Tung Po pork (braised pork belly and named after a poet) and fish, whether deep fried, braised or steamed. But she had no cooking opportunities in China because we had servants and a chef. And so, during our early days in Philadelphia she had to struggle to put appealing and varied food on the table. Nevertheless, being enormously gifted and having strong instincts and an unerring culinary memory, she quickly learned to be an excellent cook with an astounding repertoire. Among her dishes were braised bean curd dishes ("to achieve tastiness they must be highly seasoned and served piping hot," she was fond of saying); Nanking pressed duck, which could rival the famed Peking duck; pork kidney with shrimp; meat-filled dumplings; and braised whole fish accentuated with garlic. A gregarious woman, she enjoyed entertaining at home. Frequently she would invite some 50 guests and treated them to 20 to 30 marvelous dishes. She also was my first cooking mentor who greatly influenced my interest in the culinary arts. Among my most treasured recollections was our cooking side by side for the family.

However, most likely it was her love for dining pleasure, plus hereditary and lack of exercise that proved her undoing. In 1969 she suffered a heart attack caused by blockage of an artery. After being hospitalized for 18 days and starting a strict diet, she quickly lost some weight. She was 74 and began to have thoughts about her mortality. She would tell me that her own mother died of heart attack at 77 and thought she could not outlive this life span (her father died of a heart attack even earlier at 62). When her health recovered, other than looking much thinner she was her normal, active self again, doing myriad household chores and lovingly caring for Dad, Henry, and me. (David had already married the concert pianist Susan Hsieh.) Somehow, I felt sure she had many good years ahead of her. But the family did develop a heightened concern over her health and tried our best to dissuade her from over-working or doing anything strenuous.

She was soon to realize one of her unfulfilled dreams: the marriage of younger brother Henry, an electrical engineer. On September 12, 1970, he tied the knot with Lydia Chow, a bio-medical engineer, both pious Christians. And I became the only unmarried son living with my parents; it was among my happiest times with Mom, doing a host of things together: yoga, which I taught her; shopping for flowers for our garden; dining in outstanding restaurants (she still enjoyed delicious meals); grocery shopping in Chinatown; giving dinner parties; traveling to Paradise, PA, to visit Christiana Tsai (*Queen of the Dark Chamber*); and sharing my travel stories.

While she was always fascinated by my travels, one in particular terrified her. I was vacationing in a resort town near Tampa, FL. Tempted by the fine weather and beautiful beach-es in front of my hotel, I went swimming. With no lifeguard and no one else around, I plunged into the water and started to head out, confident in my aquatic ability. But unbeknown to me and with no warning signs around, the ocean had the most treacherous condition for swimming: rip current in which the extremely strong force of the water surface flowed outward from the shore, dragging whatever objects afloat inexorably deep into the ocean. Later I learned that day the rip current had already claimed the life of one person at a nearby beach. Apparently, I was replicating the victim's exact experience. After covering enough distance, I decided to head back. But no matter how hard I swam I got no closer to the shore. On the contrary, to my horror I found myself being pulled farther and farther away. Sensing the life-threatening danger, I frantically redoubled my effort but made no progress whatsoever and was overcome with total exhaustion. As water filled my nostrils, mouth, and part of my lungs, I struggled to breathe and was on the verge of drowning. Miraculously a helicopter flew by at this very instant and dropped a lifesaver, the innertube of a truck tire. But it was too far from me and therefore totally useless. What saved my life was my erroneous thought that rescue was on the way and so I started to tread water. And that was precisely the best way to cope with rip currents. With no help showing up, I slowly regained my strength and gradually waded back to the shore. Mother was so grateful to the helping hand of God that she couldn't give enough thanks.

If she came close to losing her son literally she was troubled by the fact that I seemed unable to lose my heart to some nubile woman. I was in my late 30s with no prospects in sight. But she loathed broaching the subject of my bachelorhood, remembering our conversation about "tian lun zhi le" (the heavenly joy for aging parents and offspring to live together.) At times, she was resigned to the fact that she might not live to see the day when I would settle down. Indeed, she often remarked that I had already found the love of my life because I was "married to my piano." But her journal revealed her true sentiments as she penned this 7/27/1970 passage: "I dreamt we had a gala in our house with lots of guests and happy commotion celebrating the engagement of Bing son. I saw him wearing a gold engagement ring given to him by his fiancée. I dreamt about this engagement celebration twice in the same night. I felt so very joyous and comforted and was compelled to write down these dreams." Sadly, it was a dream that never materialized during her lifetime for I was not married until many years later when I was 63.

As a bachelor son, I did have a most memorable vacation to the Far East with my parents in 1971. The first leg was in Taiwan. Father's former employer, the Bank of China, in appreciation of his years of dedicated service, rolled out the red carpet and arranged a trip of the whole island escorted by one of the bank officers. Taiwan was discovered by the Portuguese, who named it Formosa, meaning "beautiful"; indeed, it was an attractive island with an abundance of pretty sights. Especially notable was its culinary excellence. When the Nationalist Chinese fled to Taiwan from the mainland in 1949 prior to the communist takeover, countless gifted chefs also relocated there and as a result it boasted an abundance of top-notch restaurants, most of which were concentrated in Taipei, the capital.

During our stay, there one of the highlights of the trip for me was enrolling in a cooking class taught by Taiwan's Julia Child, a popular TV chef, cookbook author, and an inimitable instructor, Fu Pei Mei. When I suggested that I might translate her cookbook into English she was initially enthusiastic. Using my first published article "One from Column A" as a writing sample, I got an American publisher interested in my suggestion. But Fu, who spoke very little English, dreaded the thought of going to the States to promote the book and so she changed her mind. Nevertheless, I enjoyed her class immensely. On a few occasions she invited the city's greatest chefs to be guest lecturers/demonstrators. To see these masters at work was truly a remarkable treat. Later, back in the States, I was to tickle Mother's palate by cooking some of my newly learned recipes. She was moved to remark: "your cooking now is more delicious."

After a two-week stay in Taiwan we spent two weeks in Hong Kong, one of my favorite cities to which we had not returned since 1950. Father had a very close Fujianese friend, Zeng Ji Hua, who was a business mogul, the owner of a great conglomerate including shipping, hotels, and real estates. It had been years since we last met, and we were surprised to encounter his new wife, actually his concubine, an attractive, young woman who was many years his junior. He let us stay in one of his apartment complexes complete with a servant. Situated on a mountain, it had a gorgeous view overlooking Happy Valley Race Course. To my delight and Mother's, he entertained us with lavish banquets. In one I met the younger sister of his concubine, Annie Fung, an 18-year-old student nurse. Mother was overjoyed that Annie was very much taken with me and fervently hoped that I had finally found my match. While I was not similarly disposed, I enjoyed dating her. (We met again years later and did come very close to taking marital vows in the '80s.)

Renting a car and struggling to drive on the left, the British system, I traveled all over with my parents, visiting our old residence in scenic West Hong Kong, which brought back memories of my passion for the piano; my high school in Stanley, recalling my love for soccer, my first taste for tennis and the incomparable beef chow fun I had enjoyed in an eatery nearby; some of the top tourist spots such as Victoria Peak, with its commanding vista of Hong Kong, Kowloon, and the straits with a plethora of ships large and small of every description; Aberdeen, known for its floating restaurants; Clear Water Bay, one of the prettiest beaches. One enchanting excursion was visiting the Lantau Island where the chief attraction was the monastery and its extraordinary restaurant.

There the monks' religious fervor was matched only by their passion for and talent in cooking and its vegetarian cuisine was first rate.

On occasions when Father was calling on his numerable friends, Mom and I spent some precious time together: Feasting on fish, shrimp and crabs—all cooked live—at the Li Pai Floating Restaurant in Kowloon; swimming at Repulse Bay, the most scenic beach; visiting a gigantic Buddhist temple in Kowloon where she outdid herself—despite having suffered a heart attack—by climbing the steep steps to the towering top. All in all we enjoyed each other's company in a most intimate, pleasurable way that epitomized the pure love between an adoring son and his aging mother. In her journal she noted she was so appreciative for my "profound filial piety for giving her so much joy" on this vacation. Actually, I was the one who should be grateful for my happiness and treasured memories.

Notwithstanding her good times on this vacation, her thoughts were never too far from her premonition that her life would be limited and that she would have only one more year to live when she would reach 77, the age her own mother died. She went as far as shopping around and bought funeral clothes. And a year prior she had bought an interment site in a Philadelphia suburb, the Valley Forge Memorial Garden, which she liked because it was beautiful, devoid of headstones, and looked like a well-maintained lawn with trees and a lake.

Upon returning home, Mother would occasionally remind us of her presentiment, which I refused to take seriously. But on Mother's Day, the following year, I had a fleeting moment of foreboding myself. After the whole family, including the married couples of David and Susan, Henry and Lydia, took her to Lem's Tea Garden for a celebratory meal, we had a hymn singing session together. In the midst of one song I suddenly felt very sad and was on the verge of tears as if some horrible tragedy was to happen. It was a feeling that lasted only seconds, and soon I thought I was just being overly sentimental.

In June 1972, Mother was planning to accompany Dad to Silver Bay, the YMCA conference and retreat center on Lake George where he had had an accounting job and she a waitressing job in the children's dining room every summer for the past six years. Before her departure she felt compelled to do two things as if they would be her last legacies: Having a green thumb, she had already made our back garden the envy of all our neighbors. Now she wished to make our house even more beautiful and so she asked me to help her buy a few dozen flowers which she painstakingly planted on our front lawn. Then she wished to donate her culinary service to the Chinese Church in Chinatown, which she had been attending. It had been the practice of the church to provide lunch for the congregation after the Sunday service. Mother volunteered to cook, and Minister Chuang Wen Sun happily obliged. It was a taxing job as she spent hours preparing a multi-course extravaganza that only a person with her talent, energy, and thoughtfulness could accomplish.

A week or so later it was departure time for my parents. Henry and his wife Lydia offered to drive them to Silver Bay. While I initially was concerned that there might be some risks for a heart attack survivor to be away in the hinterland for three long summer months, David, the surgeon, wasn't worried. And so, my mind was eased and I bade adieu to Mom with the full confidence that she would return safe and sound.

In the meantime I was busy planning what was to be my first grand tour of Europe. I had signed up for an American Express six-week escorted tour to about a dozen countries. In my previous trips to Mexico, Bermuda, the Caribbean, and elsewhere I always took countless photos and gave parties showing my travel slides, and Mother never failed to express her appreciation. So she was looking forward to a similar slide presentation.

To celebrate her 77th birthday, her Silver Bay colleagues gave her a surprise party, during which they brought out an ersatz cake and dropped it in front of her as a joke. But she was so jolted by this thoughtless gag that she suffered an emotional shock. That night she started to feel intense heartache. Except for secretly telling Mrs. Lucille Pan, one of her best friends, about her pain she kept it quiet. Only when it became unbearable did she let us know. And so on a Friday morning David drove to Silver Bay to bring her back. Strangely, I thought it was a mild heart attack and that she would recover. But on her way back home she told David she expected she would not survive and that she was ready to meet the Lord. But even after sister-in-law Susan told me "You better get down on your knees and pray," I thought Mother would come through all right as she did with her last heart attack.

On the following day, I should have rushed to Methodist Hospital to see her but I had two overnight guests, friends of my then girlfriend whom I couldn't very well kick out too early. Plus, I was still not worried about Mother's prospects for recovery and stupidly took my time. When I got to the hospital David told the worst news of my life: Mother had just died. I ran to her room and touched her cheek with mine; it was still warm. But she was no more. Knowing she was dying, she must have been wondering why I wasn't at her bedside at this critical moment, and I hated myself for not getting to her sooner. How could a person so alive, vibrant, full of goodness and dear to me suddenly leave us forever? Why is death such a cruel finality? I could only react with tears, profound regret, and grief. David was not affected similarly. On the contrary, he remained calm and reprimanded me for crying. This was not a sad occasion but a joyous one, he said, because Mother was going to meet her Heavenly Father in a better world. But I was inconsolable and devastated; I just wept and wept and wept.

With Father still in Silver Bay, I returned home that day to our empty four-story house which had never felt so bleak and lonesome, where my desolation and depression grew as day turned into night. I struggled in vain to fall asleep, unable to escape from the pervasive realty even for a brief moment. During much of my insomnia I tearfully jotted down my jumbled thoughts in a notebook, recounting Mother's love, goodness, humanity, abiding faith, our wonderful times together, and pondered over the preciousness but transiency of life, the mystery and ugliness of death. When dawn's first lights streaked through the window, how I wished what had happened was just a nightmare, a passing bad dream and not real.

Later I reread her penultimate Chinese letter to me from Silver Bay. I quote one in part:

"My dearest Bing Heng son,

Two weeks have gone by since we last saw each other. (I had just visited her.) I think of you every second of the day. Only by earnestly asking our omnipotent Heavenly Father to bless your future can I get unlimited comfort and happiness . . . I often thought of Harry." (Still mourning his passing, she recalled what he had told her before leaving for Communist China in 1951): 'I'm not the only son. There are three others to be with you.' At the time I wasn't touched by the sentiment. But now, during the December of our lives Dad and I came to realize what Harry had said was the absolute truth. Still, I have infinite regret that he was victimized by Satan."

In her last letter dated July 7, 1972, nine days before her death she wrote:

"I'm so happy you'll be traveling to Europe for 43 days. I'm sure you will be bringing a notebook to record your experience so that I'll know all about it. It's my great regret that I cannot join you on this journey. I remember our happiness and enjoyment together when we vacationed in Hong Kong last summer, dining and sightseeing to our heart's content.

"It's my fervent hope and belief that while you are having fun you won't forget God's blessings and when you face unexpected danger remember God will give your strength to overcome everything, just as the time when you almost drowned in Florida. When we meet again at home we can once again enjoy tian lun zhi le.

"I'm so happy your journalism professor asked you to be a guest lecturer. I'm also looking forward to carefully reading your first published article ('One from Column A.') Perhaps it (the English) would be too difficult for me to understand. Bon voyage."

Instead of embarking on my vacation, which was to start three days after her passing, I spent that day attending her funeral service officiated by Pastor Chuang. With an open casket, she had a horrible makeup that looked false and artificial and accentuated her death. We sang several of her favorite hymns including "What a Friend We Have in Jesus" and "Sowing in the Morning." I wrote a eulogy but was too broken up to read it and asked someone else to do the job.

"Mother is a simple and good person. She has few pleasures and her greatest joy is her family. To her every one of her sons is like her only son on whom she lavishes a monumental love that can only be the rarest of gifts from God.

"A devout Christian and a remarkably selfless mother, she seldom thinks about her own well-being, worries about her comfort or complains about her pain and suffering. Instead, she devotes her whole energy to caring for us—not just physical care but also spiritual care, nourishing a constant thoughtfulness, concern and prayer.

"Her love is not limited to her immediate family for it extends to all relatives far and near, embracing even the great granddaughter whom she has yet to see. As the only woman in a home of four boys and a husband, she has a quiet strength that has sustained her well in adversities and misfortunes. She also has a boundless energy that enables her to accomplish the most amazing feats even in her old age, from painting the house on a tall ladder to climbing the roof to fix a leak.

"She is more than a great mother, devoted wife and loving relative, but a great human being, always gentle, gracious, generous, and warm to whomever she comes into contact. She has a special affection for children with a special way of reaching them. Having taught kindergarten for fourteen years and babysat for countless little ones, she has brought infinite joy to them and their grateful parents.

"She has a passion for flowers. Through years of effort she has made our garden the most beautiful one in the neighborhood. Not long ago she planted some thirty new flowers. Today they are growing well, bearing her signature, her love, her smile.

"We are heartbroken by her departure. Surely nothing can fill the void she left us. But it is a consolation that she has lived a good life, a full life, and a proud life, and we are grateful for having been part of that life. As we say goodbye to her we know that her love is reciprocated by a thousand loves, and her heart is returned with a thousand hearts. Her spirit will always be with us and God rest her soul in peace."

FATHER (1894-1980)

Eight years later Dad died at the age of 86. While I was extremely close to Mom, I felt differently toward him. The reason was he tended to keep his emotions inside, giving the façade of being aloof and inaccessible. In reality, he was as thoughtful and loving as Mother, so eminently manifested in his deeds. He enrolled me in in the best schools in Chongqing and Shanghai where he hired tutors to rectify my deficiencies; financed my musical studies despite his profound misgivings; aided my fledging Chinese food business with his accounting expertise; and provided me with a generous trust fund and inheritance. I wish I had been a better son and shown greater appreciation for his exemplary fatherhood.

Peter Wei Lin hailed from China's southern province of Fujian. His father was an indigent Protestant minister who at one point could afford only one pair of pants for his two sons, and Father's younger brother was the lucky beneficiary. Suffering the loss of his mother when he was only four, he had to cope with an indifferent stepmother and left home in his teens. With his religious roots, Father became a highly devout Christian, which influenced him profoundly and helped make him a man of principle, integrity, and compassion.

Graduated from the Baoding Military Academy second in his class, he also attended the Huang Pu Military Academy, the Chinese counterpoint of West Point. He then joined the army's artillery division, fully expecting to be a career officer. But to his disappointment he discovered there was too much corruption and quit. After marrying the former Priscilla Wang in 1918, he became an intern at Young Men's Christian Association (YMCA) in Tianjin where he met the great Chinese-born American missionary Frank Wilson Price. They were to become great friends. It was through his help that Peter was able to come to the U.S. to study. En route he had a stint teaching Chinese laborers at YMCA in France. During this time Mother gave birth to first son David, who met his father for the first time nine years later. That was why David's Chinese middle names were Yao Pei, meaning to be raised from afar.

After graduate studies at Yale University, Father transferred to Columbia. He worked his way (including summer jobs at Silver Bay, the YMCA conference and retreat center on Lake George, NY) to get his MBA. Just before returning to China he developed appendicitis. Having no money for the surgery, he was so grateful and moved by the doctor's free service that he changed his mind about pursuing a business career. Instead, he wanted to be a doctor and remain in the U.S. to study. But mother strenuously objected. After spending nine long years raising David while earning meager wages by teaching, she wasn't about to wait seven or more years for him to become a physician. So he reluctantly returned to China. Later he took satisfaction that two of his sons did realize his unfulfilled aspiration: David and Harry both became doctors.

After teaching statistics Father joined the Bank of China, one of the country's largest with branches throughout China. In time he rose to become director of the trust department headquartered in Shanghai. In 1941 the Sino-Japanese war forced him to relocate to free China in Chongqing with his bank. It assigned him to the organization and supervision of transport on the vital Burma Road which linked Burma with China's southwest to convey supplies during World War II. It was "a duty which he performed with incorruptible honesty and responsibility," as noted in a tribute to him by Frank Price, the missionary, on occasion of my parents' golden wedding anniversary (1918–1968).

When the Bank of China moved to Taiwan in 1949 due to the Communist takeover, it asked him to be its president. But he turned down this high honor. Seeking a better future for his family, he migrated to America with Mom, youngest son Henry, and me. He settled in Philadelphia to join two older sons, David and Harry, who had come here earlier on student visas.

Carving a new career, he opened an office in New York City and commuted, daily tending to his import business of tungsten and hog bristles, two of China's greatest products. After this failed he tried to find employment in the City of Brotherly Love. But it was a difficult endeavor because of his over-qualification and high position in China. Eventually through the help of a missionary friend he landed a job as an accountant in a mortgage company. A tireless worker and conscientious provider, after compulsory retirement age he continued to toil in accounting, part time in the city and full time at Silver Bay during the summer for a number of years. He brought Mother along to keep him company and got her a job working in the children's dining room.

Poor Dad suffered the agony and pain of loneliness in 1972 when Mother passed away. Two years later at the age of 81 his future was in doubt, still sound in mind but frail and in need of someone to look after him. Oldest brother David, who was about to emigrate to Western Canada as the elder of a Christian sect, didn't think I would be a good candidate because I was preoccupied with too many projects. Instead, he thought a nursing home might be in his best interest. But after visiting he came home sobbing for a couple of days realizing what a terrible place it would be to live out his life. David not only agreed but surmised that Dad might not survive beyond a few months. The conclusion was that as the bachelor son living with him, despite my crazy schedule, I would still be the logical person to shoulder the responsibilities.

Not without profound, regrettable lapses, I tried to care for him as a dutiful and grateful son. I kept a vigil over him, tended to his needs and at one time got help from a live-in Japanese man, a student of Christian ministry. Whenever possible, I took him with me to my restaurant so that he could have a good dinner, spend some moments chatting with my chef Che, and taking home plenty of food. When he had difficulty going to or coming down from his second-floor bedroom and fell a few times (luckily not too seriously) I got a carpenter to modify our stairs and installed an automatic chairlift. As his health became progressively worse, I was greatly relieved when David returned from Canada to help care for him. One day he developed high fever of 104 degrees and shivered in cold. David rushed him to his Methodist Hospital and discovered he was on the verge of catching pneumonia and might not have pulled through in his weakened state. Thankfully he recovered after an eight-day stay.

However, all too often I displayed a terrible lack of thoughtfulness and consideration. I seldom tried to engage him in conversations. Indeed, we two almost never talked to each other. For a period, I inexplicably was hostile and mean to him (but felt bad enough to "ask God to forgive me," as noted in my sporadically kept journal). At 83 he began to shows signs of dementia. As it worsened two years later, the thought that he would need help bathing and shaving never entered my mind. It was David who took up the chores and put me to shame. On December 19, 1980, his senility was at its worse; he looked pale, helpless, and seemingly unaware of what was going on (but he could still recognize me). That evening I cradled him in my arms and tried to feed him an orange. Being selfish and impatient, I was rushing him. And in the middle of ingesting he died in my arms. I shuddered to think that I might have hastened or caused his death. But when David checked on him, he said Dad died of "massive cerebral vascular thrombosis" or a stroke. It did not lessen my feeling of guilt. Subsequently, whenever I think of the events of that evening and the times I was nasty to him I am filled with remorse. I wish I could undo my unforgivable behavior.

My edited and excerpted eulogy:

"From a humble beginning as the son of an impoverished Protestant minister, he rose to be one of the most distinguished bankers of his generation. But despite his accomplishments and lofty position as the director of Bank of China's trust department, he remained an unassuming man who touched others with his grace and kindness. He never seemed to have an enemy or harbor ill feeling towards anyone. Instead, he recognized only the good in everyone. Small wonder he made friends easily and bonded with a multitude of individuals of all ages and stations in life, from Dr. Alfred Williams, distinguished and longest-tenured president of the Federal Reserve Bank of Philadelphia, to humble young college students. They were especially on his thoughts around the holiday season when he stayed up till the wee hours night after night, writing Christmas cards that numbered some 500.

"Father was also a man of integrity. In his long career as a banker and during his service to the government in transport management (the Burma Road) there were plenty of temptations. But he stayed pure, honest, and benevolent and earned the moniker 'Buddha' among his associates. As he joins Mother in eternity we are grateful for having been part of his exemplary life."

TEACHING (1968-1982)

I came from a family of teachers. My father taught statistics, my mother kindergarten and elementary school, and my brother David senior surgery students at Jefferson Medical College. In addition, Mom's two brothers were both distinguished educators: Wang Shi Bing, the army general, was founder and president of the Air Force Youth Academy; and Wang Shi Lin, dean of Xia Men University. Thus, it may well be a matter of family tradition for me to follow their footsteps. The actor in me was also attracted by the elements of theatricality: the teacher being the writer, director, star, and producer all rolled into one with a built-in live audience to boot.

In 1968 when I got laid off by DuPont, which obviated my daily, time-consuming commute from Philadelphia to Wilmington, DE, I had more time on my hands. Because of my predisposition to and my proselytizing zeal to spread the joy of Chinese cuisine, I was inspired to teach the subject. At that time, there was no Chinese cooking class anywhere in Philadelphia, and I became the first such instructor. The Young Women's Christian Association (YWCA) was my chosen venue, and my application was heartily welcomed. Initially, the class size was relatively small as I introduced such topics as:

- Soy sauces: Imported brands are preferred. They are made by fermentation, a six-month process, resulting in a rich, effective condiment. The domestic brands are made chemically, and hence, far cheaper but inferior.

- Cooking oils: Corn, salad, peanut oils and the like that have a relatively high boiling point, which is essential for stir-frying and deep frying, whereas sesame and olive oils are too delicate for these purposes.

• Cooking wines: Chinese rice wine and dry sherry are both suitable; stay away from wine that's too sweet.

• The most common ingredients include ginger (especially effective in countering the foul taste of fish), black mushrooms (great garnish), long grain rice which is more tasty than Uncle Ben's and Minute Rice.

• Cooking utensils: A 14-inch wok or skillet is the most practical size. An iron wok conducts heat faster and is the choice of professionals but rusts easily. A stainless-steel one is acceptable.

• Chinese cleaver: An indispensable tool. For cutting, slicing, mincing, chopping, it has no equals. However, one must exercise great care or easily get hurt because the blade is so sharp.

Regional cuisines, with representative examples:

1. Cantonese. The emphasis is on natural flavor. Steamed fish, pepper steak, chicken with X.O. sauce, and the famed dim sum.

2. Shanghainese. Known for its "red cooked" dishes such as "dee pong," or pork shank, and dim sum specialties including soup dumplings or xiao long bao, scallion cake, and pork bun that are different from its Cantonese counterparts.

Sichuanese. Spicy-hot selections like twice-cooked pork, whole carp with hot bean sauce, General Tso chicken; non-spicy ones include steamed pork with glutinous rice and camphor tea duck.

3. Fujianese. Famed for its seafood dishes and its use of fermented red rice paste. Stir-friend rice noodles

and "Buddha Jumping over the Wall," comprising such ingredients as shark's fin, sea cucumber, and abalone. (Genesis of the name: allegedly a Buddhist monk was so enticed by its aroma that he violated his vow of vegetarian diet by jumping over a wall to devour this tasty dish.)

4. Beijingese. Peking duck, mou shu pork, dumplings, lamb hot pot.

• Cooking techniques. They total over a dozen. The more common ones include steaming, roasting, deep frying, par-frying or "guo yue," stewing, braising, blanching, and the well-known stir-frying. For the last, ingredients are cut into bite-sizes that have two advantages: 1. It allows for the blending of two or more components—including vegetables—in a given meat or seafood dish, giving a multidimensional effect, better aesthetics, contrasting texture, and a more balanced, more healthful diet. 2. The possibility of cooking over very high heat for the shortest time resulting in vegetables that are crispy, meats succulent and tender with flavors sealed in.

In teaching such favorites as beef with peapods, shrimp with lobster sauce and won ton soup, I discovered I had a wonderful rapport with my students, and that there was no greater joy than to impart the knowledge of something I loved to well-motivated enthusiasts. One gave a five-course dinner before the semester was even over. Another was a handicapped woman who enjoyed the course so much that she enrolled in three more semesters. Having mastered some 80 selections, she was proud to give a challenging 18-course feast for dozens of guests, doing all her preparation and cooking in her wheelchair. Her courage, passion, and determination were an inspiration to her fellow students and really heartened me.

After food writer Lesley Kruhly came calling and did a lengthy story in the *Evening Bulletin* with photos and recipes, I began to attract capacity or a full class of 28 students in most semesters.

Just before an upcoming semester one man insisted on enrolling even though the class was full. He was a Teutonic blond who introduced himself as a professional chef and winner of an Olympic cooking competition representing Germany. Because he was so determined, earnest, and persuasive, I made an exception and allowed him to squeeze in the class.

Tell Erhardt proved to be an exceptional student, being very attentive, quick to raise questions and show appreciation in his thick German accent. He also turned out to be a gracious friend as he invited me to his home to enjoy his Olympic award-winning dishes. When marrying the former Miss Philadelphia Janet Nicoletti, an American-born Italian, he gave a highly nationalistic reception at the Kona Kai restaurant where he was a chef. It was emblazoned with the flags of Germany and Italy and a long table comprising a stunning array of specialties from the two countries.

A showman with an outsized personality, Erhardt soon began to appear on local TV shows, then on *Live with Regis and Kathie Lee,* and went on to become one of the pioneering celebrity chefs with his own popular TV show on PBS, *In the Kitchen with Chef Tell.* In addition, he taught cooking, marketed a line of his own cookware, and owned restaurants in the suburbs of Philadelphia. In one of them President Nixon, resigned from office then, was his patron who befriended him and sponsored his U.S. citizenship (he was an illegal immigrant.).

An unexpected visitor to audit my class was Joan Specter, wife of Pennsylvania senator Arlen Specter. She had her own well-known cooking school and so I was humbled by her visit.

She especially liked the two recipes I was demonstrating that evening. Days later the *Evening Bulletin* published a story about her and it included my two recipes. As a return courtesy and to honor her husband as a distinguished lawmaker (selected by *Time* magazine as one of the 10 best senators), I invited the couple to my Jade Palace restaurant for dinner.

In 1970, having tasted the thrill of teaching at YWCA, I felt the urge to expand elsewhere. I was especially drawn to the prestigious cooking program at the China Institute in New York. To earn a teaching position there was fraught with hurdles. It was headed by Florence Lin (no relation), who was a famous cookbook author and occasionally interviewed by the *New York Times*; she had very rigid standards and an elite, small staff. I was sure I'd have little chances of success if I tried on my own. Luckily, I had an influential godfather, Dr. S. W. Kung. It was through his effort and connections that I succeeded. With this appointment I continued to teach at YWCA.

The kitchen at China Institute was conveniently equipped with a large mirror tilted at such an angle that students in the last rows could see the preparation and cooking of the teacher. My class comprised two groups of 30 students each, including teachers who took it for accreditation. Weekly lugging a suitcase full of ingredients from my Philadelphia home, I lectured/demonstrated with enough portions to constitute a small dinner for everyone. Augmented by a grocery tour and lunch in Chinatown and a farewell multi-course banquet dinner, the course was so much in demand that enrollment required a one-year wait.

For the Chinatown tours, I consolidated my two groups of 30 students into one of 60. Many of them capitalized on the grocery store visit to fill their culinary needs. The owner of the best store, located on Mott Street, was so grateful for their patronage that he gave me a prized Mongolian fire pot. A competition of his, on the other hand, went ballistic at the onrush of the throng. To my utter humiliation and embarrassment, he viciously attacked me in front of my students for "disrupting" his business and kicked us out—without even giving me a chance to explain. In retrospect, I should have been more sensitive to his concern. After all, he had no idea my students were there to do business.

During one semester, my fellow cooking teachers and I were astonished and elated to be invited for lunch by the multitalented comedian, dancer, singer and actor Danny Kaye ("The Court Jester"). He was about to be inducted into the international gourmet society Chaine de Rotisserie (of which I was a member as proprietor of my own restaurant), and he needed input from us so-called "experts" to put together an original menu. Expectedly, he dominated the conversation and regaled us with captivating stories. An ardent Chinese cook, he told us when entertaining he habitually prepared an eight-course meal and that he could do 30 dinners without repeating anything.

Another surprise was my short-lived liaison with a student. I had just finished an evening class. Before returning home, I happened to strike up a conversation with a young female about Tennessee Williams' *Cat on a Hot Tin Roof,* then on Broadway. On the spur of the moment, we decided to see the play. We were both moved profoundly, followed by a fervent discussion analyzing and admiring this marvelous drama. Since we seemed unable to end our highly enjoyable conversation, she invited me to her apartment to continue. It was so riveting, lasting late into the night. It then happened spontaneously and impulsively: we began to embrace and kiss, culminating inexorably in an amorous denouement.

However, I had no interest in developing our relationship, because I already had a girlfriend back home, and I didn't believe in playing around. I should have had the decency and courtesy to explain my situation but regretfully did not. I might well have come across to her as a lecherous, insensitive brute, prone to seducing women and one-night stands. I hope I did not hurt her feelings too much—if she indeed expected a blossoming of our relationship. At any rate, I had a guilty conscience.

Otherwise, I was on very good terms with my students. Some gave me presents at the end of the semesters. A few told me my cooking tasted better than the luncheon they had in Chinatown when touring there. One of them, Al Myers, and I became lifelong friends. Another, Jim Grossman, took the class with his wife Sarah. Long after I had stopped teaching at the China Institute in the mid-1970s, he ingeniously tracked me down some 30 years later around 2005, after I had relocated to the Los Angeles area. A retired journalist, he said that he and Sarah had enjoyed my class and were still using my recipes. Another enthusiastic student was the mother of famed cellist Yo-Yo Ma. She told me she had audited other cooking classes at the China Institute and that she enjoyed mine the most. She took such a liking to me that subsequently she invited me to her home for lunch.

The enthusiasm of these students sparked me to seek teaching at a more prestigious venue in Philadelphia: Temple University's Institute for Continuing Studies (ICS) in center city. When that came through I gave up my YMCA post. The syllabus of the beginner's course was similar to that of my New York class, complete with a grocery tour, lunch, and a graduation banquet dinner in Chinatown. I had a full enrollment almost from the very beginning.

My students, who were required to grade their teachers, had been most generous, invariably giving me the highest marks. One year, Temple's newspaper featured me as "teacher of the year." With my success, I became the only one to teach cooking all year round in the spring, summer, and fall semesters.

In subsequent semesters I added several other courses, including:

- Vegetarian Cooking with such selections as bean sprout salad, broccoli with hot garlic sauce, peapods with water chestnuts, and fried dumplings.

- Chinese Sauces. To my best knowledge it was a course that had never been given anywhere, and no such cookbook existed. Yet Chinese sauces are one of the most distinctive features of its cuisine, and perhaps nothing defines the dishes more eloquently. Consider the savory taste of sweet and sour sauce in the popular shrimp and pork dishes, the pervasive allure of black bean sauce that accompanies spareribs, the tantalizing effect of the fiery sauce in kung pao chicken, and the elegant egg sauce in lobster Cantonese. They represent part of myriad Chinese sauces that help make its cookery popular the world over.

This course also represents a novel approach to studying. Instead of learning dish by dish, which is arduous and time-consuming, by learning the basic sauces, one can apply them to a wide variety of selections. Take black bean sauce for example: it is applicable to clams, snails, beef, shrimp and scallops; "red cook" sauce is applicable to chicken, pork and beef tripe, Chinese radish and sea cucumber; Yue hsiang sauce is applicable to pork and eggplant.

One distinct advantage of the Chinese sauces is that they are generally not an additive but an integral part of the dish. This is achieved: One, by thickening the sauce with corn starch so that it binds to the dish. Two, by simmering the sauce for a long time so that it becomes absorbed by the dish. This integrated taste is a lot more satisfying than making the sauce as a separate entity and then laying over the dish as in other cuisines. Mastery of the sauces also makes the cooking more consistent, and the reason some Chinese chefs make master sauces daily is so that no matter who does the cooking, the result will be the same.

• Less Familiar Chinese Dishes. Examples: Cantonese pork pie, meat ball soup, beef with eggs.

My best student was Marc Rauer, a computer science professor. After finishing beginner's class, he signed up again, fully expected to repeat the whole thing. Since I had plenty of recipes, I devised a new set of them. When that course ended, he signed up yet again, and then a fourth time. And so I ended up revising the recipes four times to accommodate him. Subsequently, when I offered the aforementioned classes, he enrolled in them all. In addition, he had private tutoring with me and became a good friend of mine. (His passion for Chinese cuisine was only matched by his love for felines. Annually he gave a luncheon party honoring his two or three cats and invited some 70 guests for whom he offered aprons adorned with the picture of a cat. He repeated this routine for three years in a row and engaged me as his caterer each time.)

I also taught a seminar in Commercial Acting (of which I was just hitting my stride in New York as a fledging actor) and a class in Restaurant Management (among the topics was public relations, a great marketing tool on which I capitalized to great advantage of my restaurant, the Jade Palace).

At one point ICS appointed a new supervisor. Unfortunately, Ellen Ravin detested me owing possibly to a clash of personalities, or more likely, my ethnicity. Some examples: when I misplaced the kitchen key, I had to wait two semesters for a duplicate, meanwhile, gaining entry only through the security guard, a tedious process. When Pennsylvania state required verification of my employment, Ravin became furious and attacked me for wasting her time. She also had a habit of leaving me little nitpicking notes in the kitchen. Since her hostile attitude was unconducive to my teaching, I made the mistake of complaining to Gillian Gilhool, her boss, but it backfired and further alienated our relations. Bent on reconciliation and as a peace offering, I invited them both for lunch.

Ravin refused and phoned me instead:

"Things are not working out. I want you to stop teaching."

"What?" I was stunned.

"I don't want you to teach anymore."

"Why?"

"We don't get along. And I want you out."

"Don't my students have any say so? After all they gave me excellent reviews every

semester."

"But I'm the supervisor. You have no choice but to quit."

"I won't."

"I insist."

"I love teaching. I came from a family of teachers, and I will never give up. And you can't force me out."

She resorted to a new tactic some days later, sounding surprisingly friendly: "I want to make a slight change this semester. Since you always enjoy a full beginner's class, I would like you to give other cooking teachers a better chance to compete."

She suggested that instead of starting my fall class in September, as did the other teachers, I postpone my starting date to November. Not realizing the dark scheme, I did not object. When November came, for the first time the enrollment fell short of the minimum requirement. She instantly fired me.

I got so angry that I fired off a two-page letter to Temple University's president Peter Liacouras, whom I had met once at a dinner party of which I was the caterer. He didn't take any action or reply. Having no other recourse, I ended my long tenure the victim of politics, subterfuge, and possibly racism. However, nothing could diminish my joy of teaching and my happy memories at Temple and elsewhere.

COMMUNITY SERVICE (1965–1969)

In the 1960s I was eager to serve the Chinese community as the newly elected president of the Chinese Students and Alumni Association (CSAA). It actually embraced practically all the Chinese in Greater Philadelphia as well as those in the neighboring states of New Jersey and Delaware, numbering several thousand. They represented the intelligentsia, professionals, college and university students who resided outside Chinatown. Residents of Chinatown, numbering over 100, were like a separatist group. The majority did not have the same educational opportunities. They were all of Cantonese origin and engaged primarily in the restaurant, grocery, and gift shop businesses and were all members of the Chinese Benevolent Association (CBA). Except for shopping, dining, and the few who attended Catholic and Protestant services in Chinatown, CSAA members had very little to do with CBA members. My partnership with restaurateur-chef King Chen during the embryonic stage of my won ton soup business was most likely the first exception.

It was a well-known fact that Chinese were like a pan of loose sands: "yi pan shan sha." There was no unity, no cohesion among us, especially between the better and the less educated classes, and between people speaking different dialects and from different regions. I was determined to use my office to forge solidarity among the diverse diaspora. The first thing I did was try to join the CBA, the Chinatown faction, but I was afraid it might reject me because I was an outsider. Instead, the organization was overjoyed by my initiative to break down the Berlin Wall between us two Chinese factions. I began to attend CBA monthly meetings along with leaderships from the various family and business associations. And the welfare of Chinatown became my concern.

My biggest worry was the Pennsylvania Department of Transportation's (DOT) plan to expand its Vine Street Expressway. In total disregard of the well-being of Chinatown, it called for the erection of two exit ramps on Ninth and Eleventh Streets, and the destruction of part of the Holy Redeemer Church and School.

Chinatown already had two physical barriers, with the Convention Center bordering on the south, and the Vine Street Expressway on the north, just three blocks apart. If the two exit ramps were to be erected, they would form two additional barriers to the east and the west. In other words, this enclave would be boxed in on four sides. No less insidious was the DOT's proposal to partially destroy the Catholic church and school. Established in 1941, it ministered to the religious, cultural, social, and educational needs of the Chinese in Greater Philadelphia and abutting states.

During an emergency meeting, the leadership was all set to accept what seemed to be an inevitable fate. I, however, disagreed and made an impromptu, impassioned speech, paraphrased as: "Chinatown is facing its worst crisis in history. We are subjected to a thoughtless, cruel, racist policy that has no place in a democracy. Yet you are unable to muster the will and courage to save our community; you capitulate too easily and accept injustice too readily. I, for one, will not give up. We have our rights and we will exercise them. By raising our voices, maximizing our protest effort and fighting to the bitter end, we shall overcome."

My exhortation worked. We speedily organized a march

from Chinatown to the Pennsylvania state building on Spring Garden Street. Meeting the DOT officials, I—along with others—denounced the expansion plan. This gained much publicity and became the start of a protest movement. As more activists—including those who vowed to lie in the path of the bulldozers—joined our fight, we eventually thwarted the PA state's ill-considered proposal.

As publisher and editor of the CSAA newsletters, which were always in English, I made them bilingual so that Chinatown residents could not only read the publications in Chinese but be encouraged to attend the various functions that I planned. They included social, cultural, and recreational programs.

An especially successful one was a whole day cruise on the Delaware River attended by a huge turnout from both CSAA and CBA. I rented a large ship. One deck was for mah-jongg playing, a second deck dancing, a third socializing, and a fourth sunbathing. To add to the enjoyment, I asked King Chen, owner-chef of the Pepsi restaurant, to prepare box lunches of dim sum. For visual delights on the cruise, which went south toward Chesapeake Bay, we took in such sights as Philadelphia's famous Navy Yard, a 1200-acre of ship building/repair and research facilities; Pennsylvania towns like Chester and Marcus Hook on one side of the Delaware River; and little South Jersey towns like Camden, Collingswood Sewell, and Bridgeton on the other. When we were returning to the port after a fun-filled and relaxed day, Philadelphia's skyline, dominated by the imposing city hall, the tallest building then and topped with the statue of William Penn, never looked more beautiful against the backdrop of an enchanting sunset. As the sojourners alit they all seemed well contented with smiling faces.

An even bigger event was the Chinese New Year celebration. I planned to organize a grand gala highlighted by a spectacular banquet catered by New York's best Chinese restaurant, Shun Lee, which I frequented and was rated four stars by the *New York Times*. Not being in the catering business, Shun Lee, however, did not own the needed trucks and facilities, one of the most critical being portable Chinese ranges, the so-called candy stoves. Without their intense fire power, no large-scale cooking would be possible. Hence, I was faced with some logistical problems.

Looking for two such stoves was not easy. I investigated the possibility of buying them and propane gas tanks. But the costs were prohibitive. Another option was to rent them. However, no such rental companies existed. At one point I thought I had to scrub my catering plan. Before giving up I had a feeling that Chinatown might be the answer. By knocking on quite a few doors and checking with my contacts there I discovered a restaurant having exactly what I needed: two portable candy stoves. The owner, Frank Hing, generously lent them to me and with his plumbing skill hooked them up gratis to the kitchen gas line at the dining venue.

My choice was International House (IH) with which I had a very close relationship, having served as president of the Students Council and founder of the IH Glee Club and IH Soccer Team. International House boasted a large auditorium, a convenient location only six blocks from Chinatown, and a very reasonable rental fee, indeed the least expensive of all the places I had investigated. While the IH lacked banquet facilities and was not sure such a function was feasible, I convinced them otherwise by my proposed plan to rent the needed round dining tables and dishware.

On the day of the New Year celebration a volunteer drove his station wagon to Shun Lee to pick up two chefs, ingredients for over 100 guests, cooking utensils, and serving platters. Everything went well without a hitch as the chefs arrived in early afternoon to do the preparation, and dinner was ready at the appointed hour. Despite the limitations of the IH kitchen our talented chefs treated the full house guests to some 12 ingratiating dishes the likes of which Philadelphians had never savored. At the end of this memorable extravaganza, happy guests gave me—the more deserving chefs should have made an appearance—a big round of applause.

After the tables were cleared and rolled away, volunteers turned the dining hall into a theater where an evening of entertainment was presented. I wrote a short romantic comedy in Chinese, *An American Education*—my very first— especially for the occasion. (In successive years, even after the expiration of my presidency, CSAA would present a new comedy of mine in English annually as part of the New Year celebration.) This evening ended with a dance that allowed young professionals like me and students from the various colleges and universities (Penn, Temple, Drexel, Bryn Mawr, Villanova, etc.) to mingle and indulge in the delight of foxtrot, jitterbug, waltz, tango, cha cha, etc.

To remind us of our proud heritage I sponsored cultural programs with slides from New York's Museum of Art showcasing China's greatest artworks from the various dynasties, and invited prominent artists to give talks and demonstrations. One program featured a husband-and-wife watercolor team, with one painting tree branches adorned with flowers and the other complementing them with birds. In addition I put together a CSAA song book containing such favorites as "How Can I Not Think of Her" and "Flower Drum Song."

I was also active in a Chinese fraternity called FF. Founded in 1910, it had chapters in major U.S. cities, Shanghai, Hong Kong and Singapore, with the motto "fellowship and service." For the second part of this motto I, as chairman of the local lodge, came up with a fund-raising idea to benefit an orphanage in Hong Kong: a charity ball. I rented the huge auditorium of Drexel University's Student Activities Center, hired an 11-

piece band, and displayed Chinese paintings in the anteroom. For our guest of honor I invited Pearl Buck. She was well-known for her ties to China where she was born to a missionary father and penned *The Good Earth,* a novel about life in a Chinese village. Largely on account of this epic drama, she won the Nobel Prize in literature. In her later life, she relocated to Bucks County and headed the Pearl S. Buck Foundation and an adoption center for abandoned Amerasian children fathered by American soldiers stationed in the Far East.

She arrived at the charity ball with a man known as the "Dancing Master," Ted Harris, as portrayed in a not-too-flattering *Philadelphia* magazine article. He was an Arthur Murray dance instructor with whom she spent a small fortune taking lessons. In welcoming her and Harris, I introduced myself as sponsor of the ball but was surprised she made no effort to be sociable; just a word of "hello," a quick handshake and walked away. When the band started playing, she surprised me further by her dancing. Despite being overweight, she did the jitterbug, cha cha and other dances with agility, grace, skill and exuberance. Obviously, Harris had taught her well as the two commanded the dance floor. The ball turned out to be a great success, raising enough money to add a wing to the Hong Kong orphanage.

Frequently visiting New York to meet with friends and have a good Chinese meal, I got acquainted with the China Institute. Founded in 1926 by a few distinguished educators including John Dewey and Hu Shih (known especially for his advocacy for vernacular written Chinese), its purpose was to "advance a deeper understanding of China through programs in education, culture, business, and art." It boasted a prominent art gallery and popular classes in history, music, philosophy, language, art, literature, etc. It also had an acclaimed cooking program to which I was highly attracted and was elated to join its teaching staff in 1970.

In addition to providing community services to Chinese students and professionals with programs such as lectures, dances, and movies, the China Institute's biggest event was the annual convention in upstate New York at scenic Silver Bay on Lake George. It always attracted several hundred Chinese from numerous states during the Labor Day weekend. There were such diversions as athletic activities, lake cruises, concerts, movies, picnics, and lectures with topics varying from "The Art of Movie Making" by famed actress Tan Pao-Yin, to "Chinese Men's Physiology" by Tony Award winner David Henry Hwang (*M. Butterfly*), to "The Romance of Chinese Cuisine" by me.

One highlight was the annual beauty contest of which I was one of the organizers and the emcee for several successive years. To make it entertaining, I tried to be humorous and devised a few tricky but droll questions for the finalists, including the following:

"In ancient China, some people thought taking too many baths were harmful to one's spiritual and physical well-being and so they limited bathing to just three times in their lifetime: at birth, at wedding, and at death. If your intended husband is like that how do you encourage him to cleanse himself more often?" which brought some interesting answers to the delight and amusement of the audience.

I also told jokes including one concerning an American tourist's frustration in buying a $1.25 fan in a Chinatown gift shop (as reported earlier in my chapter on Jade Palace).

Impressed by whatever attributes I might have and the fact I had been president of Philadelphia's Chinese community, the China Institute's board of trustees at one time were considering me a likely candidate to succeed its outgoing president, Richard Hsu. It was an august and coveted position, and I was highly flattered. It would have been a great way to continue my interest to serve the community and advance a greater appreciation of China. Regrettably I was busy running my Chinese food business while taking writing courses to fulfill my aspiration of becoming a journalist and reluctantly turned down the golden opportunity.

CHAPTER SEVEN (1962–2009)

Won Ton Entrepreneur

If variety is the spice of life, thankfully I have been able to indulge in myriad enthralling endeavors including three that came about not by design but by chance: attending Arthur Miller's *The Crucible* inspired me to become an actor, the publication of my first magazine article turned me into a journalist, and the fortuitous perusal of an article about a business tycoon challenged me to be a businessman, more specifically, an entrepreneur.

The last did not come about without some careful soul searching. For a long time I had abhorred business. It seemed to appeal to our baser instincts, our lust for money, the proverbial root of all evils, breeding greed, dishonesty, corruption, and all too often brought out the worst in humanity. Just a few personal experiences: auto shops that milked me for unnecessary repairs and inflated bills; an Aspen, CO, lawyer/businessman who cheated me in a real estate transaction; contractors who swindled me working on my house; a utility company deliberately overcharged me despite evidence to the contrary. Even in ancient China of the four categories of professions, business was ranked the lowest.

Then I read the amazing—and unlikely—story of food magnate Jeno Paulucci.

A Minnesota native and second-generation Italian-American, he came from a penurious family. After working in the grocery business, he aspired to be an entrepreneur by manufacturing and marketing canned bean sprouts. However, no bank would lend him the needed capital. It was only through the help of a friend that he got a $2,500 loan to get started and founded his Chun King Company in 1947 (named after China's wartime capital then, Chung King, spelled Chongqing today).

He was a diligent worker and superb salesman who began to get truckloads of business way beyond his local territory. Spurred by one success after another, he went on to develop a line of Chinese products including canned chicken chow mein, his best seller, chicken chop suey, water chestnuts, and soy sauce. Ironically, chicken chow mein and chicken chop suey were unknown in China and believed to have originated in America.

With increased business, Paulucci got additional help from funny adman Stan Freberg, who created highly effective and humorous TV ads. In time, he built a gigantic empire and enjoyed a 50% market share. Subsequently he sold Chun King to R. J. Reynolds for a cool $63 million dollars in 1966. He next got into the frozen food business and became a noted philanthropist.

I first came across chicken chow mein in 1951. I was a student at the Juilliard Music School in uptown Manhattan (before moving to Lincoln Center). Having lunch in a nearby Chinese restaurant called Lucky, I ordered this dish out of curiosity. It was something I had never seen before: an unappetizing looking mélange of chicken and three gooey vegetables—bean sprouts, celery, and onion—so overcooked that they lost their crispy textures, which violated one of the Chinese culinary tenets. This mixture was served over what was called "chow mein noodles" of which bundles of noodles were deep fried to a crispy finish.

With great curiosity and interest, I dug in and found it not without merit. When the three vegetables were overcooked together, they somehow created a synergistic effect with an enticing aroma and taste. And when the chicken and the mushy vegetables were served over the crispy chow mein noodles, the whole thing offered the delight of textural contrast, which did reflect the yin/yang principle of Chinese cuisine. That may be the reason for a long time it was the favorite selection in Chinese restaurants.

Paulucci's success story got me thinking. If a Midwestern Italian-American could achieve such phenomenal success with a pseudo-Chinese food product, maybe I'd have a chance to emulate him. With my ethnicity and erudition in Chinese cookery, of which I was a devotee since I was a youngster, perhaps I could commercialize an authentic line of Chinese food.

Meanwhile I gained a softened outlook about business and a new insight into entrepreneurship. There is no denying that business is as necessary to society as water is to fish. It promotes trade, powers economy, creates jobs, provides valuable products and services, and stimulates innovations and inventions that steadily improve the quality of life. What's more, the overwhelming majority of businessmen are conscientious and law-abiding, not least my beloved father, a most honorable banker nicknamed "Buddha" for his honesty and integrity.

Another important consideration: to be an entrepreneur of new products puts one in a different and loftier business category. One must be a visionary who identifies an unmet consumer need, takes the risk, and expends time, effort, and money to fulfill that need in the cutthroat marketplace. If successful, one is rewarded with not only financial gains but also the satisfaction of seeing the germ of an idea translating into a reality. This creative joy is no different from that of an inventor who transforms an inspiration into a tangible product, a composer who turns a blank manuscript into a symphony.

I thought if I joined the company of these men as a Chinese food pioneer I would have a lot of fun and enhance my voracious appetite for life, despite the high fatality rate of new products (about 80% according to one source) and my total ignorance of business. If I should fail I might lose my shirt but I had something to fall back on: my day job as an analytical chemist at Merck.

Two big questions facing me were "What would be my new product?" and "How best to manufacture it?"

Frozen food definitely had an edge over canned food. While both processing methods inevitably impaired the flavor, the former did not do as much damage to the taste. However, canned food had some distinct advantages: less expensive to develop, manufacture, package, store, ship, and market. Having little capital, I thought it would be prudent to opt for the more economical route.

As to what would be a good candidate for my venture, I was in a good position to decide. A frequent patron of Chinese restaurants, I came to know the public taste pretty well. It was highly conservative then. The more exotic and sophisticated hot and sour soup, kung Pao chicken and mou shu pork were still relatively unknown. Among the most popular selections by far were egg rolls and won ton soup, and next to them, pepper steak and sweet and sour pork. Egg rolls would not be a good choice; being deep fried it could not be easily sterilized and packaged as a canned product.

Won ton soup, on the other hand, could be an excellent consideration. Transcending the traditional concept of soup, it's almost half a meal, an excellent first course that tickles the palate in a most delightful way and paves the way for whatever entrée that follows. Won tons, literally meaning swallowing cloud in Chinese, are dumplings whose fillings can be minced pork alone, or combined with shrimp, or with such vegetables as watercress and spinach, or any other ingredients one fancies. Won tons can be deep fried, but are more commonly served with a hot, tasty soup. It enjoys certain universal appeal having its counterparts in the Italian tortellini and ravioli, the Jewish kreplach, the German gefilte noodle, and the Polish pierogi. And to my best knowledge there was no packaged won ton soup anywhere in the states or elsewhere. Since it was time consuming and arduous to make, I could mass produce this specialty to meet a consumer need while enjoying a proprietary position.

For a fledging entrepreneur like me, the best—and only— way to get started was through contract packing. But finding such a packer before the era of Google was not easy. After extensive research, I finally found an ideal one by the name of Venice Maid. Located in Vineland, South Jersey, it was near Philadelphia where I resided, only a little over one hour's drive. This company was one of the largest canneries in the country, which not only manufactured its own line of Venice Maid brands but also packed for other companies, some of which were industrial giants. When I phoned John Pepper, the CEO, about my proposal of commercializing won ton soup he expressed interest in exploring the possibility and arranged a meeting.

On my first visit to Vineland, the first thing that struck me was the strong tomato aroma permeating the air long before my arrival. The relatively small offices were part of the canning plant where I met John and his two brothers, Larry and Vincent, president and treasurer of Venice Maid respectively. The three were highly gracious, friendly, and helpful and did not fit my stereotypical image of throat-cutting, unscrupulous businessmen. They were enthusiastic about my proposed venture.

"What kind of filler would your won tons contain?" John Pepper asked.

"The typical Chinese restaurant filler is pork, which is what I have in mind."

"But isn't it true that the prime customers of Chinese food are Jewish?"

"Definitely."

"Since many Jewish people don't eat pork, I suggest you use chicken filler."

"But it's slightly more expensive."

"It would be worth it. If I were you that's what I would use."

I had no trouble embracing his suggestion.

"If you were to pack for me do you have a suitable soup for my won tons?"

"Yes, we make a very good chicken soup called Chickerino." Brewed for a long time with chicken backs and necks, it made a highly favorable impression on me.

"So, all we need from you are the won tons and your own labels," he added.

He further suggested that we limit the number of won tons to four per can. A novice would-be businessman, I pretty much deferred decisions like these to him.

Giving me a vote of confidence, John said: "You have an excellent idea. I believe there is a market for you, and we'd be happy to be your packer."

I was thrilled and found certain irony in this joint venture. Like Jeno Paulucci, the Peppers were American-born Italians. While Paulucci made a fortune on pseudo-Chinese products I was hoping to make a fortune on won tons, which may be related to ravioli or tortellini through Marco Polo. On my visits to Italy many natives told me they believed that pasta came from China. One tourist guide, Mrs. Primavera, a Chinese-

Italian resident of Venice, informed our group when Marco Polo returned to Venice from China, he brought with him several Chinese servants/cooks, which may give more credence to the linkage. Food historians may doubt the connections but there is no dispute that Chinese pasta and Italian pasta bear some eerily striking similarities, for example:

- Won ton and tortellini are 100% identical in the way they are made: It calls for placing filler in the center of a square wrapper, sealing it to form a triangle and then gluing the two side arms together. And both pastas are served with broth. The only difference is in the sizes, tortellini being a trifle smaller.

- "Da been," literally big pie, is shaped, sized, and baked just like pizza.

- "Fah mein," or hair noodles, are like the Italian angel hair, except the former is thinner.

- "Mao err," or cat's ear, resembles the ear-shaped orecchiette.

- Various types of Chinese noodles can find their twins in spaghetti, fettuccini, and linguine.

Whatever the real connections, John Pepper's willingness to be my contract packer was not without some risks. Trusting me fully, he didn't investigate my financial resources which were extremely limited, my business experience and marketing savvy which were nil, my FICO, my credit rating, which was unacceptably low. He didn't even ask me to sign a contract. His only requirement was a minimum 1,000 case order. In return, he would store my product for free and then ship my order with its own trucks or common carriers to anywhere in the U.S. and charge me only for the quantity ordered. He also helped me by asking one of his top food brokers, Frank Jelinek, to represent me.

Before I left, John Pepper took me on a tour of his plant where huge quantities of tomato products were being canned—the reason for the strong tomato aroma I detected earlier on my way to Venice Maid. It was fascinating to watch the automated process of making raviolis, Venice Maid's specialty. A gigantic mixing bowl blended durum flour, eggs, water, and oil to form well-kneaded dough. An extruder turned the dough into sheets which went to a pasta machine containing the filling and voila, out came individual raviolis. The operation was smooth, fast, and efficient, like the automobile assembly line I saw in Detroit. How I wished my won tons could be manufactured similarly. It became one of my challenges. For the time being the only way to make won tons was by hand, a slow and costly process.

For my intended production of 1,000 minimum cases, which would require some 50,000 won tons, I would need a labor force to wrap the won tons within the shortest time possible, say two days. It would be difficult for me to recruit the necessary workers, the prime source being Chinatown. At that time, I was not yet an active civic leader there and so my contacts were not good. As a frequent restaurant patron, I did get to know one owner well: King Chen of the Pepsi restaurant. He was also a talented chef whose specialties included dim sum. Having learned to speak Cantonese in Hong Kong, I was able to communicate with him in his native tongue. When I told him about my proposed won ton soup venture he thought it had great merit and expressed interest in joining forces with me. Indeed, being a Chinatown resident with friends galore, he not only could supply all the won tons I needed but was interested in investing money to be my equal partner. Despite his lack of English comprehension, I took him on without much deliberation.

Before scheduling a production at Venice Maid, I had to

tend to a lot of details:

1) Incorporate our partnership, the best advantage being limited liability. If our company should fail and bankrupt the most we could lose was the net asset of the corporation and our personal assets would not be touched. There were also tax advantages. The owners needed to pay only taxes on net profits after deduction for salaries, dividends, and other expenses.

2) Think of a corporate name. Since I had lived in Hong Kong, graduated from high school there, loved this beautiful island and considered it one of the world's gourmet capitals, I opted for Hong Kong.

3) Register my product with the United States Department of Agriculture (USDA). That was how I discovered no other packaged won ton soup existed in the States as USDA had no such prior registration, and I had to define what won ton soup was. Later when international food distributors became my customers they assured me that mine was the first of its kind in the world. My relatives in China told me the same thing.

4) Worry about the USDA's requirement that a federal food inspector be present when producing meat-containing products and the manufacturer had to put him on the payroll. This would make my startup costs high and operation impractical. I was planning to have a factory to make the won tons. After scheduling my first production I wouldn't know when the next production would be. And I doubted if I could hire an inspector periodically as needed with lots of gaps in between. However, I discovered if the product contained less than 2% meat, the inspector require-

ment could be waived. And fortunately, my finished product met that requirement. So I got around the technicality.

5) Choose a brand name. I opted for "Da Tung" which means the commonality of mankind, recalling Confucius' famed saying, "within the corners of the four seas, all men are brothers." To add to the appearance of authenticity I decided also to inscribe the brand name "Da Tung" in Chinese. A good friend of my mine, T. T. Chang, director of Philadelphia's Chinatown YMCA, who happened to be an excellent calligrapher, graciously took on the job.

6) Design a label. With my suggestion and the input of a lithograph photographer, we came up with a pretty picture: a matching set of an ornate spoon, dish, and bowl abutting a pair of pink chop sticks against a bright yellow background (changed later to red). It's eye catching and seemed to be a good stimulus for impulse buying.

7) Search for a small factory in a commercial zone that could accommodate about 60 workers with enough space for a walk-in box. I found just such a place on Front Street not far from the Delaware River. That street was close to a residential area that later became a plush neighborhood known as Society Hill. The rent was not high and it was very near Chinatown and not far from my home.

8) Draft a contract between Hong Kong, Inc. and Venice Maid. Though I had no business background I had enough common sense to worry about the possibility that Venice Maid might unscrupulously pack a similar won ton soup for my would-be competitors in

case my venture became a success. And so, I brought my lawyer Raymond Heuges to Venice Maid. John Pepper saw no problem that as a pioneer I would need a legal document to protect me and so we signed a contract. However, Heuges did not draft a strong contract. It stipulated that either Venice Maid or Hong Kong could annul the contract with a short notice. So I really didn't have a full protection. But since I wholly trusted Pepper's integrity, I didn't press for an iron-clad contract.

All this time I was able to keep my day job as a chemist at Merck. Using my spare time and taking "sick leave" (virtually every Merck chemist took advantage of the so-called "three-day virus" whether sick or not; it was an accepted perk) as needed I was able to accomplish all the above.

Now I was ready to schedule a production at Venice Maid. True to his promise, my partner Chen got all the workers he needed to wrap the won tons in our factory. I asked him to do the job within two days as any longer would impair the freshness and Chen had no trouble producing some 50,000 won tons. To make sure the won tons would not fall apart upon much handling we used an alternate method of making them, preferred by many Chinese restaurants: Place chicken filling in one corner—and not the middle—of a square wrapper. Next roll it toward the opposite corner. Halfway through, bring the two side arms together and seal them with eggs. To prevent the won tons from sticking together, our biggest worry, we coated them with generous amounts of cornstarch before loading them into corrugated boxes.

On the eve of the scheduled production Venice Maid sent a refrigerated truck to pick up the won tons. Very early the following morning Chen and I drove to Vineland to witness the birth of the world's first packaged won ton soup.

To my relief none of the won tons got stuck together. On their historic journey to be canned, they were first blanched and then transported to a circular turntable where female workers used a semi-automatic process to place four won tons into each can. After a dispenser fed hot chicken soup into the cans they were sealed, which had to be completely airtight. Otherwise, botulism, one of the deadliest toxins known to men, would result. The canned food then underwent the retort process at 250 degrees Fahrenheit for one long hour to make sure the product was totally sterilized. After cooling, naked cans (called shiners) of the soup got dressed with my pretty Da Tung labels and the canning process was complete. It took just a few hours to produce some 1,000 cases.

Naturally Chen and I were eager to taste our won ton soup. Our verdict: It was highly palatable. Though the chicken filling shrank a bit, it was still quite acceptable. The won ton wrapper was nice and thin, even after the long retort process. The chicken soup, as tasted earlier, was incomparably good, indeed better than its counterpart in most Chinese restaurants. The two truly made a perfect match. I easily concluded that it was a winner. And all others, including the Peppers and the plant manager, Larry Haas, agreed.

Now the tough part: How to take the soup to the marketplace, primarily supermarkets, and secondarily specialty and fancy food stores, and entice them to buy. Supermarkets were particularly difficult to break into. Because of the convenience of one-stop shopping, they never had to worry about a lack of customers, even during the height of a depression. For that reason, every food manufacturer wanted to be a supplier. By the same token, the competition was utterly fierce. Buyers generally had little interest in accepting new products unless they were backed by an extensive advertising campaign comprising both TV and newspaper ads. Another way to interest the buyers was outright bribery, the offer of free goods. If a supermarket chain had 200 stores, the typical offer would be one case free per store or 200 cases. I certainly didn't have this kind of budget. If the new product had real merit the buyers might accept it with an offer of one case free with purchase of five or 10.

An alternative for me was to rely purely on the attributes of the won ton soup and the salesmanship of my broker. At that time, I had just one: Frank Jelinek, the one John Pepper recommended. A discriminate salesman who often reviewed restaurants for the trade paper, he was not an easy man to please. After tasting the soup, he said it was "very good" but made no prediction as to the chances of success.

Some of the first feedback I got was from my Chinese fraternity brother Steve Ip. He was an enthusiastic supporter of my business from the very beginning. An avid hunter of deer and pheasants, he would invariably give dinner parties and did the cooking after bagging them. On one of his hunting trips he brought with him several tins of freshly processed Da Tung won ton soup. After a day's shooting, he settled into a lodge with his Caucasian friends and was getting ready for dinner. The conversation went something like this as he related to me:

"I have a surprise for you," said Steve, a gifted cook, to his fellow hunters.

"What?"

"Won ton soup."

"You mean you are going to make won ton soup for us?"

"I'm going to serve it, but I don't have to make it."

"How?"

"I've got something you guys never had before: canned won ton soup."

"I never heard of such a thing," said one of the fellows.

"It's a brand-new product. I know the manufacturer. He's a fraternity brother of mine."

Opening one of the cans, Ip said: "You'll find exactly four won tons. That's what he told me." But to his surprise and chagrin one fellow hunter found only two won tons. "Let me try another can." This time there were not four but six won tons.

Ip was at a loss to explain. It appeared that Venice Maid did not have good quality control with its semi-automatic process. It involved the transferring of the won tons from a turntable into the cans partially by hand, which lacked precision. This disparity in the won ton count did not detract from the enjoyment of the diners who expressed hearty approval. But Steve's story worried me about the reaction of those who bought the product and might find only two skimpy won tons and feel cheated.

Meanwhile I decided to do a little product demonstration on my own. It was around early November of 1962 when I first canned my won ton soup. As Thanksgiving was approaching I opted to capitalize on the long weekend to test my product with the public. And Snellenburg's, a Philadelphia downtown department store, agreed to my proposal in return for sales commission. To assist me was my violinist buddy Michael Ma, a 13-year-old Taiwanese-born prodigy. A student at the Curtis Institute of Music, he was living at my house and often played duos with me as a pianist.

On this Black Friday, we found ourselves passing out hot won ton soup and eagerly waited for the reaction. Among the throng of shoppers, numerous tore away from the frenzy of bargain hunting to taste my pride and joy and the general comments were very positive. Indeed, one after another began to buy the soup which kept Michael and me very busy.

I felt relieved when my partner Chen arrived to watch us in action.

"Will you help us out?" I asked.

"No."

"Why not, because you don't have the time?"

"No."

"Then why?"

"I don't feel like doing this sort of thing."

After pressing him further I discovered his reasoning: It was beneath him to sell won ton soup like a common street hawker.

"It may not look too dignified, but if I am willing to do it why should you mind?" I asked.

He was still unmoved. With one word leading to another we started to quarrel, getting angrier and angrier. Soon, like newlyweds we were thinking of splitting before the honeymoon was even over, and over such a trivial matter. I was being small-minded and pig-headed and he was no less stubborn.

Undeterred, Michael and I managed to carry on for three full days and sold some 18 cases. I was exhilarated by the results. But my euphoria was tempered by Snellenburg's suspicion that I underpaid the commission, even though I showed the manager my meticulously kept sales record. "How do I know if this is the true record?" he asked, reviving my earlier loathing about business.

In the next few days I carefully analyzed my relationship with Chen. If a little thing got us so far apart, when bigger problems came along we were bound to have more serious differences. His inability to communicate in English would further complicate our operations. When I accepted him as an equal partner I really didn't think things through.

When we next met, I told him it would not be in our best interest to remain partners. But since he made an invaluable contribution to help me get started and I was not an ingrate I bent over backward to give him the right of first refusal. In other words, if he felt that strongly I offered him the right to buy out my share and find another partner, notwithstanding my nascent exuberance of being an entrepreneur and my initial accomplishments. He graciously let me buy him out. After a period of coolness, we resumed our friendship until his death in 2014.

How would I handle the next production? I had no ready answer. Worse comes to worse, I could take my annual two-week vacation from Merck and try to round up as many won ton wrappers as possible. It would be difficult but not impossible, or so I thought. Meanwhile, there was nothing I could do except to wait for results—if any—from my broker Frank Jelinek.

While the normal commission was five percent, Jelinek asked for seven percent to be my master broker whose additional job was to appoint sub-brokers in areas not covered by him. I consented. He did not require any contract as he seemed to trust me and vice versa. He struck me as an honorable, trustworthy gentleman whose proven salesmanship with Venice Maid gave me peace of mind. However, a few months went by without hearing from him, and I began to worry. It was quite possible I might have to eat my own 1,000 plus cases of won ton soup for the next 50 years.

My worry turned out to be misplaced. Justifying his reputation as a talented salesman, he began to place one order after another starting in January 1963. I was especially pleased that he landed two super accounts, Giant and Safeway chain stores in the greater Washington, D.C., and Baltimore areas. Better still, he made these initial sales without any free goods. In other regions he was equally successful with distributors like Key Foods, Rome Paper, and Phillipsburg. Meanwhile he appointed a sub-broker by the name of Agazarian who covered the greater New York area. He also got orders from a host of outlets including Waldbaums, Big Apple, and Buy Low. In addition, with my appointment of a Philadelphia broker, Joe Dougherty, I was able to do business locally and among my customers were Trymor and Haddon House. The latter proved to be especially valuable as it began to distribute my product to specialty and fancy food stores nationally.

When I got re-orders from all the buyers it was a sure sign of approbation.

What I didn't expect was that my earlier abhorrence toward business would come to haunt me. When Jelinek and I first met, he offered to do the initial billing for me to help me get started. I agreed to this strange arrangement because of my lack of invoicing experience. While he promised to turn over the proceeds as soon as possible, he did not. Despite my repeated reminders he kept stalling with one excuse after another. I soon discovered he was up to an insidious plot. Seeing the potential of my business and my inexperience, he tried to use the payments as ransom to coerce me into giving him my company shares so that he could be a part owner. This greed and his unscrupulous tactics utterly revolted me and I refused to offer him even a single share. The upshot: I had to sue him to recover my money but ended up paying my attorney the standard fee of a third of the collected sum.

I had no trouble appointing a broker to cover the Baltimore and greater D.C. areas: Robert Lehm, a young man and a dead ringer for Elvis Presley. Every time I rode with him on our sales trips I felt he might break out into renditions of "Blue Suede Shoes," "Jailhouse Rock," or the like. Between him, Joe Dougherty, Agazarian, and a little selling on my part when I could take time off from my Merck's chemist job, the Da Tung won ton soup was steadily making inroads. To gain entry to chain stores I occasionally had to offer one case free with purchase of five or 10. With increasing sales and the depletion of my inventory it was time to schedule another production. But how was I to do this single-handedly with the loss of my partner, King Chen?

To supervise the production, I would need three days: two

for the wrapping of some 50,000 won tons and one to deliver them to Venice Maid as no truck was available to pick them up. So I reported a "three-day virus" sick leave to Merck and it was granted as expected with no questions asked.

Ordering the two main ingredients of ground chicken and won ton wrappers challenged my ability to estimate. The quantity of the one had to correspond to that of the other. If there were insufficient wrappers, the excess filler would go to waste, and vice versa. Fortunately, being an analytical chemist and having a fairly good head for math I made a near perfect, educated guess.

As to finding the needed labor force, initially I was not too worried. I heard from the grapevine that Chinatown was suffering unemployment. I thought I could kill two birds with one stone: creating jobs while getting the workers I would require. Unfortunately, the unemployment problem was not real. On the first day of my scheduled two-day production I recruited only a few Chinatown residents. I also put my dear mother Priscilla and a couple of her lady friends to work, totaling about eight and representing a fraction of the 60 or so I needed. Waiting in vain for others to show up, I began to despair. It didn't help that some of the lady wrappers took their sweet time to produce, occasionally slowing down to chitchat, totally oblivious to my time constraint and my pleas to speed up. At the end of the day I was thoroughly dejected.

Early the following morning I felt worse when my frantic efforts to recruit more workers failed miserably. My relations with Chinatown were just developing, and I soon exhausted my connections. And so, I got the same eight helpers making very small progress.

In great despondency, I stepped out of the factory to take a short walk, breathe some fresh air, and clear my mind. Having far too few won tons for the minimum 1,000 case order, I would have to call off the production while fearing some repercussions. And what would I do with the won tons already made and the plethora of ingredients in the walk-in box? (My factory had no freezer.) They were surely destined as wastage. I started to have great regrets of getting into the business.

But just as in my army days when confronted with seemingly impossible obstacles, I did not give up. Instead, I searched for inspiration and possible solutions and like a flash of lightning a fresh idea struck me. I remembered that once when I was in a Pennsylvania Unemployment Office I saw a room full of people, virtually all African Americans, anxiously looking for work and waiting to answer possible calls from employers who might phone in. It's a long shot but why not try to utilize these people? Accordingly, I called one of the offices asking to speak to the manager. A woman answered.

"I need people," I said.

"Good. How many?"

"As many as you have."

"Are you sure?"

"Positive."

"For how many days?"

"Just one day."

Apparently surprised, she asked: "To do what?"

"Make won tons."

She wasn't sure what she had heard and made me repeat. "Yes, to wrap won tons, the kind of won tons you get in a Chinese restaurant."

Sounding more and more incredulous, she said: "But my people are not Chinese; They don't know how to make won tons."

"Don't worry. I'll teach them."

"Is it hard?"

"No, not too hard."

"How much would you pay?"

"Minimum wage ($1.15) and I'll pay cash. I need people right now at this very minute.

And remember, send me as many as possible."

The manager didn't know how many of the unemployed would take up my strange offer but promised to try her best and asked for my factory address.

Within about 30 minutes a few arrived. My standard operating procedure for them was wash hands first, put on an apron, sit down, and learn the routine. Again, I chose the restaurant way of making won tons to minimize their chance of falling apart. My new employees had no trouble learning although their pace was very, very slow initially. But gradually they picked up speed and when I clocked it they were averaging about 100 won tons per hour. Not great but acceptable.

Soon a number of others reported for work. After a short time, an even greater throng arrived. In time my factory became what was probably Pennsylvania's hottest place for the unemployed. I was amazed to see a long, unending procession that started to inundate my factory with no end in sight. I was instantly reminded of a segment of Walt Disney's epic animation, *Fantasia*, featuring Paul Dukas' "The Sorcerer's Apprentice," with Mickey Mouse in the title role. Using his master's magic hat, he turned a broom into a robot with two hands and taught it to fetch buckets of water as ordered by his master. When the robots began to clone themselves by the hundreds they formed an army of unending procession marching inexorably towards their destination, just as what I was witnessing.

By noon my factory still had a long line waiting outside. Instead of turning the crowd away I told them if they wanted to wait or come back later they could replace those who had to leave and that my factory would be open probably till midnight.

Shortly afterward, the PA Unemployment district manager stopped by to see what exactly was going on and if I had a legitimate business. She was stunned to behold an incredible sight: Except for a few Chinese workers there was an all-black team, male and female, sitting shoulder to shoulder on long tables, furiously making won tons in a newly learned skill unlikely to help them get another day's job elsewhere. The district manager beamed approvingly.

For a few hours, I was aided by my friend Aloysius Lee, owner of the Oriental grocery store in Chinatown and a former Chinese restaurant waiter who often had to make won tons as part of the job. Having done it so many times, he developed an incredible speed that one had to see to believe. Like an automated process, a culinary Vladimir Horowitz, he was churning out the pasta at the rate of some 400 pieces hourly. He really didn't need this job and was doing me a great favor, and so I gratefully paid him $4 an hour.

Meanwhile I was elated to see the mountains of ingredients in the walk-in-box rapidly diminish. I was convinced by day's end I would have more than 50,000 won tons as needed. Indeed, just before midnight the walk-in-box had nothing left. Sending everyone home, I needed one person to help me clean up and transfer the boxes of won tons into a U-Haul that I had rented. A very attractive African American teenager of about 18 or 19 caught my attention. "Would you like to make a few more dollars by helping me?" I asked. "Sure," she said.

When we finished a little after midnight I had a sudden inexplicable, amorous urge, although I had had such a long, long, tiring and trying day and at such a late hour. I was not a lustful guy or one prone to seducing women. On this magical night, I was surprised I didn't try to rein in my overpowering desire. If she didn't give me the slightest encouragement I certainly would restraint myself. But when I looked at her with obvious passion she didn't turn her eyes away. Instead, without saying a single word she easily communicated to me through her facial expressions that she was attracted to me and that she was responsive to acting spontaneously toward a physical union. Strangely, the thought of going to a motel never occurred to me. I simply pointed at one of the long tables and awaited her answer. It would have been a crude, unromantic, horribly poor substitute for a bed but she nodded. We both felt a powerful impulse and that this was the right moment. I had never made love to an African American woman and thought it would be a beautiful interracial carpe diem to climax our mutual attraction.

But alas, before we proceeded I chickened out. I just had too much on my mind. Would some of the won tons fall apart? Would I have enough energy to drive to Venice Maid at the crack of dawn and not fall asleep? Would our lovemaking result in any complications? And suddenly I felt uncomfortable. Regretfully I said, "I better take you home." When I parked my car just outside her West Philadelphia home my passion was still strong, and I felt the pang of unconsummated love. Acting as a perfect gentleman, I tenderly asked her if I could fondle and kiss her and she gladly said "yes." We both let ourselves go and made the most of this rare, ephemeral intimacy.

When I got home it was already wee hours on this last day of my "three-day virus." After grabbing a little sleep I drove the U-Haul to Vineland and made it before the scheduled production hour at seven A.M. I was relieved none of the won tons got stuck together, or fell apart, thanks to the good work of my one-day employees. As before the production went speedily and smoothly.

But I resolved not to produce won tons this haphazard way ever again. My only alternative was to find a method to mass produce them with a high-speed automatic process, and ideally one that could work with Venice Maid's ravioli machine, since ravioli and won tons involved the same principle of stuffing dough with filling. If I were to succeed it would be difficult or perhaps impossible to make them the conventional way with two side arms of a triangular won ton wrapper glued together. What if I skipped this sealing process by simply making triangular won tons? They would look a little different from the usual but I felt the consumers might not find them too objectionable.

It became my challenge to develop such a detachable won ton die that could be hooked up to the ravioli machine. John Pepper was skeptical about the feasibility but referred me to his mechanic/die specialist. This man was not sure either.

"If you're willing to take a chance and pay me $3,000 I can try to make such a die. But I give no guarantee it'll work," he said. A risk taker, I agreed to his terms and waited eagerly for him to finish the job.

At a family dinner when I discussed the possibility of making triangular won tons with my oldest surgeon/brother David, the smartest son of the family, he had his doubts.

"People will not buy triangular won tons because the appearance would violate their concept of what won tons look like," said David, who was 15 years my senior and had always been like a father to me.

I countered: "If a round pizza is changed to a square shape but having the same flavor I believe people would still buy it." My mantra was: "If a rose by any other name smells just as sweet, a won ton by any other shape tastes just as great."

As soon as the won ton die was completed I scheduled a little test run at Venice Maid. Using a typical ravioli filling and dough for the purpose of our experiment, the machinist attached the die to the ravioli machine. We both were anxious to see the results as he set the machine initially at a very low speed. The die did successfully make the triangular won tons but we got worried when quite a few got stuck on the die. The problem disappeared after he made some minor adjustments. He then gradually turned the machine to maximum speed and to our relief dozens of won tons tumbled down with no sticking problem. We succeeded in perfecting the first automated process of producing won tons in history. I was filled with an ineffable joy and the pride of being an entrepreneur.

Before my next production, I had to make some important decisions:

1) Change the makeup of the won ton filling. Since I felt my product had broad appeal to the general public and was not limited to Jewish patronage, I devised a new recipe based on my own original recipe using a combination of ground pork and cabbage. To expand the recipe into an industrial scale formulation required much testing and mathematics, which I successfully accomplished.

2) Instead of four won tons per can, I increased to 11 to give the consumers better value and because the triangular won tons were slightly smaller than the handmade ones. With a totally automated process, Venice Maid assured me each can should get 11 won tons, plus or minus one.

3) Since ravioli dough and won ton dough had virtually the same ingredients, I could use the former to encase my won tons. But I didn't care for its thickness; I wanted my won ton dough to be as thin as possible for better taste and to minimize the problem of doughiness to which both raviolis and won tons were vulnerable after sitting in the cans for a while. After making some adjustments I got what I desired.

With everything falling into place and the dwindling of my inventory I scheduled another production. This time all I had to do was simply make a phone call to Venice Maid. While the earlier test run was successful, no one was 100% sure a full-scale production would not cause any problems, especially with my new formulation. There were none as I witnessed the realization of my dream, the rapid manufacturing of won tons devoid of human hands. The die worked perfectly, turning out hundreds upon of hundreds of them at lightning speed. Occasionally I brought a few newly made won tons to Venice Maid's on-site lab to check the thickness of the dough and weigh the filling and both met my specifications. When canning was complete I tried out my brand-new, triangular-shaped won tons with pork filling and the same chicken broth. The taste was highly satisfying as before.

As to how the marketplace would react, happily I heard no complaints from the customers, brokers, or buyers and there-fore I suffered no decrease my orders. On the contrary, I actually enjoyed ever-increasing sales.

To expand my business, I tried my hand at something I knew very little about but thought could be an effective marketing tool: public relations. It was just before the annual National Food Brokers Convention in New York in 1967. Despite my deficiencies in English I submitted an article on spec to the *Food Trade News*. It chronicled my path from an aspiring concert pianist, who was Van Cliburn's classmate at Juilliard, to an analytic chemist at Merck, to an entrepreneur who commercialized the nation's first packaged won ton soup. *Food Trade News'* editor saw fit to publish my article promi-nently on the front page accompanied by my photo.

The story caught the eye of the top buyer of Liberty Import, an international specialty and fancy foods distributor. He approached me and wanted me to be his purveyor. Unexpect-edly, I found myself in the strange position of being sought after by a buyer instead of the other way around. After placing one order he asked me to pack the soup under Liberty Import's own Bonavita brand and included it in its product catalog.

Soon becoming one of my best customers, Liberty Import succeeded in distributing my soup in the U.S., Europe, and elsewhere.

With the success of the consumer market, I next looked into the institutional trade which serviced restaurants, hospitals, schools, and various other dining establishments totaling several billion dollars' business annually. To accommodate this trade I needed a modified won ton soup. The product development turned out to be relatively easy. I simply devised a slightly different formulation and procedure which called for placing 70 won tons per 50 ounce can with the same chicken broth except it was now concentrated. All one had to do to serve was to heat the contents with the addition of one can of water.

As expected, I easily broke into the institutional trade because of the product merit and that it met a great consumer need with no competition. The nature of this trade was such that manufacturers did not have to worry about advertising, promotions, or giving free goods to get an order. A simple presentation to the buyer would suffice. That was how I easily sold to smaller distributors under my Da Tung brand. Then I acquired three big ones: S. E. Rykoff, Monarch, and John Sexton. The first was a very large distributor based on the West Coast. The second had branches in a number of regions including Philadelphia and Detroit. The third was the nation's largest institutional distributor which serviced some 50,000 customers and had its own manufacturing plants. Soon I began to pack for these distributors under their labels.

I also expanded into the vending business. With a simple presentation I acquired the two biggest customers in the industry: ARA and Macke. Both liked the novelty and convenience: with the insertion of a quarter, one could instantly get a single serving of hot Da Tung brand won ton soup. The public liked it too and I was hoping it would be another rousing success. When sales started to decline I resorted to a costly dining and wining party to which I invited a large group of Macke executives with their implicit understanding of placing orders. But they turned out to be freeloaders who failed to reciprocate the courtesy. I really shouldn't blame them too much because my product did not have sustainability and was not compatible with the vending business. And no amount of entertaining would have saved the soup from its premature demise. After all, ultimately it was really the consumers who had the final say so on the life or death of a new product.

Eying the growth of my consumer and institutional businesses, John Pepper approached me at one point with an offer I didn't like at all: to buy my won ton die, not outright but gradually by giving me a "die allowance" with 10 cents deducted from each case of the consumer size ordered and 20 cents from the institutional size.

"Why?" I asked.

"I want to make sure you don't take your die to someone else to make the soup," he said.

"Why would I do a thing like that?"

"We appreciate your business and just want to protect ourselves; we are not trying to pack for other customers," he assured me.

I really felt like rejecting his offer which sounded a little fishy to me. But during a moment of weakness I decided not to put up a fight, trusting his honesty instead.

Meanwhile I had more pressing thought on my mind. I wanted to expand my product line and turned to the poss-ibility of developing another specialty which no other manu-facturer had packaged: sweet and sour pork. This has always been one of the most popular Chinese dishes and for good reasons. The meat, which is coated lightly with cornstarch, is deep fried, giving it a lightly crispy external texture contrasting with a soft internal texture. The garnishes consist of a colorful blend of such vegetables as yellow pineapple, green peppers, and orange carrots. Adding enjoyment is the sweet and sour sauce, which seemed to have a universal appeal. In short, this dish was a marvel of visual beauty and contrasting textures and tastes.

Unlike big companies such as DuPont and Procter & Gamble, which had to go through market research, panel discussion, focus group test marketing, and endless meetings before launching a new product, I simply relied on my own judgment and went full steam ahead with my idea. The product development, however, was quite daunting. To mass produce the coating of the pork and the deep-frying processes would be too complicated and impractical. Bypassing these steps, I developed a new, original recipe at home which kept the same proportion of pork and similar vegetables with the same sweet and sour sauce, a 50/50 combination of vinegar and sugar. The finished dish tasted very good to me. To ascertain the viability of this prototype, I conducted a taste testing with a small group of people and their responses were highly encouraging. My next job was to expand the recipe to an industrial scale. Working at my home kitchen and Venice Maid's on-site lab, I perfected the requisite formulation and procedure.

The pork would be cubed and vegetables cut to the proper bite-sizes and blended with the sauce in a gigantic vat, cooked and fed into individual cans. I did not use the leanest pork because the cost would be too high. Instead, I opted for pork that had a little fat, but that turned out to be a winning quality. When the fat was rendered under the hot retort process it had the effect of a marbled steak, adding a wonderful taste and enhancing enjoyment.

For the first production, I had enough faith that the product would be suitable for the consumer as well as the institutional markets and so I packed 15-ounce cans sweet and sour pork for the former and 50-ounce cans for the latter. My instincts turned to be correct: I was able to gain entry into both markets, and customers like Giant Food were doing particularly well.

With two products on the market, I could have gone all out to be a full-time businessman: appointing a national network of sales force, calling on the trade, considering suitable ways to promote and advertise. But somehow my earlier reservations about business still lingered and more importantly I lacked the killer instinct of a gung-ho entrepreneur. Instead, I chose to be a part-time entrepreneur, which ironically violated my motto: "Whatever I put mind to, do it with the fullest passion, commitment and dedication."

Be that as it may, I kept my chemist's job. After Merck closed up its Philadelphia operation and moved to faraway West Point, PA, I found the commuting too strenuous and time consuming. Hence, I applied for a job at chemical giant DuPont and in particular its explosives department, which was located in nearby Gibbstown, South Jersey. Thanks to the highly laudatory recommendation of my Merck boss, Walter Eberbach, I was hired. My assignment was to develop analytical methods with emphasis on micro-chemistry.

This job gave me a chance to delve into a little non-chemical activity during lunch breaks. As a youngster in Shanghai, one of my greatest passions was cricket fighting. The labs in Gibbstown were located in the countryside surrounded by grass and rocks. It's the cricket chirpings that refreshed my teenage memory and inspired me. From their music making I knew where to find and capture them. Using lab beakers as the fighting arena, I was having a ball with this diversion. Soon my colleagues started to emulate me and shared my fun as we turned our lab into to a veritable coliseum for gladiators.

Unfortunately, I did not have the same enthusiasm for my chemist's job. After working at DuPont for three years—and Merck for five—I began to find lab work stifling and lacking in creativity. Galvanized by my experience as an entrepreneur I did, however, gain a fascination for marketing. There was so much about it I would love to learn from the perspective of Fortune 500 companies: a more sophisticated approach to new product development, product management, advertising, market research, merchandising, and promotion. I knew DuPont's headquarters in Wilmington, DE, had a consumer products marketing division in its fabrics and finishes (F&F) department. It became my fervent hope to find some way to transfer there.

But the likelihood was virtually nonexistent. If it had an opening in the first place the ideal candidate would be a business graduate, preferably an MBA in marketing. My only chance was through a powerful connection. Luckily, I had just such a connection.

My FF Fraternity brother Steve Ip, the avid hunter, happened to be a fellow DuPonter (also schoolmate of my brother David at St. John's University in Shanghai where he earned a BA in economics). He began his DuPont career with a summer warehouse job, part of which was to sweep the floor. After getting his MBA from Temple he joined DuPont as a salesman in the F&F department. His first assignment was to sell industrial paint to a big customer, Bethlehem Steel.

Looking down on Ip, the buyer half-jokingly and half mockingly said: "DuPont must be pretty hard up to send a Chinese laundryman to sell paint." A lesser man would have been enraged by the racism. Instead, Ip smilingly retorted: "If I can't make any sales at least let me do your laundry." Touched by his humility and sense of humor, the buyer atoned for his prejudice by giving Ip a very big order. They soon became fast friends.

Steve Ip was like a real brother to me. He was a warm, high-spirited, giving man. Endowed with a terrific personality and a humanity that touched people in a special way, he was also a gifted communicator and raconteur who loved nothing better than to collect and tell jokes—especially the off-color kind. Every time I saw him he invariably had a new one and nobody could tell it with his panache. Not surprisingly, he went on to become DuPont's top salesman, beating every record and winning every award imaginable. And so he carried a lot of weight.

Asked to assist me with my quest for a marketing position at F&F, Ip not only helped set up an interview but heartily endorsed my application. I traveled to Wilmington, DE, DuPont's headquarters, where I had a good meeting with Ken Browning, vice director of F&F's consuming products division. Although big corporations generally were not too keen about hiring people with an entrepreneurial background, fearing they might be too independent and not good team players, Browning thought otherwise. He liked my practical experience, saying he was "impressed" and that: "anyone who could succeed in the highly competitive soup business as you did has made quite an accomplishment."

By coincidence, DuPont's executive committee not long ago had issued an edict to develop consumer products for the mass merchandising outlets such as supermarkets. Hitherto its consumer products were limited to automotive products such as Zerex antifreeze, garden products, and Remington Arms, sold in specialty stores and representing a minuscule part of its industrial sales. Now DuPont was bent on exploring the mammoth and lucrative markets of household products, emulating the marketing successes of companies like Procter & Gamble and Lever Brothers. Accordingly, F&F created a new products development group, an elite team comprising five members including Bill Wright, Greg Fleming, Ed Glass, and

N. T. (Peter) Shields—none of them were chemists. Just then it needed a sixth member and Browning offered me the job at the end of the interview.

While we six had the title of new products assistants, our responsibilities were that of a product manager: to bring a new idea to the marketplace. The ideal candidate would be one that filled a consumer need, enjoyed a proprietary position, and was something virtually every household could use.

My bailiwick was to scout for new product ideas using a two-prong approach: One, search for an unmet need and then try to match it with a DuPont technology. Two, conversely, identify DuPont technologies that could be developed into suitable new products. The first approach was accomplished by soliciting suggestions internally from our own marketing, advertising, market research, sales, R&D personnel, and externally through brainstorming by our three advertising agencies, N. W. Ayer, Tatham, Laird & Kudner and Batten, Barton, Durstine & Osborn (BBD&O). The second approach was by far the more important and fruitful. I and two chemists, Leslie Cohen and Andy Ratkowic from F&F's Marshall Lab, were members of a scouting team. We would visit various DuPont labs throughout the country, sometimes flying on DuPont private jets. In time we made it to about 80% of the 40 plus labs.

My standard spiel was to give a presentation, outlining our intended markets that included laundry and paper products, health and beauty aids; defining our criteria, two most important being a unique technology and a unique consumer benefit that satisfied a need; and touching on the various phases of new product development from concept to proto-type to test market to commercialization. After the presentation, our team would inquire about the specialties of the chemists to see if there were any appropriate technologies. If so, I would submit them to DuPont's Marshall Lab to conduct initial studies to determine the feasibility of developing a prototype.

My position turned me into a serious marketing man. I was especially attracted to advertising. The creative and inspirational copies of good print ads appealed to the writer in me; the clever TV ads, especially the humorous ones, appealed to my comic bent. And to me the two ad agencies that exemplified the best in the business were Ogilvy & Mather and DDB. I was also entranced by the marketing strategies of innumerable new products such as Procter & Gamble's Bold laundry detergent, which successfully identified its brightness as a salient feature; Alberto Culver VO5 Hair Dressing, which started in 1958 and in a few years through its aggressive marketing and advertising elevated it to the number one brand in the country; and Contac, which was selling at a premium price but utilized unique packaging and a smart ad campaign to win the favors of consumers.

For self-improvement, I took courses in accounting and business law at the University of Delaware, and also was grateful to DuPont for providing me the opportunity to enroll in an invaluable business writing seminar with its emphasis on effective, terse prose, and to attend a seminar at the American Management Association in New York where I rubbed shoulders and exchanged ideas with fellow marketers.

I didn't fare too well on my marketing position. Despite my dedication and hard work, no suitable new products were developed. My five colleagues, who were working on products in various post-conceptual stages, did no better. In the eyes of my supervisor, Orville Wetmore, I bore the brunt of failure. In evaluating my job performance, he attacked me so viciously that he puzzled me beyond belief. His criticisms: I was lacking in motivation and initiative. Ironically, John Palermo, the Marshall Lab supervisor assigned to scrutinize and develop the dozens of technologies and ideas I had submitted, complained I was too aggressive, pushing him too hard, too often, having too much initiative. When I showed Wetmore's evaluation to my colleague Bill Wright, he was stunned by his vitriol and contempt. My explanation: Wetmore was prejudiced against my ethnicity with a lack in perspicacity to boot. Indeed, I detected his thinly disguised bias toward me right from the beginning when we first met some 20 months before.

Utterly incensed, my only course of redress was to complain to Ken Browning, Wetmore's boss. In analyzing the situation, Browning would have fired me if Wetmore's assessment of me had validity. Instead, he was very sympathetic, assuring me that he had never doubted my initiative and competence. To smooth things out he arranged a luncheon meeting at the DuPont Hotel for the three of us. The upshot was that I would report not to Wetmore any more but to my colleague Pete Shields. It was a humiliation but a humble pie I was willing to eat for the sake of my continued interest in marketing.

Within a few months, DuPont's executive committee decided that the mass merchandizing markets were too costly, too competitive, and too difficult to penetrate. Our New Product Development Group became a casualty and dissolved. While my five colleagues were placed in other marketing positions, I was not. Wetmore told me that he did try to get my old chemistry job back at the explosives department in Gibbstown but failed. Browning was nice enough to invite me and Wetmore to a farewell lunch before I became an ex-DuPonter in 1969, to the obvious delight of Wetmore.

With the end of my tenure at DuPont—three years as a chemist and two as a marketing man—it was a time of reckoning: What would I do with my life now?

I had three options:

- Looking for a chemistry job; but I was burnt out and

had no more interest.

- Trying to get an MBA majoring in marketing at the Wharton School of Finance. The vice director of admission was impressed by my entrepreneurial background and DuPont experience and said: "You have excellent qualifications. If you get a minimum score of 500 on the GMAT we'll accept you." It was a tempting offer.

- Devoting full-time to my company, Hong Kong, Inc.

I was 35, still single, and therefore had no family burden. I could certainly afford to spend two years to complete the MBA program. But I wasn't sure how far could I advance with such a coveted degree. Having been treated so abysmally by Wetmore, would I suffer a similar fate in another company? Racism still abounded, and I might well suffer a similar fate elsewhere. Moreover, I suspected that many companies might find the idea of having a Chinese executive a little uncomfortable. Almost none were known to have such positions in the 1960s. It could be a matter of a paucity of candidates. The preferred professions among the Chinese were scientists, engineers, physicians. So they had little opportunity to prove their capability.

I, nevertheless, had some reservations about the corporate climate and culture: the rigid caste-like system, rat race, bureaucracy, difficulty to make waves. With my own company, Hong Kong, Inc., I was the top man, responsible to no one but myself. I called all the shots and had the last word. Furthermore, there was a lot more I could do with my business. I was finally committed to being a full-time entrepreneur.

The first priority was to be a hands-on executive by calling on food buyers. I long forgot I had spent two summers during my college days in Philadelphia as a door-to-door salesman, the toughest kind of selling. As a Fuller Brush man, my routine was to place catalogs in 50 homes the first day. The second day I would call on these homes with free samples, hoping to take orders in cosmetics, brushes, personal products, and other home aids. Though it was not easy work, I rather enjoyed going to people's homes and talking to housewives about the benefits of my products.

I also sold electric appliances and furniture for United Homes Furnishing Company. It had a small sales force, and I turned out to be the best producer. The owner, Paul Dinnerman, who initially valued me as a hungry, hustling salesman, soon befriended me, frequently inviting me to dine out and to his plush home on the Mainline. Both he and his new Italian wife Juliana were classical music lovers and were thrilled to hear me play on their grand piano and my soloing with the DuPont Chamber Orchestra. With the experience of these two summer jobs, I discovered I had a great affinity for selling.

Come to think of it, selling actually has certain broad appeal. In a way everyone is a salesperson of some kind. We all sell ourselves, our ideas, our creations, trying to win friends and influence people. In the higher realm, selling can be as challenging as a writer attempting to attract the attention of readers, a presidential candidate hoping to win the hearts and minds of voters.

The art of selling is elusive and varies from individual to individual. Mine was perhaps different from many others. Instead of hammering and boring the buyers with how great the products were, which they no doubt heard all day long from hardnosed, pushy salespeople, I purposely avoided talking about my products at the outset. Instead, I would try to entertain them and talk about other things that they might be interested in: Chinese cuisine, some amusing anecdotes, my colorful background and love for music, some aspects of Chinese civilization and philosophy. When the buyers and I were on the same wavelength, they became so relaxed and well-disposed that I could sell them the Brooklyn Bridge. This approach worked time and time again and was appreciated by both the buyers and the brokers who accompanied me. For an example, one Boston buyer told me that I made a "great presentation" when I hardly talked about my won ton soup and yet he placed a good order.

Using a similar approach, I did well in my home base of Philadelphia. It had such chains as Food Fair, Penn Fruit, and Acme. Working on my own, unaided by my broker, I got the soup into all of them.

With other buyers I didn't always have the benefit of making a leisurely presentation. Instead, I had to make my point with a few terse sentences within the briefest time. One such challenge was A&P which was one of the largest super-markets in the country with over 2,000 stores. To sell to any of its branches, the first step was to get approval from its headquarters in the Graybar Building in New York City. The top buyer was a busy man who had no time or interest in social chitchat. I had to gently persuade him of the merits and successes of my won ton soup within a few short minutes. Fortunately, my presentation was successful and won his headquarters' approval. However, this did not mean the various A&P stores would automatically place orders. To make sure its branch in the Philadelphia area would do so, I spent week after week visiting the managers of every one of its 100 plus stores. It was an arduous effort for which I was well rewarded.

Elsewhere, with phone calls or letters I gained such distributors as Selected Specialty in Kenilworth, NJ; Specialty Foods in Tampa, FL; Wine & Schulz in Louisville, KY; Zucker-man in Cornwell Heights, PA; A&A in Carlstadt, NJ; Gourmet Goods in St. Paul, MN; and American Roland in New York City. I enjoyed selling so much that I also called on institutional end users like the *Philadelphia Inquirer*, my alma mater University of Pennsylvania, and retail outlets in Chinatown such as Wing On and Asian grocery stores.

As an alternative to calling on the trade, which was time-consuming, I recalled my earlier success of PR with Liberty Import. How I wished to do more with this marketing tool. Short of taking such a course at a journalism school at, say Temple, I didn't know how to proceed. Luckily, just then I was introduced to the owner of Confucius, a Chinese restaurant in New York. She had a publicist who, she said, had improved her business greatly and thought he could help me, too. With much anticipation, I came to be acquainted with PR expert Leslie Kuhn. A graduate of Columbia University's Journalism School and president of the International Press Associates, Kuhn was a gregarious and garrulous older man who spent some four long hours detailing how he gained fame and success for his innumerable clients all over the States.

Easily convinced by his potential, I became his new client. For $2,500, he would embark on a six-month campaign with newspaper articles, radio, and TV interviews as well as getting me into Who's Who in America, which I declined as I thought it was not necessary. In his proposed contract I quote in part: "I intend to introduce you as a man of ability and originality. What with your musical, artistic, and scientific background as well as your manifest successful experimentations in the culinary field you are bound to develop a fuller understanding and richer appreciation of Chinese food in general and your own products in particular."

For press releases and brochures, he wrote this headline: "Benjamin Lin: FROM UNCANNED CLASSICAL MUSIC TO DA TUNG WON TON SOUP and SWEET & SOUR PORK IN CANS." Some excerpts: "This Shanghai-born epicure is an accomplished pianist, analytical chemist and dramatist and the undisputed Brillat-Savarin of Chinese kitchen yore." Getting carried away, he added exuberantly: "Mr. Lin, an apostle of poetry, creativity, palatability and zest in music as well as in won ton soup is genuinely witty, subtle and informative, and he is bound to charm everyone with his comfortable profundities on Mozart, Mendelssohn, Mussorgsky, and Mandarin cuisine—not to mention the attractive and delectable recipes which he has himself evolved. According to the expert opinion, the later are memorable both economically and gastronomically..."

Admittedly the blurb was done with flair but a little too florid and pretentious to my taste, and I was more than a little embarrassed. But I wasn't about to argue with a PR pro or attempt to exercise a little editorial judgment. At any rate, true to his promise Kuhn got stories about me and my products into a number of newspapers including the *Philadelphia Inquirer*, *Bulletin*, and *Daily News*, in which Nels Nelson called me a "Renaissance man." He wrote: "Benjamin Lin, the father of canned won ton soup, may be the only man in West Philadelphia who can sit down at a Steinway grand and play a tone Peking duck and lobster Cantonese."

Pointing out I succeeded in changing the manufacturing of won tons from the slow hand-rolling operation to an automated process, he talked about my various other interests: studying acting at Hedgerow Theatre; making my acting debut, a non-paying job as a Chinese cook, in *Action in the Afternoon* (a live TV Western produced locally on the back lot of KYW); doing portraits; and writing plays, having seen all five produced by amateur companies.

Intrigued by my comedy *Mr. Wong: Or How I Learned to Love the White House,* in which the theme of universal brotherhood was espoused, Nelson summarized the plot. He concluded the piece with "an impertinent visitor speculated whether Chinese food as a bridge to universal understanding would stand the test of time. As they say, an hour after you've eaten in a Chinese restaurant . . ."

"A myth," said Lin. "There are many myths. The Chinese viceroy (on his first visit to the U.S.) who invented chop suey, probably did so because he became desperately hungry one hour after attending an American banquet."

In addition to getting me a guest appearance on the Joe Franklin radio show, Kuhn's biggest effort was to secure an invitation from the Bentley College in Waltham, MA, as the speaker on "The Marketing of Chinese Food."

Bentley was noted for its excellence in accounting and management. So I was quite honored by the invitation and happily waived any lecture fee. Under the coordination of its public relations director, William Steinhardt, there were excellent advance publicity and arrangements for a press conference. In my half hour speech I detailed the growing interest in Chinese cuisine as evidenced by:

- The proliferation of Chinese cookbooks.

- The enthusiastic reaction to a Chinese cooking show entitled *Joyce Chen Cooks,* coincidentally produced in Boston not far from Bentley College.

- The rapid spawning of Chinese restaurants every-where and particularly in New York which boasted some 2,000 in 1968.

- The impact of processed Chinese food industry, growing at 15% yearly and at two and a half times the rate of overall foodstuffs.

As to what accounted for the Chinese food explosion, I attributed it first of all to the intrinsic appeal and greatness of the cuisine and cited additional reasons:

- American GIs, who were stationed in Asia during

World War II, brought back their enthusiasm for the cuisine.

- Growing migration of the Chinese to the U.S.

- Our affluent society which encouraged people to try more sophisticated food.

- The shrinking world.

- The rising number of working women and the availability and convenience of processed Chinese food.

- The aggressive advertising and promotion of large manufacturers, especially Chun King.

I then mentioned La Choy, a subsidiary of Beatrice Foods and Chun King's biggest rival, and the smaller Chinese food manufacturers to give an overall picture, complete with some sales and advertising figures. Dwelling on my main theme, I discussed at length the marketing of processed Chinese food in the supermarkets including newspaper and TV advertising, and promotion schemes such as cents-off coupons, self-liquidating premiums (in which the product's cost is recovered through a retail sale of the product), and end-cap display. I also discussed the institutional trade, the fancy food trade, and the private label business.

For a little human interest, I related how I was inspired to become an entrepreneur by Jeno Paulucci, who turned an initial $2,500 investment into a gigantic empire that he sold to R.J. Reynolds for $63 million 19 years later.

The speech was scholarly but dry. I should have lightened it with a little humor and a joke or two. Nevertheless, it was a huge success. The students paid rapt attention and gave me enthusiastic applause with many taking notes. The press conference that followed also went well, generating several news stories including one in the *Christian Science Monitor*. In the *Sunday Herald Traveler,* Janet Christensen quoted me: "Cooking is a source of pleasure for me. Sometimes when my friends give a party I cook. Once I made my Chinese shrimp toast and the hostess got so mad—they (the guests) ate all my hors d'oeuvres and none of hers . . . When the busy bachelor decides to take the fatal step and marry, who will do the cooking is a moot question. 'It depends on how talented my wife is, said Lin with a smile.'"

Gaining appetite in public relations, I was hoping to get an interview in the *New York Times* and the *Washington Post.* Kuhn said the papers were too big and beyond his ability. So I tried on my own. The *Times'* celebrated food writer Craig Claiborne politely declined because he was about to retire. (But later, he did agree to be my restaurant's guest of honor and helped create a stir as detailed earlier.)

With the *Washington Post* I succeeded with a simple phone call. I advised its food writer Elinor Lee I was about to attend an upcoming food brokers' convention in the nation's capital, and that my multifaceted life—not least my entrepreneurship—might make a timely and pertinent article. She agreed and wrote a three-quarter page profile with the headline "The Won Ton Wizard." It touched on my passion for the piano, how I got interested in Chinese cooking, my aspiration of having a TV cooking series, and my commercialization of the world's first canned won ton soup and sweet and sour pork. Since the Washington area was my best market I couldn't be more jubilant with the article and my first successful PR effort.

Not long afterward I was saddened by the sudden death of Kuhn; I believe the cause was a heart attack. He gave me my introduction to PR, taught me such things as writing press releases, how to develop an angle and what he called finding "a peg to hang a hat on" to trigger the imagination of an editor.

I vowed to carry on with my own PR.

One secret I learned was that often it's more effective to use verbal instead of written communication as evidenced by my experience with the *Washington Post*. That was how with another phone call I got a story in the *Trenton Times*. Sharon Schlegel quoted me: "There are five Chinese schools of cooking. Each is totally individual. Being brought up on the Shanghai school, which is difficult to find here, I was forced to learn to cook to satisfy my desire for certain dishes. To measure up to Ben Lin standards, a Chinese dish must meet the tests of appearance, aroma and flavor." And two secrets to the success of stir-frying are "maximum preparation and minimum cooking." She also included my recipes for shrimp with green peas and bean sprout salad and some tips: "following a recipe word for word is not important . . . [It] is only a guideline to a truly good cook—your sense of what is needed must be the final judge."

With the approach of the Chinese Water Festival (commemorating the death of a popular and patriotic poet who protested the corruption of the government by drowning himself), yet again with one phone call I successfully used the occasion as a "peg to hang my hat" to meet with Winfred Phillips of the *Baltimore Sun*. At one point I said: "I eat, therefore I am" and she used that phrase in her lead paragraph. As a great lover of crabs and in deference to Baltimore's fame as the "Crab Town," one of the recipes I offered was the dipping sauce comprising soy sauce, sugar, vinegar, ginger, and wine. She liked it so much that she later included it as one of her favorite recipes in a book she penned.

However, my PR exhilaration was soon tempered by a terrible setback.

As my institutional won ton business with John Sexton increased dramatically with orders from its branch offices including Philadelphia, Cincinnati, Mississippi, Massachusetts, and New Jersey, I started to receive even bigger orders directly from its Chicago headquarters. Then all those orders suddenly stopped.

I called the headquarters buyer to find out why.

"You charge us too much money. I know what Venice Maid charges you and I think your gross margin is too high," he said.

What transpired was that Venice Maid a little earlier had sent a copy of an invoice intended for Hong Kong, Inc. to John Sexton allegedly by mistake. So the buyer knew exactly what I was paying for the product. Absolutely incensed, I asked Vince Pepper, Venice Maid's treasurer, how and why this had happened. Without even apologizing he said it was an honest mistake made by its bookkeeper Marie. Whether he was telling the truth, which I seriously doubted, the damage was done. While the usual profit margin for manufacturers was between 20% and 25%, mine was higher. But considering all the development and marketing costs I had incurred, the margin was not unreasonable. However, the Sexton buyer didn't try to negotiate for a better price. His final words to me were: "We are not going to buy from you anymore."

Guess where Sexton was getting the won ton soup from? Venice Maid!

Years ago, when John Pepper offered to buy off my won ton die gradually by deducting cents off from each case ordered, I was strongly opposed to his strange proposal. But after he assured me he had no ulterior motive except trying to keep my business I reluctantly consented to trust his truthfulness. But my trust was entirely misplaced. Now, using the won ton die I had developed, the formulation I had perfected, the business I had established, and against the verbal and written assurances that he would not pack for my competition, he was doing just that.

When I confronted Pepper with this despicable deed and accused him of violating our contract he suddenly became a victim of amnesia. "I didn't know we couldn't pack for Sexton," he said. "I don't remember ever having signed a contract with you." He changed his tune after looking at the contract that I had brought with me.

"I want you to stop doing this and compensate me," I demanded angrily.

He offered a ridiculous five percent "commission" for my lost business but refused to stop packing for Sexton, which had long been one of his biggest customers on other canned goods.

My immediate thought was litigation. However, it was easier said than done. At that time Venice Maid (VM) had just been acquired by Connelly Containers, an even bigger corporation listed in the New York Stock Exchange. Its legal team would be formidable. Furthermore, since my contract with Venice Maid stipulated that either party could annul it simply with an advance notice, VM could easily jettison me—if it should lose the lawsuit—and pack for anyone it pleased. And by this time Venice Maid had long paid off my won ton die. I would surely end up as the real loser.

After discovering there were no other suitable private label canneries for me anywhere in the country, I had the option to stop doing business with Venice Maid and end my entre-preneurship or hang on to my hateful relations with them. I chose the latter, inasmuch as my retail won ton soup con-tinued to progress well. But the emotional cost to me was immeasurable and once again I was filled with disgust for business and businessmen.

I was to suffer other consequences. Since Sexton was such a gigantic company and obviously getting a lower cost of the soup, it began to outsell my other institutional customers. Eventually I lost them all.

To add insult to injury, I had to endure yet another humiliating experience. Whenever there was production of my won ton soup and sweet and sour pork I habitually went to the plant to see how everything was progressing. On one of these trips I ran into Venice Maid officer Mike Leonard. On very friendly terms with each other, we chatted a little. He happened to be carrying two cans of freshly produced lobster bisque.

"Take them home. You'll enjoy them," he said.

As I was walking in the plant with the tins in my hand I bumped into Larry Haas, the plant manager. We had met numerous times, and he knew I was a valuable, long-time customer. But on this occasion, he looked at me with a stern face and contempt and lectured me, pointing at the lobster bisque: "These are the property of Venice Maid. You are not supposed to take them without authorization." I had difficulty believing what I was hearing. He was actually accusing me of being a thief! To jump to this rash conclusion without giving me the benefit of the doubt or the courtesy of asking how I got them was a sure sign of racism. I was too stunned to reply coherently. By the time I recovered and told him the lobster "was given to me," he did not believe me and quickly walked away. I should have complained to Mike Leonard right away but got distracted by the production of my won ton soup at hand and soon forgot the incident. Not long afterward Haas ended his tenure at Venice Maid, and I never had a chance to straighten out this racist pig.

An ongoing process for Hong Kong, Inc. was to expand my sales force. I accomplished this by attending the annual food brokers' conventions in New York where I had a chance to interview prospective candidates. Another way was to appoint them through the food brokers' directory. In time I built a network of 32 brokers. Consequently, the soup was distributed virtually from coast to coast. In addition, my long-time client Haddon House continued to sell the product in fancy food stores nationally, and another, Liberty Import, was distributing it internationally.

To drum up business for the won ton soup, I did some

advertising and promotion. I ruled out television; it was just too costly and my sales volume did not warrant it. Instead I designed and wrote a lot of small newspaper ads for limited markets and was eager to see their effectiveness. But after a campaign when I noticed no improvements in sales, I pulled the ads out. I next turned to the common practice of offering cents off coupons in newspapers. Stores owners/managers were supposed to collect these coupons from paying customers and be reimbursed by the manufacturers. What I discovered was that far too many dishonest businessmen abounded. They were in areas where the won ton soup had no distribution whatsoever but by clipping coupons from newspapers they claimed to have actually sold the product and tried to collect money from me.

I made no effort to promote or advertise my sweet and sour pork because it was not as popular or widely distributed. Nevertheless, the pork was a solid success in limited areas and enjoyed a monopoly for a good five years. Eventually it became a casualty of market forces because the cost of pork was just too high to be viable. So I let my inventory gradually run out. Toward the end I had a few cases of the institutional size sweet and sour pork that I could not dispose of. Rather than letting them go to waste, I searched my mind and thought of an unlikely outlet: Philadelphia's Holmesburg Prison. Positive this dish had never graced its dining rooms, I was hopeful the buyer might have an interest. Sure enough he liked the pork and the price, which I was selling at cost, and I sold all my remaining pork. It gave me the amusing thought that my exotic dish would surprise the inmates and perhaps brighten their day a little as they repaid their debts to society.

Not ignoring my product development, I tried out three items. The origin of the first had to do with my intimate friendship with Paul Dinnerman, whom I first met as his salesman selling electronics and home furnishings. He later became a co-owner of the Silo chain stores, a giant electronics retailer with numerous branches. As his company kept growing I got him interested in the possibility of a joint fast-food operation. Based on the most popular Chinese restaurant appetizer, the egg roll, and that all time American favorite, the hamburger, I developed a new specialty that fused the two: Using ground beef blended with diced onion and soy sauce as the stuffing, I wrapped it with egg roll skin and then deep fried. Everyone who tasted it loved it. And for a while my invention seemed destined for a bright future. But Silo's management eventually decided that a fast-food operation was too great a departure from its regular business and rejected my idea.

I next turned to pepper steak, mindful it was highly popular in Chinese restaurants and might have possibilities. I opted for the frozen process this time and found a New Jersey manufacturer that would pack this item for me. Using sliced flank steak, I cut it against the grain for better tenderness, marinated it with salt, soy sauce, and wine, and lightly coated it with cornstarch to retain its succulence and garnished it with green pepper. I stir-fried the ingredients at home and brought the finished dish to the frozen food company. After the quick-freeze processing, the steak was reheated for my tasting. I liked it and thought it had strong commercial potential. But before proceeding headstrong into this endeavor I had to weigh the pros and cons.

True, pepper steak would be a nice addition to my product line. Since there was no such product canned or frozen on the market, I would enjoy a proprietary position. Moreover, being such a favorite restaurant dish, it would require little introduction to the public and meet a consumer demand.

On the other hand, with the high fatality rate of new products (80%) I still had to bear considerable risks. Having been burnt by VM, I was not too keen about the idea of relying once again on another contract packer. And finally, the cost of commercializing and marketing frozen food was still too high for me. So despite what I thought was a tasty product I reluctantly gave up this venture.

The other product that I turned my mind to was bean sprouts. Zestful, succulent, and versatile, they made for a good stir-fried dish, delightful garnish for beef, pork, chicken, shrimp, and a wonderful salad. And for those into pseudo-Chinese dishes, the sprouts were an indispensable component for chow mein and chop suey dishes.

Canned bean sprouts had, of course, not only been a supermarket staple but also a fast moving one. That's how Jeno Paulucci started his Chun King Co. before becoming a giant in the grocery business. But the canning process took a heavy toll on the sprouts, making them become limp and lose much flavor.

Why not produce and market fresh bean sprouts?

They would be full-bodied, nice and crispy, and taste better. I knew such packaged product already existed in selected areas in the U.S. and Canada and reportedly did well. Yet no such vegetable was distributed in Pennsylvania and its neighboring states. And so I could be filling a vacuum, a great consumer demand. The sprouts were very easy—and even fun—to produce: simply soak mung beans (the best was from Thailand) in water overnight. Then drain and transfer to a perforated container kept in the dark and sprinkle water every four hours (around the clock for best results) for about four days and each pound of the beans would yield eight of the sprouts.

By chance, around that time I got acquainted with William Yang, who was interested in my proposed venture. It was something that we could start economically: no need to rent a factory or buy expensive sprouting machinery and sprinkling system. Instead, I could rely on Yang's willingness to mass produce the item in his large basement with the use of perforated garbage cans. He was also willing to do the packaging, and all we required was a machine to seal the vegetables in plastic bags. There was also no need to incur the expense of renting a refrigerated warehouse because we could produce only as ordered. To be conservative and cautious, I wanted to begin small, primarily serving food chains based in Philadelphia. If successful we could always expand our areas of distribution and our production facilities.

Finding little sales resistance, I easily got the Da Tung brand bean sprouts into such chains such as A&P, Food Fair, Acme, and Penn Fruit. With initial success, I expanded the distribution into Grand Union and Safeway in neighboring states.

While I realized bean sprouts were highly perishable, I didn't think that would cause any problem. Their shelf life of about 10 days under refrigeration should be enough time to be sold. It, therefore, came to me as a surprise when a Penn Fruit buyer called me in for an emergency meeting. He was very unhappy.

"What's wrong?"

"Your bean sprouts."

"There was nothing wrong with them," I protested. "They were freshly produced and immediately shipped to your warehouses."

"Just look at them," he showed me a few bags. "That's what I found in all our stores."

What I saw was shocking. The sprouts were not only wilted but each had tails about six inches long like human hairs, all curled up inside the plastic bag in a tangled, ugly mess. I knew from experience if I kept fresh bean sprouts in my refrigerator too long they would just rot but never like what I was witnessing. I immediately suspected the reason.

"Didn't you keep the bean sprouts under refrigeration?"

"No. We have cooling system in our produce department

for certain vegetables. But not for bean sprouts; we don't have the space for them."

"That's what happened. Without refrigeration, the sprouts just kept growing erratically if you didn't sell them within a week or so."

"That's too bad. We can't carry any produce so perishable; I'm afraid we can't do business with you anymore."

That was a terrible blow. But more bad news was yet to come. My other distributors also began to complain about the perishability, similarly made worse by the lack of, or otherwise inadequate, cooling system, and/or the slow sales movement. It's obvious there wasn't enough consumer interest. It would have helped if I had imprinted recipes on the plastic bags and resorted to such merchandizing tools as in-store display signs. Without these efforts the bean sprouts just weren't moving fast enough for my buyers and in time they all stopped ordering. Consequently, my bean sprouts venture didn't live beyond five months.

Did I have any regrets? Absolutely not. Business, like life, is full of triumphs and setbacks. I hope I've learned to accept failures just as gracefully as successes. If anything, my bean sprouts endeavor, like all my other failed ventures, has certainly enriched my life. One final consolation: Because our initial investments and startup costs were so small, with the profits we made Yang and I lost virtually no money.

At this point in the mid-1970s, I no longer had the interest of developing new products and entertained the possibility of building a Chinese food empire. I was satisfied with just the retail won ton soup. It was still enjoying a monopoly. I had seen this product in packaged, dehydrated form in Chinese grocery stories, but it did not last very long. My canned won ton soup remained unique. While far from doing truckloads of business, it continued to expand slowly. And I frequently wondered when an imitator would jump in.

That day finally came.

In an anguished tone, one of my Midwest brokers called me. "Why are you selling your soup under a different brand?"

"I did no such thing."

"What about the Ty Ling brand won ton soup?"

"Never heard of it."

"It's identical to your Da Tung brand in looks and taste. I thought you were packing the soup for another company."

"Positively not!"

"At any rate, I've lost your account. The buyers were obviously getting a better deal from this other company."

"Sorry you lost our business. Let me investigate and I'll get back to you."

It took me much effort to get hold of the Ty Ling won ton soup because it had not been distributed in my area yet. It was the same size as mine in fourteen and a half ounce tins. When I scrutinized the label I couldn't believe my eyes. It had no originality at all but was a copycat and clearly intended to challenge the supremacy of my product and confuse the public: its picture displayed a bowl of the soup accompanied by a pair of chopsticks that was a very close imitation of my label. The brand "TY LING" was written in Chinese brush stroke fashion in yellow color against a red background exactly like my "DA TUNG" brand; it even copied my cooking directions verbatim with the words: "Do not add water. Just pour the contents into a saucepan, heat and serve" and my serving suggestions of "adding chopped scallion to enhance the flavor."

Upon opening the can, I found the shape of the won tons was triangular, just like mine, obviously made from the won ton die that I had developed. It differed from my product only in the won ton filling. It was chicken, which was my original formulation instead of pork. But there was very little discernable difference in taste between the two meats after the canning process. The distributor of the Ty Ling won ton soup was Reese Finer Food, one of the biggest specialty food distributors in the world with hundreds of its own Reese brands and a line of Ty Ling brand oriental products.

I could well imagine what had happened. Attracted by the success of my won ton soup, this company could have asked me to be the sub-contractor as did Liberty Import with its Bonavita brand. Instead, it chose to go straight to Venice Maid to get a better price and cut me out. Having no integrity, Venice Maid was all too happy to acquire a bigger customer, knowingly violating our contract, and unconscionably ignoring the consequences to me.

Enraged, I didn't realize Venice Maid could sink so low a second time. Having cheated me once by stealing my institutional customer John Sexton, it blatantly was swindling me again, using my won ton die, my formulation, profiting from my hard work as a pioneer to build the business, to betray me, despite having made a ton of money from me for over thirty years. Venice Maid's shameless, duplicitous act brought back my profound loathing for business with its inherent lust for profit, its temptation to be dishonest, greedy, and unscrupulous.

I called for a meeting at Venice Maid. Present were the two Peppers, CEO John and President Larry, and plant manager Charles LaGrossa, who had replaced his predecessor, the racist Larry Haas. After I presented my case they acted faintly surprised. Denying they had done anything wrong, John insisted they were only doing legal business with Reese Finer Foods and there was nothing untoward about it. At my request, Ty Ling and Da Tung won ton soups were heated and brought to our meeting. The Venice Maid contingency reluctantly admitted the two were virtually the same product.

"Why did you do it? What about our contract and your promise not to pack a similar product for any other party?"

Despite my protest, John Pepper admitted no culpability

and refused to accede to my demand not to pack for Reese. To compensate for my lost business he again offered to pay me a ridiculous five percent commission, as with John Sexton.

"That's not acceptable!" I left the meeting in a huff.

Apparently fearing I was considering litigation, Venice Maid set up a meeting between me and a highly placed executive from Connelly, the company that had acquired Venice Maid. I thought he was going to settle the Reese problem in a more equitable way. Instead, this man subjected me to the most heavy-handed, humiliating, intimidating, racist treatment by launching into a diatribe; he brutally lectured me that VM had been doing me a great favor all this time by being my packer and warned me not to do anything rash or suffering dire consequences. I should have told him "Fuck you; you go to hell!" But I knew throwing a temper tantrum would not bring about anything productive. I simply kept a cool head and walked out of the meeting without saying a word. John Pepper had the nerve to pull me aside, saying, "I hope he was not too rough on you."

My logical step was precisely what Venice Maid feared: Initiate legal action against VM and possibly Reese, too. Through referral I found a big time New Jersey lady lawyer who was a former judge. But I failed utterly to make any headway. Despite all evidence to the contrary, she maintained I did not have a solid case. Unlike intellectual properties such as scientific and other inventions which could be patented and protected, food was something that enjoyed no exclusive rights. Any food manufacturer could copy its counterpart and come up with an identical product with impunity. So I couldn't sue Reese. As to Venice Maid, to prove they stole my idea or copied my won ton formulation would be very difficult, the lawyer thought. "It would involve costly tests by food technologists. Yours could be a very expensive proposition, and I have no guarantee that we'll win," she said.

These words sealed my fate. I was the victim of an atrocious industrial crime, and I had no one to turn to. For a time I again thought of salvaging my business by going to another contract packer. But as before, I could find no one else with the same capability as Venice Maid. Even if I did I could not compete against Reese.

In the coming months Reese Finer Foods, being a much bigger corporation, was obviously getting a better price and expanded to my other areas of distribution. My other brokers gradually all had the same experience as that of my Midwest broker: The Ty Ling won ton soup easily squeezed out the Da Tung brand and in time I was down to only one customer, Haddon House of New Jersey, the national fancy food distributor. It kept my company from going out of business by ordering on a regular basis.

In the near future there was an ultimate irony. When Venice Maid purchased new, ultra-fast ravioli machines it abandoned its older models. But the latest machines were incompatible with my won ton die and so the cannery could no longer produce triangular won tons. Since Venice Maid was still willing to pack for me, using the ravioli die and for smaller, minimum 500 case orders, I reluctantly decided to accept a radical alternative: Won tons that took on a bastardized shape, looking no different from raviolis.

While my heart was no longer in the business anymore, purely to satisfy the orders of Haddon House I chose to continue. As expected I got complaints from a few end users who told me my won tons did not look like won tons. Nevertheless, Haddon House did not experience any decline in sales and Harry Anderson, the owner/buyer, never even questioned how or why my won tons were transformed into raviolis in appearance.

Anderson, who had been one of my first customers tracing back to 1963, in most likelihood would order from me indefinitely. He kept this up for the next eight years. Hong Kong, Inc. was probably the only corporation in the U.S. that survived and stayed in business for that length of time with just one lone account. Finally, it was time to call it quits. In 2001, after relocating to the Los Angeles area to further my interest in acting, I dissolved my company and bade farewell to my entrepreneurship. Venice Maid was no more either, at least under its original management. After merging with Connelly Containers it was acquired by Hanover Foods Corp. in 2004.

Though I never realized my aspiration of building a Chinese food empire, I had embarked on a journey that made me a proud participant of American capitalism and the American dream. Although being an entrepreneur may be just one facet of my life, it stood out as one of the most enduring occupations, and in many ways the most satisfying and meaningful. Despite my business naiveté and inexperience, I turned a vision into reality by giving birth to two products that had never existed on the market. Of the more successful one, I revolutionized the way it was made, penetrated into outlets across the land and abroad, and steered it through thick and thin for 40 long years before I executed a coup de grace.

I hope I gave consumers some enjoyment, a little pleasure at the dining table, and a glimpse into the marvels of Chinese cuisine. In return, my entrepreneurship freed me from the day-to-day routine, the eight-to-five rat race, the drudgery of pushing for a paycheck, and afforded me the ability to be the free spirit that I yearned to be. It gave me the leisure and flexibility to explore, pursue, and indulge in so many other endeavors. It was indeed a lucky day when I stumbled on that Jeno Paulucci article. Hats off to Jeno!

CHAPTER EIGHT (1970-1981)

Journalism

As founder and marketer of my Chinese food company, I utilized public relations to advance sales. Initially aided by a professional, I in time became adept at it and succeeded in getting the story of my entrepreneurship into a number of newspapers, including the *Washington Post*.

Since my home base was Philadelphia, where my business venture had already enjoyed good news coverage, I was hoping to do more in 1970 by getting an interview from *Philadelphia* magazine. It was a prestigious, award-winning city magazine whose readership was sophisticated, well-educated, and well-heeled. Though it was a long shot, I sent a letter of request and enclosed some newspaper clippings about myself. Rosalie Wright, assistant managing editor of the magazine, replied: "You seem to be such a Renaissance man we can't decide which would be more interesting—a story on you or by you."

Subsequently opting for the latter, she asked me if I would be interested in writing an article on the Chinese restaurant scene. As an epicure who dined out regularly, I certainly knew the subject well. But I wasn't sure if I was equal to the task. Having flunked English composition for foreign students at

Columbia University, I had since gained enough fluency to pen skits and comedies in the 1960s. However, I knew nothing about writing an article. So I put Wright's request on the back burner, but every once in a while I thought it might be a worthy challenge.

I kept procrastinating and some two months later I got started with the proposed title "One from Column A." Still suffering doubts about my command in English, I mailed my manuscript and felt for sure it would be rejected. To my utter surprise Rosalie Wright wrote: "After reading your article all the editors were salivating. We liked the piece a lot. Would you accept a $100 fee?"

The article was published in the August 1970 issue, introducing me with a tiny bio: "Benjamin Bing-Heng Lin was born in Shanghai, studied piano at Juilliard, acting at Hedgerow, chemistry at Penn. He markets Chinese food."

I began with an amusing anecdote about Mrs. S. Liang, co-owner of the Jade Palace restaurant. Also a talented chef, she was well versed in the several schools of Chinese cooking and endowed with a large repertoire. On her first day of business shortly after her arrival in this country she understandably was eager to dazzle her customers with her skill and versatility. However, to her utmost disbelief and embarrassment, a customer ordered something she didn't know how to prepare: chicken chow mein.

"It was not a complicated or unusual dish," I quote. "But on the contrary, a simple one which has long been considered the most popular Chinese dish in this country and requires only a minimum skill to prepare.

"The only trouble is that it isn't Chinese.

"Neither known in China nor akin to any authentic Chinese dishes, it is believed to be an American invention. How it has acquired its Chinese identity is a mystery that no doubt requires the mind of a Margaret Mead or the skill of a

Charlie Chan (another American invention, I am afraid) to solve.

"Be that as it may, Mrs. Liang wasted no time to master chicken chow mein and lived happily thereafter."

I continued with my observation that most Chinese restaurants here made a distinction between their American and Chinese clientele when it came to ordering. "Such favorites as chop suey and egg foo young never grace the Chinese menu because they are not Chinese. Conversely, such exotica as snails, fish maw, and fried squab are not featured in the American menu because they are considered too native or odd to be enjoyed by Philadelphians. Other dishes may be of Chinese origin but adulterated by the exclusions of certain ingredients, which may be offensive to the more delicate and less sophisticated Yankee palate, or by the addition of certain ingredients which may be of special appeal. The omission of black beans in lobster Cantonese and the use of bacon in butterfly shrimp are two such examples.

"There are even two versions of egg roll. So popular is the celery-filled American version that few restaurants bother to make the more costly, authentic version.

"Such disparity between the East and West may be objectionable to purists or gourmets but it enriches our language by engendering a most catchy and droll phrase 'One from Column A.' It is designed to guide Americans in ordering by grouping certain dishes together but hardly translatable into Chinese."

I went on to survey the Chinese restaurant scene with a brief review of seven eateries (including Mrs. Liang's Jade Palace) and my recommended dishes.

An additional bonus from the publication was being invited to the magazine's rare but elegant Christmas party where I met publisher Herb Lipson, also owner of *Boston* magazine and the recipient of numerous awards. Among the guests were the editors and other freelance writers whose articles had impressed me and made me proud to be in their company.

Thus stimulated, I instantly got interested in journalism and considered taking some courses. I first looked into Penn, my alma mater, where I got my BA in chemistry. Its Annenberg School of Communications, headed by renowned writer and columnist George Gerbner, was one of the best in the country. However, it offered no writing courses. On the other hand, Temple did have a journalism department as part of its Annenberg School of Communications and in September I enrolled in a class, which, not surprisingly, was magazine writing.

The professor was Joseph Carter, a white-haired, bespectacled, avuncular gentleman. He told the students to write a total of five articles with the explicit purpose of trying to publish. "No matter how well you write, unless you find a home for your articles you won't get an A," he cautioned. Relying on *Writer's Market* as a guide, we submitted our first assignments in self-addressed stamped envelopes (SASE) to various magazines but none of us had any luck. Carter turned stern and even a little angry, castigating us for our failure and exhorting us to do better.

For my next effort, titled "Peking Duck a la Beethoven," I espoused the unlikely thesis that classical music and Chinese cuisine might be two worlds completely apart but they shared some common chords and seemed to be rooted in similar soil.

Edited excerpts: "If I were Leonard Bernstein, I would no doubt do a program based on my findings in a 'Young People's Concert' on TV, featuring various dishes to illustrate my hypothesis. However, lacking any far-sighted sponsor, I must rely on my writing which probably serves the purpose better anyway, because it would be hard to concentrate on good music when there is excellent food around just as it is almost impossible to enjoy a delectable Peking duck while attempting to listen to, say, Beethoven's last string quartet.

"To be perfectly honest the genesis of my idea was not triggered by the piano trifle 'Chopsticks,' a piece known the world over and requiring only two chopsticks, or lacking that, two index fingers to execute, though I must give its composer credit for his unwitting insight. The inspiration actually came to me in my dual capacity as a musician and a lecturer on Chinese cuisine. I discovered that my discussions on certain principles and intricacies were much more lucid when I resorted to musical term or analogy.

"In a given Chinese dish seldom is one ingredient treated as an independent, self-sufficient entity. Instead, it is usually cut into bite-size and mingled with two or more similar sized counterparts. When different components are cooked together the resulting dish blends the characteristic taste, aroma and texture of each to form a new, integrated entity. In musical terms it is like a chord, achieved by playing different notes on different instruments simultaneously, resulting in a more sensuous experience and greater dining pleasure.

"In contrast, most American dishes (with a few exceptions like beef stew and succotash) are cooked with no accompanying ingredients, be they meat, seafood or vegetables. They are, therefore, analogous to music without harmony, which paradoxically, is the trademark of traditional Chinese music.

"If you dig the musical form of 'theme and variations,' you will find a perfect parallel in the famed medley of Chinese dishes called 'one duck four flavors.' They are really nothing but a duck theme with four variations: Out of the same fowl four completely different dishes emerge. Like Brahms' Fourth Symphony, these variations are so subtly structured that the original theme is barely recognizable. Yet, if you analyze carefully you'll find the unmistakable link.

"The first course is the duck skin appreciated for its crispness. Next comes the duck meat which takes on an entirely different taste and texture. These two courses are often served together and sandwiched in steamed doily with scallion and hoisin sauce. The third dish is the remaining duck, shredded and stir-fried with various vegetables. The fourth variation is the ingratiating soup made with the carcass.

"Just as symphonies represent the epitome in music in terms of size, use of instruments, complexities and tonal color, the formal Chinese banquet is the ultimate in dining pleasure. It is in a class by itself, big in scale, complicated to prepare and requires several hours to consume.

"In such a banquet nine to over 20 selections are served course by course. The first is always the assorted cold platter (in the in more elaborate banquets, it's the first four courses). It may include tidbits of aromatic beef, abalone, meat in aspic, jelly fish, which are like a symphonic overture or introduction, lightweight fare designed to stimulate your appetite. The quantity of each is limited so that you won't fill yourself at such an early beginning, just as an overture is swift-moving and never too weighty.

"Then come the individual dishes which are likened to different movements of a symphony. They are tools to show off their creator's imagination and technical virtuosity, contrasting in mood, emphasis, rhythm and pace.

"Like a good composer who may have an abundance of ideas but cautiously guards against jamming too much stuff down the audience's throats all at once, a good chef would serve just enough dishes, and then switch to a soup which, of course, changes the whole eating rhythm from chewing to sipping. This is both a welcome and necessary change to prepare the guests for other great things to come.

"These may range from sea cucumber, 'lion's head,' eight jeweled duck, sautéed crystal shrimp and red-cooked whole fish, each a thematic wonder, harmonic intrigue, contrapuntal delight.

"Toward the end of the banquet, a second soup is served. It will be entirely different from the first soup, which may well have been a light chicken broth. Now it becomes a thick puree, possibly the shark's fin soup or bird's nest soup.

"Like a symphonic finale which must hold its own no matter how magnificent the previous movements are, the last course—the dessert—must also rally to the occasion. Moreover, it must be a climax unto itself to bring the feast to a fitting end. This mandate is generally fulfilled by 'eight precious rice pudding,' which is, indeed, a whale of a dish, made of glutinous rice and eight colorful ingredients. It is both an aesthetic delectation with its artistic arrangements and superb taste. An alternative is glazed banana, of which the fruit is coated with caramelized sugar and dipped into icy water just before serving, cold on the exterior but hot inside.

"Throughout dinner the most exquisite tea, rice wine or the fiery mao tai (a Chinese liquor) is interwoven like a Wagner leitmotif.

> "When you are finished with a good banquet it's like coming out of a marvelous concert: Euphoria fills your every cell and you feel that life is really great. Such is the sensual and spiritual pleasure of music and Chinese dining. What a shame Beethoven was not born a Chinese epicure. Had this been the case, how much richer the musical and gastronomical worlds would have been with perhaps a symphony inspired by the heroics of a banquet or a creative dish in the order of a Peking duck a la Beethoven."

I submitted my article to *Music Journal*, a national magazine. This time the manuscript was not returned via my SASE with a dreaded form letter of rejection. Instead, the editor was pleased to accept my whimsical piece. The news brought a smile to Professor Carter. He congratulated me as the first student to succeed and urged my classmates to emulate my breakthrough.

Before long I scored again with *Philadelphia* magazine: Philadelphia's Chinese grocery stores as the topic. Excerpted and edited:

> "Just five of them, they are landmarks in Chinatown, an attractive stopover for tourists, and a vital culinary link to the 3,000 plus Chinese in the tri-state area of Pennsylvania, New Jersey, and Delaware. These residents are mostly first-generation immigrants whose quality of life would be drastically diminished if they could not indulge in their native cooking with the requisite ingredients. The patrons also include a small but growing number of Americans who are fascinated by the joy of Chinese cooking, with its universal appeal, health benefits, and dramatic stir-frying technique.

"The five stores are invariably small, crowded and overstocked, with little semblance of order or organization. The majority still relies on the ancient abacus. Other than the minimal advertising in Chinese newspapers, they use none of the marketing tools: no window display, trading stamps, discounting, merchandizing gimmick. And few go for the psychological prices of, say 39 cents, 49 cents or 99 cents, but rather 40 cents, 50 cents or $1.

"But they do offer the personal service that are all too rarely found these days. The customer is patiently waited upon from the time she (or he) steps into the store till shopping is completed.

"Behind this façade of anachronism, there is some very scrutable logic. The personal attendance may be time-consuming, but it is really a matter of necessity because locating desired items amidst a sea of merchandise is a task best left to the experts.

"An average food shop probably carries enough variety to rival a supermarket, enough exotic food to dwarf the best gourmet shops and enough ready-to-serve food to challenge a delicatessen.

"The stock includes some of the essential Chinese foodstuffs:

• Black mushrooms. In their dried form, they are as dead as fossils. However, after being soaked in warm water, they bloom to full life, with an expanded body and a celestial aroma.

• Chinese vegetables. They are trucked from New Jersey or Long Island in warm weather and Florida during cold seasons to ensure a year-round supply. The better-known ones include bok choy, ginger root, winter melon, and radish. Their prices vary according to their availability. Fluctuating the most are the dainty snow peas: from 80 cents to about $8 per pound.

• Fresh water chestnuts air-freighted from Taiwan, still bearing the mud of that country. Also, the famed dessert, "eight precious rice pudding," in cans and "thousand-year-old eggs" (a misnomer. The Chinese don't know it by that name.) which are duck eggs, aged and coagulated in alkaline solutions for about 90 days.

• Fresh litchi nuts flown from Florida (August only).

• Shrimp sauce, oyster sauce, and dark and light soy sauces. A judicious use can enhance the taste immeasurably.

• Dried noodles from Japan, abalone from Mexico, and Chinese sausages from Canada.

"There is also myriad fresh, ready-to-serve foods prepared right in the backroom kitchen. They are the pride and joy of the proprietors who are not only businessmen but also talented culinary artists, providing such Cantonese staples as barbecued pork, soy sauce chicken, flavored tripe, and various sweet and salty dim sum specialties.

"One of the biggest operations is the growing of bean sprouts. All that is necessary is relatively little space, humidity, darkness, and patience. Water is sprinkled on mung beans (placed in perforated containers) every four hours for three to five days. When fully sprouted each pound of the beans would grow to six or more times their weight.

"One especially popular grocery store is Wong On (1005 Race Street), the oldest and does the most business. On Sundays customers must take a number and wait their turn. While bean sprouts, like Oriental faces, may all look alike to uninitiated Americans, they do differ in appearance; they can be long or short, fat or skinny, fresh and juicy or old and shriveled. Wing On's weekly production of about 2,000 pounds surpasses all others.

"Oriental Mart (909 Race Street) offers background music by Brahms, Mahler or the like because owner Aloysius Lee (he helped me in my won ton production mentioned in an earlier chapter) loves classical music and often tunes his store radio to WFLN. 'We have the largest merchandise, totaling over 19,000 items,' asserts Lee. His grocery is the most international in scope with many selections of snacks, prepared frozen foods; canned and dried goods, including the macrobiotic *mu* tea, from Japan; and numerous specialties from India, Korea, and the Philippines. Two of his more unusual items are:

• Balut eggs, which are partially incubated eggs with most of the external and internal organs already formed. They are favorites of the Filipinos and some Cantonese.

• *Hoy Gaw Bien,* which is a well-known aphrodisiac among the Chinese. It is made from the penises of certain seal dogs (which could copulate many times a day and dramatically increase men's sexual prowess even in their advanced ages, according to owner Lee).

"The remaining grocery stores are graced with such tempting goodies as su my, shrimp dumplings, egg rolls, and pig knuckles. So who needs trading stamps?"

When I told Professor Carter that *Philadelphia* magazine had accepted my manuscript he was so thrilled that he offered me the incredible honor of guest-lecturing in one of his subsequent classes.

Meanwhile there was yet another honor—and surprise—arising from my "Peking Duck a la Beethoven" article. Robert Sherman, program director of WQXR, radio station of the *New York Times*, invited me to be his guest. I had a delightful time chatting about my article and other facets of Chinese cuisine. At one point I mentioned that contrary to public knowledge there were a host of Chinese deserts including the ones I mentioned in "Beethoven." In a day or two, Oscar Collier, a literary agent, phoned me, saying he would like to represent me if I wrote a cookbook on Chinese desserts. Such a project would require much research, meticulous testing, and accurate measurements. I was just too busy with my myriad endeavors during that time. Consequently, I missed my chance and in time forgot all about this offer.

In the next three years I continued my education at Temple and took virtually every undergraduate writing course. To onlookers I must have seemed an oddity: A man pushing 40 sitting among classmates who were some 20 years younger. But the disparity in age did not make me feel out of place. My fellow students treated me as one of their own, and I had no trouble blending well with them, eagerly trying to absorb everything the professors had to offer and carrying out my assignments. Luckily, my age was no detriment to my capacity for learning and I was glad to be back in academia.

My next course was "Interpreting Contemporary Affairs," in reality editorial writing. It was taught by Mark Isaacs, a highly persuasive and effective professor who possessed a quick mind and sharp wit, whose own writing impressed me as having great flair, an ease and agility marked with catchy phrases and colorful expressions befitting the estimable copywriter he was once. He was not above advising students to using "partial truths" to make a point or mask certain vulnerabilities. I was indebted to him for introducing me to *The Federalist Papers*, essays written by James Madison, John Jay, and Alexander Hamilton to promote the ratification of the constitution; writings by the great journalist and social critic H. L. Mencken, and the abolitionist Frederick Douglass, among others. In editorial writing, he emphasized that the writer should do more than merely assert his opinion but also to persuade and effect action where applicable. And his mantra was AIDA, which he called the "old advertising hag":

A - to attract Attention

I - to arouse Interest

D - to Develop the pitch

A - to ask for Action

For our final he let the students pick their own topics. It was during the Vietnam conflict. As one adamantly opposed to this unjust war, I had been particularly incensed by the duplicity of the Nixon administration and the common belief that lives of yellow-faced Asians were cheap. Titled "The One-sided Peace," my essay lamented the plight of North Viet-namese civilians whose lives were lost, homes destroyed, rice fields defoliated at a time when President Nixon made the pious claim that the war was winding down while increasing our bombing raids, resulting in over one million casualties. While Nixon was credited with bringing most of our fighting men home and seemingly marching toward peace, war was still waging in Vietnam. "Peace, like war, can never be one-sided," I wrote, adding that "has Nixon altered the course of the war or merely altered its character? Has he reduced the levels of killings or merely changed the color of the corpses?

"Mr. Nixon's entire strategy is based on a highly question-able program called Vietnamization, which means that our fighting men are being replaced at a lower cost in blood to us. It is a policy compounded of hypocrisy, inhumanity, short-sightedness, and moral bankruptcy. It maintains in power an inept, puppet regime in Saigon that muffles dissent, jails peace advocates, and shows as little interest in negotiated settlement as it does in holding elections."

Toward the end of my piece I called for peace activists to unite, broaden their base, and rally behind Senator Edmund Muskie to unseat Nixon.

Of the 60 or so editorials from the class, Professor Isaacs picked 16 including mine, edited and published them in a booklet called *New Views*. Commenting on "One-sided Peace" he wrote: "Benjamin Lin takes a passionate view of Vietnam-ization and called for political action to end it. Mr. Lin plays the classic role of the orator, the pamphleteer, the crusading editor. He will not be content with winning nods of agreement; he wants action now."

Among other courses I took during successive semesters:

- Photography. Under the guidance and encouragement of the personable Edward Trayes I learned to enhance the aesthetics of a picture, marveled at masters like Ansel Adams and Margaret Bourke-White, carried out challenging assignments with such themes as "texture," and did a dissertation on food photography highlighted by interviewing one of the best-known practitioners in New York.

- Short story writing. It was an extension of my earlier interest in writing comedies and skits in the 1960s.

- Review writing. The professor was a working professional, the music critic of the *Philadelphia Inquirer*, Samuel Singer. I got to review a wide spectrum of areas including the arts, political speeches, editorials. Commenting on my review of an Andre Watts piano recital, Singer flattered and humbled me with these words—no doubt tongue in cheek: "You are not supposed to write better than your professor!"

While I enjoyed and aced these courses, I continued to tend to my other interests: running my Chinese food business, contributing occasionally to *Philadelphia* magazine, and teaching Chinese cooking at Temple University and the China Institute in New York. A new development was to become a TV chef. I got started partially due to my newfound interest in show biz and partially as an extension of my PR effort to publicize my canned products.

My debut took place locally on WCAU-TV, a CBS affiliate. I was, along with singer, actor, and band leader Rudy Vallee, a guest on the *Betty Hughes and Friends* show. Hughes was the wife of then New Jersey's governor, Richard Joseph Hughes. With a can of each of my won ton soup and sweet and sour pork next to the cooking range, she introduced me as "president of Hong Kong, Inc., producer of the Da Tung Chinese foods." Instead of a wok I used a 14-inch skillet because it heated up faster. However, it wasn't fast enough. The few minutes' waiting time seemed interminable, and I felt embarrassed with nothing else to do. Otherwise the demonstration went well. I enjoyed the experience immensely and my confidence as an entertainer was bolstered by the producer's letter saying "Thanks again for a great show. We're still getting requests for the recipe for Shrimp with Green Peppers."

In 1972 after my vacation in Taiwan where I studied with the country's most famous TV cooking star and author, Fu Pei Mei, I was invited by Edie Huggins to be her culinary guest, again on WCAU. A versatile person, Huggins was a former nurse and actress and one of the first African Americans to be a TV reporter, broadcaster, and hostess of her own program (she eventually enjoyed a 42-year tenure with the WCAU and received numerous awards). Both members of ethnic minorities, we had a mutual empathy and resonance and easily developed a good rapport.

I was eager to demonstrate a fish recipe I had learned from Fu Pei Mei. This time I took the trouble of heating my skillet before the program began. This way, I wouldn't have to waste any airtime before my cooking. However, Huggins and I kept talking and by the time I began my demonstration the skillet was so hot my addition of a little oil instantly created a fire. It was a horrifying sight that scared everybody and nobody seemed to know how to deal with the inferno. Good thing I had enough common sense not to douse water onto the skillet; it would have made the situation worse. Instead, I covered the skillet with a plate and the burning stopped. And fortunately, it was not a live show. Huggins rescheduled the taping.

At this taping the crew helpfully placed a large fire extinguisher next to the cooking range. Only we didn't have to use it as everything went hunky dory without mishap.

I next branched out to Baltimore. I had to travel by train for my car was in the repair shop. After the TV show as I was waiting for a taxi, a sedan stopped by. Three young women were inside.

"Do you need a ride?" the driver asked.

"I sure could if it's not out of your way."

"Where are you headed?"

"The train station."

"Hop in."

Introducing herself as Kathy (a pseudonym) and a nurse, the driver was very friendly and curious to know what I was doing in Baltimore. She and I soon began to talk in earnest. She seemed to take real interest in me and I found her attractive. At one point she asked me if I would like to go to a party later.

I was flattered by her invitation. But tired from getting up early that day, the travel from Philadelphia, lugging a heavy load of cooking utensils and ingredients, and the TV demonstration, I was eager to return home. So regrettably I took a rain check. We exchanged telephone numbers, promising to keep in touch.

In the ensuing weeks we did talk on the phone on occasions and entertained the possibility of getting together. Just prior to that time I had a girlfriend who used to live in the Philadelphia area until a job in New York took her away. Subsequently, I discovered long distance romance was not conducive to our relationship; there were signs of deep fissure, and we eventually broke up. I didn't think another long-distance romance would be fruitful and wasn't sure my relationship with Kathy would go beyond a platonic one. But somehow when she expressed interest in visiting me in Philadelphia and asked me to reserve a hotel room, my sense of adventure and unwillingness to hurt her feelings made me welcome her.

Arriving in late morning, Kathy didn't pick a good day because I had a couple of journalism classes to attend in the afternoon and loads of reading and writing assignments in the evening. With no time for lunch we proceeded to lovemaking almost immediately. Afterward I had to hurry to Temple University and left her in the hotel. I should have squeezed some time out from my busy schedule and invited her for dinner. But I didn't extend her the courtesy, being preoccupied with my homework. I was really being a selfish brute, a heel, with no regard for her sensitivity, sincerity, and good intentions. I never forgave myself for treating her that way. Although I still phoned her once in a while—surprised she was still willing to talk to me—we never met again.

As I continued my TV appearances I was fascinated by the first cooking program on commercial TV: Graham Kerr's

Galloping Gourmet. It inspired me to pursue a cooking program of mine own tentatively titled *The Wokking Chef.* The timing was good. President Nixon had just made his unprecedented trip to China in 1972. The heavy TV coverage of the elaborate banquets showed that there was more to Chinese food than chicken chow mein, won ton soup, and egg rolls and stimulated a strong national interest in Chinese cooking in general and in the more sophisticated dishes in particular. At that time *"Yan Can Cook"* was getting popular but it was on the Public Broadcast System. I was hoping to air my proposed program on commercial or cable TV. Eventually I gathered enough recipes for 52 shows and got Comcast interested in the possibility. We went as far as taping several segments. But Comcast decided not to go any further and my inability to find a sponsor made me give up my aspiration.

Still, the fun of demonstrating on TV was hard to resist and so, I brought my show to Washington, D.C., and continued to make appearances on various Philadelphia stations. One day I got a surprise call from Elaine Tait, the *Inquirer* food editor, who had done two stories on me through the efforts of my PR specialist Lesley Kuhn.

"I hope you can help me," she said. "The producer of the Barbara Walters show (called *Not for Women Only*) asked me to recommend a Chinese chef to be her guest." Thinking of me as a strong possibility and having sampled my cooking, she, however, wanted to make sure I could rise to the occasion. I pointed out that I had been a seasoned TV performer and was positive I would be equal to the challenge.

Convinced, she made the recommendation and soon the producer phoned me. "We'd be happy to have you. Arrive the day before the taping. We'll put you up at the Waldorf Astoria and invite you for dinner."

Just then in 1974 Walters was already a big star and the first broadcaster to earn a million dollars in salary. To be the guest of such a celebrity would certainly be a high point in my life. But it also turned out to be one of the lowest.

Arriving by train at Penn Station in New York, I decided to buy a ticket first to see the hit musical *Pippin* starring Ben Vereen the following day, and took a yellow cab to the theater. When I reached for my wallet to purchase the ticket I could not find it. Instantly I realized what had happened: After paying the driver, I picked up my business suit but left my wallet on the seat. Hoping against hope, I rushed from the theater to the street to find the cab but it had already disappeared. In great panic I thought of calling the yellow cab company but knew it would be useless as the cabs were individually owned. I had some $200, credit cards, a social security card, and a driver's license in the wallet. The discovery of the loss was one of my most traumatic experiences, a horrible feeling of despondency, regret, terror, and worry.

Penniless, I had to walk from the theater to Waldorf Astoria. The producer and his assistants did their best to console me and gave me $20 to tide me over. But my day was ruined, and I was in a foul mood which words of comfort and the sumptuous dinner could not abate. Would I survive this trauma and recover enough composure the following day?

I slept surprisingly well. When I appeared on the set at NBC I was able to put the memory of the day before behind me and excitedly get ready for the taping. For this program I picked the simplest and the most conservative recipes: rice, egg drop soup, and pepper steak. Needing some crushed garlic, I added to the theatrics by placing a Chinese cleaver flat on the bulbous plant, raised my right hand high above the shoulder, and banged on the cleaver with a swift martial arts chop, accompanied by a thunderous battle cry "HIYA" likened to a kung fu master breaking several layers of heavy boards with his bare hand.

Totally stunned, puzzled, and even a little scared, Walters

said: "Wha-what was that?"

"I was just trying to crush some garlic."

At the end of my cooking, Walters and I tasted the food and chatted. Known as an incisive, probing—and sometimes tough—interviewer, she proved to be a pleasant, amiable, unassuming hostess who made me feel right at home. She asked no personal questions, only some culinary ones. She also made me field questions from the audience. I dealt with them easily. The taping went so well and was so enjoyable that I loved every minute of it. Indeed, it was an intoxicating experience that got me increasingly attracted to show biz.

My show biz venture, however, did not detract from my enthusiasm in journalism as I continued to take other writing courses at Temple. My progress and presence as the only Chinese in the journalism department attracted the interest of its chairman, Dr. Bruce Underwood. He astonished me with this question: "Would you like to consider teaching at Temple?" It was the remotest thought on my mind. At this point I was content being an entrepreneur running my Chinese food business while keeping busy as a cooking teacher in Philadelphia and New York and doing some acting when an opportunity presented itself. While journalism appealed to me greatly, I had no greater ambition than being just a freelance writer— and I was doing just that as I continued to contribute to *Philadelphia* magazine. But being open-minded, I listened. He thought I might add something to the journalism department and suggested a long-range program for me: enroll in the graduate department first. Then get a Ph.D. from the University of Missouri, and finally return to Temple to teach.

I began to look back at my life. Having failed in my quest to be a concert pianist and finding my job as a chemist less than inspiring, I was nevertheless enthralled by my entrepreneurship. But I also discovered the ugly side of business, the greed, cutthroat tactics, and dishonesty. I realized I was still at the crossroads of my life trying to find my true calling, a profession that I could commit to totally.

After serious consideration I decided Dr. Underwood's suggestion had definite merit. I came from a family of educators: Father, Mother, and eldest brother David were all such practitioners. As for me, I had treasured my role as an army instructor years ago, and more recently as a Chinese cooking teacher. I certainly considered teaching a marvelous and noble profession and thought being a professor of journalism could be a satisfying and stimulating career and embraced Underwood's proposal. So in the spring semester of 1974 I became a candidate in the master of journalism (MJ) program.

In one of my first graduate classes I got acquainted with Ben Compaign, publisher of the *Collegiate Guide*, an annual guide to Philadelphia's various business establishments. He asked me to review a few of the best Chinese restaurants during the summer, the deadline being August. I was not sure I could carry out the assignment as I had planned a long trip to Europe and thought most likely I would not be back in time. But an accident on that trip cut short my vacation and hence I was able to review just one restaurant, which serendipitously opened up a sideline for me as a restaurateur. Since this journey marked another turning point in life, let me provide some details.

Long interested in Europe, I initially planned to go on an American Express packaged tour. It would have been my second such attempt. I had to cancel the first due to my mother's death. This time I again was planning on an escorted tour. My good friend Joan Ruggles, however, talked me out of it. She had been a seasoned traveler, had lived in Europe, and was so persuasive that I agreed with her that it would be a lot more fun and adventurous to travel independently.

To my elation my scheme worked out perfectly. I had no trouble finding accommodations the last minute even though it was during the height of travel season in June. I used local transportation to get around and train to go from country to country. I stayed in each city—including London, Brussels, Bruges, and Amsterdam—just long enough to satisfy my curiosity and then moved on. And I was having the time of my life. At one point I met a Japanese student who was also traveling independently. He told me his next destination was Zermatt and easily convinced me to add that to my itinerary.

Upon my arrival I was awed by everything, including the following: 1. The excellent cuisine, not just in some fancy restaurants but in a modest one right at the railroad station where I had an excellent ox tail soup. 2. The quaint, charming little town where only horse-drawn carriages—and no automobiles—were allowed, and above all, 3. The stunning, exquisite and majestic Matterhorn.

But that evening I was dismayed to find myself in a mountaineers' cemetery where some 50 climbers had lost their lives trying to scale the Alps. Especially heartbreaking was the tomb of a New York City youth with the words "I live to climb" on the headstone accompanied by an American flag and his red ice axe.

The following day I was excited by the incredible sight of skiers weaving their way down the Alps in the dead of summer. Being a rank beginner skier but already an inveterate devotee to this sport, I decided to give it a shot. As I was renting the skis I asked the attendant if the bindings were checked and adjusted according to my weight and skiing level, a good way to break my leg if they were not. "No need to," said the Englishman. To prove his point he banged on the bindings with his fist and they released. The proper way, however, was not so haphazard but to use a specially designed machine. But neither of us knew better.

Riding in a cable car, I chanced to strike up conversation with two fellow visitors, Otto Kalb, a Swiss, and his American wife, Jane. They were extremely friendly. Before we parted company they invited me to drive with them to their home in Zurich and sail on their yacht. Surprised by their hospitality and generosity, I offered to cook a Chinese meal as a token of my gratitude. We arranged to meet after my skiing that day.

Ski conditions were far from ideal. The snow, which became frozen during the night, began to melt in the morning and by noon it would become too slushy to ski. Nevertheless, the spectacular beauty of the surroundings more than compensated for my skiing difficulty. By about 11:00 A.M. I was ready to quit. Traversing on an easy terrain, I suddenly lost balance and fell. Properly adjusted bindings should have released my feet. But mine did not. As I tumbled with my full body weight going one direction, my boots, which were chained immovably to the skis, stood in the way and it created a classical condition for twisting the knee. I knew instantly I got hurt terribly. As I lay on the snow I was hoping ski patrol would discover the accident and take me down in a toboggan, but for a long time no one showed up. Hampered by my broken leg, I managed to ski down to the base with great difficulty.

I met the Kalbs at the appointed hour. They sympathized with my mishap and suggested that we still follow the original plan of going with them to Zurich where they would take me to a hospital. On our way we went down a steep mountain with numerous hairpin turns at very fast speed in Otto Kalb's sports car. Later he discovered one of the tires had a hole with the inner tube exposed. Something untoward—or even fatal—could have happened, I thought, and counted myself very lucky not to have one accident following another.

When we reached Lake Lucerne I was so moved by the beauty that I decided—against my better judgment—to leave the Kalbs and take a cruise, broken leg or no broken leg. The cruise would take me to the other end of the lake, the town of

Lucerne, where I would spend the night. The following day I planned to take a train to Zurich where Otto would meet me. Arriving at Lucerne after dark, I had to hobble on my one good leg while carrying a 45-pound suitcase and trying to locate a hotel. I walked six or seven torturous blocks before finding a suitable one.

The following morning Otto picked me up at the Zurich train station and rushed me to a hospital. But without sufficient cash the hospital refused to admit me. It was only through the compassion of Otto who advanced the necessary money that I was able to see an orthopedic doctor. X-rays showed that my left leg suffered a broken medial lateral ligament, and he recommended prompt surgery. Knowing that knee surgery was very tricky and suspicious of this doctor's young age (he seemed to be in his late 20s) I was afraid to follow his advice. Seeking a second opinion, I phoned my Philadelphia physician Ron Jan, partner of my doctor-brother David who was away at the time. Dr. Jan suggested that I forgo the surgery and come home. Thus I curtailed my European trip, which lasted only about two weeks, and took the next flight home, struggling with a pair of crutches while carrying my heavy luggage. This could not be possible without the kindness of strangers who helped me at every turn.

Dr. Jan referred me to an orthopedic doctor, Phil Mahre, team physician of the Phillies. To my relief he recommended a different course of action. Instead of surgery he would put my leg in a cast for six weeks. Afterward I would follow rigorous physical therapy. In time the broken ligament most likely would grow back and heal perfectly, he said. It would be a slow process which I was happy to endure in place of the dreaded alternative.

One day when I was bored with my snail-paced recovery, happily an old schoolmate of mine from Chongqing's Holy Light School came visiting. Dr. Anthony Tsou was a vivacious man who, like me, enjoyed the pleasures of the table. Indeed, he was more of a foodie than I, having earned the nickname "Zhua Zhua," meaning "Grab Grab" during his high school days for his impatience to snatch good food before everyone else. With the approach of evening I decided to kill two birds with one stone by dining at the Jade Palace, my favorite restaurant, while reviewing it for my Temple classmate Ben Compaign's *Collegiate Guide* as requested. To have more fun and sample a variety of dishes, I invited my girlfriend Betty Schrom and fixed up Dr. Tsou with a date.

With my right leg still in a cast, Tsou drove us to the Jade Palace on 2222 Cottman Avenue in Northeast Philadelphia, mentioned earlier in "One from Column A." There was nothing palatial about the restaurant. Seating about 80, it was unassuming with booths along the walls and tables in the center like a typical Chinese restaurant. The owners were Stanley Liang and his wife, an enormously gifted chef whose cooking had already made a deep impression on me during my previous visits. On this occasion the meal was exceptional as expected. In the course of my interview with Stanley Liang, a full-time engineer who helped out in the evenings and weekends, I discovered he and his wife were thinking of selling the restaurant. Having long aspired to be a restaurateur myself, I ended up being the proud new owner. One irony was that I got to read my own rave review of my own restaurant in the *Collegiate Guide*, which was published after my purchase.

With this acquisition I continued to be a full-time graduate student at Temple. Choosing music as minor, I was able to return to my first love and enrolled in a number of enjoyable classes. I was no longer studying the piano which proved to be too laborious and time consuming. Instead, I took up singing with a well-known teacher, opera singer, and protégé of Jan Pearce, Philip Cho. I discovered that the human voice was indeed the most beautiful of all musical instruments, and despite my slow progress I was glad to find an alternate way to express my joy in music.

The second half of the 1970s was among the busiest—and the happiest—times of my life but fortunately I was able to set my priorities and keep up with everything. Still managing my Chinese food business, I did not dwell on it. I was no longer interested in expanding sales or developing new products; I simply relied on my established business with recurrent orders from my brokers. As proprietor of the Jade Palace I went there only in the evenings, five days a week, Wednesdays through Sundays, being assisted by my manger, Susan Che, wife of the executive chef. I taught cooking Mondays at Temple University and Tuesdays at the China Institute in New York. Once in a while I even got to do a little acting. And graduate work at Temple was not as burdensome as I had feared and three years went by very fast. The one intimidating obstacle was a comprehensive examination for which I had to cram. For a while I simply dropped everything to devote to my preparation. Of the three other candidates I passed with the best score. In 1977 I earned the MJ degree.

While I was poised to follow Dr. Underwood's suggestion to enroll in the Ph.D. program at Missouri University prior to teaching at Temple, I unexpectedly found myself without a sponsor as he had departed from the journalism department for employment elsewhere. Would the new department chair have interest in hiring me if I did get my Ph.D.? I had no idea.

For the time being my aspiration turned more to writing than teaching, and I thought my better future lay in being a newspaperman, a practitioner rather than an instructor of the craft. With my ethnic background, broad interests, predilections toward the arts and particularly music, I thought I could make some contributions to the fourth estate. Being fresh out of grad school I certainly would have no chance of getting a job with big papers like the *Philadelphia Inquirer*. Perhaps the *Courier-Post*, located in Cherry Hill, NJ, just across the Delaware River from Philadelphia, and the largest daily in South Jersey, might have an interest in me. It helped that I was not a total stranger to the paper. Following top reviews of the Jade Palace from various publications the *Courier-Post* echoed the praise, saying "We had heard of the reputation of the Jade Palace and owner-chef Ben Lin (I actually was not its chef until later,) and gave it the highest rating of four stars and featured my picture in the review under the byline of Alonzo Gristle.

Being too naïve to realize the byline was an obvious pseudonym I addressed a letter to the reviewer, enclosing some of my writing samples and asked if I could be an intern. Managing editor Bob Schryock interviewed me and granted my request.

Though interns received no pay I was eager to get practical experience: to gather news, interview subjects, develop the facility for fast writing to meet the demands of deadlines, and hopefully in some small way to create "literature in a hurry" as English poet and critic Matthew Arnold defined journalism. Unfortunately, I had a very boring beginning. My job was to write short, complimentary articles about the newspaper's advertisers, a meaningless public relations effort. I kept wondering when I would get a real writing assignment.

Finally it came when news editor Jerry Moore asked me to do a story about a fire department that painted its fire trucks yellow instead red. After interviewing fire chiefs of the three counties of Camden, Burlington, and Gloucester I completed the story relatively easily.

Moore's next assignment was to profile a woman Ph.D. whose job was to analyze air crashes with the use of black box. Her mother was so pleased with the piece that she not only sent me a highly laudatory letter but also a $10 bill. I replied with a note saying I appreciated the heart of a loving mother and her kind gesture of gratitude but that I had to return the cash because I could not accept gratuity as a journalist.

Moore also liked the article and said: "You write as well as our veteran reporters. From now on we'll pay you for your stories." So I ended up as a stringer, making a puny $50 per article but happy to carry out myriad assignments working virtually full-time.

I got another pleasant surprise from my two articles. Features editor Stanley Goldstein asked me if I would like to interview Roger Moore. I embraced the challenge. Indeed, I was more than a little eager to meet this celebrated British actor who came to Philadelphia to promote his latest James Bond adventure *The Spy Who Loved Me*. He had already made his mark in the TV series *The Saint* and as a worthy successor to Sean Connery in the 007 franchise, having starred in two James Bond movies. More than just an impartial observer, I had studied acting, made my professional debut in 1970, and joined the Screen Actors Guild in 1976. And so I was as much a reporter hungry for interesting information as a fledging actor probing for the secrets of his success.

Greeting me at the Barclay Hotel suite in Philadelphia was his press agent. I was afraid his presence might inhibit my interview. Fortunately, he didn't utter a single word during the whole time. Wearing a safari outfit, Moore seemed to be a surprisingly modest person with a ready smile. At the age of 50 he looked fit and younger. Behind his façade were jauntiness and a lively mind. For the next one plus hours he patiently answered all my questions and covered a wide range of topics. He started his career as a model, which was not surprising, considering he had such a handsome face and marvelous physique. Serious about acting, he had studied at the Royal Academy of Dramatic Arts for three terms. Later, while doing movie extra work he caught the attention of an influential person who gave him a chance to play principal roles. He eventually made it to big time with such TV series as *Maverick*, *The Persuaders!* (with Tony Curtis), particularly *The Saint* and the two Bond movies, *Live and Let Die* and *The Man with the Golden Gun*.

He didn't dwell much on my question on the differences between film and theatrical acting (later I discovered he had very few stage credits and was in a 1953 Broadway play that closed on its opening night) but did admit one could cheat a little in movies. That was the case in the riveting ski sequences in *The Spy*. They were done by a stunt man as he was not much of a skier.

He observed that he and David Niven were the only two persons he knew of who could be performing while going outside themselves, so to speak, to give a detached look at themselves and even laugh a little at their own acting.

At one point Moore and I paused to have coffee. He then lit a cigar and enjoyed it not unlike the way the super spy savoring his "stirred and not shaken" martini. Turning lighthearted, he said he didn't like to do dining scenes because he could not easily talk and eat at the same time. "I prefer bananas because I can swallow them in a hurry." To keep in shape he followed a rigorous regimen of exercises. Toward the end of our talk he introduced me to his pretty Italian wife. "She was an actress but gave up her career to raise a family," he said, adding that he took her along to locations whenever possible.

The Spy became a box office success worldwide, and Moore went on to do four more 007 movies, or a total of seven, more than any other Bond portrayer. (Moore died of cancer in 2017.)

It was, however, not always smooth sailing for me at the *Courier-Post*. To test my news reporting ability, Moore asked me to accompany a veteran journalist to cover a big political event in which complicated policies were unveiled. Without a tape recorder and being a terrible note taker, I did execrably, missing out on some salient points and failing to give a comprehensive picture.

Happily, I redeemed myself somewhat. In a subsequent assignment I wrote about the first prize winner of a sandwich contest. His winning entry was fusion cuisine in which he combined bean sprouts with some American ingredients. Interjecting some humor, I recalled Rudyard Kipling's famous observation and contradicted him by saying "East is East, West is West, but the twain did meet" in my encomium of this culinary creation. That prompted executive editor Phil Book-man to go out of his way to commend me.

In time my assignments turned almost completely to features whose editor Stan Goldstein was a gracious, gregarious, heavyset guy who had a passion for Chinese cuisine. We soon became the best of friends. He liked to call me "my Renaissance man" and gave me one juicy assignment after another.

As I looked for other writing ideas I remembered my long fascination with the Jewish affinity for Chinese cuisine. They were the best clients of Chinese restaurants and the loneliest day of the year for many of the proprietors (including me as owner of the Jade Palace) was Yom Kippur, the Day of Atonement and observed by fasting. I had heard about New York's first—and long running—kosher Chinese restaurant, Bernstein, in the Lower East Side, and a more recent one in the garment district, Moshe Peking. When I asked Goldstein if I could review it, he cheerfully consented.

On my journey to New York I pondered on the similarities between Jews and Chinese. They are the world's two oldest civilizations, share a respect for the elders, have a low rate of juvenile delinquencies, a passion for dining pleasure, and the business acumen that has made them world class financiers and businessmen. And not surprisingly in a number of Far

Eastern countries Chinese have earned the sobriquet "Asian Jews." But I never found out why Jews, more than any other ethnic minority, have the greatest enthusiasm for Chinese food. I had, however, noticed that kreplach was like won ton, blintz bore some resemblance to egg rolls, and gefilte fish had a counterpart in the Chinese fish ball.

On this review assignment I was hoping to make some salient culinary as well as sociological discoveries, perhaps examples of cross fertilization between the two cultures, and a restaurant that would attract discriminating gentiles much as kosher meats attracted some discerning gentiles.

The manager of Moshe Peking showed no surprise at the sight of this peculiar looking, unlikely Asian customer. However, I did feel out of place among the yarmulke-wearing Jewish clientele. The restaurant was well appointed, graced with a cozy, romantic ambience and the presence of a rabbi. The menu was filled with popular Chinese selections but without any innovative, unusual, or fusion dishes that I had hoped for. All the tref (non-kosher) entries were preceded by the adjective "mock" such as mock mou shu pork, mock sweet and sour pork. Wondering what a kosher kitchen was like and what kind of chefs worked there, I would have liked to have an inside look and chat with them but thought it would be too much of an intrusion and betray my mission as an anonymous reviewer. I simply proceeded to order several entrees. Unfortunately, none of them proved outstanding. I left Moshe Peking disappointed and wrote a lukewarm review.

Writing the review reminded me of two jokes:

1. A young Chinese lands a job in a kosher restaurant in New York right after his arrival from China. Training him to be a waiter, the manager teaches him to speak Yiddish. The youth is a quick study and soon becomes fluent in it. One day a couple are his guests

and are utterly delighted by his linguistic ability. As they are leaving they tell the manager how wonderful the waiter is and how they are amazed by his command of Yiddish.

"Not so loud," the manager whispers. "This boy is a FOB, fresh off the boat. He thinks he is speaking English."

2. An American Jew visits Hong Kong for the first time. Knowing that his ancestors have settled in China as early as the seventh century, that there are Chinese Jews living there today, and that this former British colony has a synagogue, he decides to attend services. Afterward he tells the Chinese rabbi how much he enjoys it.

Puzzled by his presence, the rabbi asks, "But why are you here?"

"I'm Jewish."

"Funny, you don't look Jewish."

Shortly after my Moshe Peking visit Goldstein asked me to review two South Jersey Chinese restaurants, Szechuan Wok and Peking Mandarin, unconcerned that I might have a conflict of interest since I was the proprietor of the Jade Palace, an area competitor. I would certainly recuse myself if I found anything less than complimentary. As it turned out both restaurants were very good, and I was happy to rave about them. To show the power of the press my reviews gave both a terrific boost in business, prompting a number of their counterparts to invite me for dinner. But I turned them all down to avoid impropriety or the appearance of impropriety. Goldstein and I became particularly fond of Peking Mandarin where we shared numerous lunches, dinners, and extravagant banquets because of its consistently high cooking quality and the amiable and accommodating owner-chef Uncle Lui.

Whatever spare time I had I devoted to my interest in the theater. I enrolled in acting classes from time to time, attended as many plays as possible, and when opportunities presented themselves I did a little movie and TV extra work for fun. Within the past two years I also landed two regional commercials as principal and got myself a New York agent, Jadin Wang. I was glad when she got me an audition for the soap opera *One Life to Live* on ABC.

The character was a Chinese jeweler. During those days one did not have the luxury of having the sides in advance. Having no experience or training in cold reading, I held out little chances of success.

I took an early train to the Big Apple, hoping to have sufficient time for preparation. But some 10 minutes after my arrival at ABC the casting director summoned me into her office. She did the reading with me without taping. Afterward she simply said "fine," which sounded more like a perfunctory remark than a compliment. I felt that I did a so-so job which made very little impression on her. But to my surprise she cast me.

On the date of the shoot I was treated like a VIP. A production assistant ushered me into the dressing room of one of the stars who was not working that day and brought me a hot breakfast; a wardrobe mistress fitted me with the proper garment; a makeup artist and a hair specialist fussed over the way I looked. Soon the production began. I was introduced to the director, the stage manager, and other principals with no time for pleasantries. The first order of business was blocking, i.e. the movements and positions of the actors, which in turn, helped determine the positions of the cameras, usually two rolling simultaneously.

The rehearsals were short and efficient. The director spent almost no time on interpretations and nuances. I had 10 lines as a guest star and was not nervous. Unlike movies and commercials which normally required tedious take after take, soap operas, which aired a different episode every day, by nature had to be produced quickly. And before I knew it my scene was over.

I told a few of my colleagues at the *Courier-Post* about my gig which produced much excitement. One of them immediately put up a big sign next to the newsroom's TV saying "watch Ben Lin starring in *One Life to Live*" on such and such date. As if I didn't garner enough glory, Goldstein asked me to write a first-person story about this experience.

An offshoot of *Courier-Post's* restaurant reviews was a weekly column called "Specialties of the House" of which I became a regular contributor, covering many of the better restaurants, Chinese and otherwise. It had been quite some time since I last wrote about Szechuan Wok and food editor Ruth Otis accepted my proposal to pay a second visit.

This time I was, however, a little intimidated. From personal experience, I knew that the kitchen of a Chinese restaurant could be such a pressure cooker where tempers easily flared and fights were not uncommon. But nothing quite prepared me for the horrible story I heard from a former waiter of Szechuan Wok: During a heated argument with one of his kitchen help, owner-chef Yang (a pseudonym) became inordinately enraged. He picked up a cleaver, aimed at his employee's head, and threw with what had to be ferocious force. It was a good thing chef Yang missed his mark slightly, which could have been fatal. Nevertheless, Yang did turn the poor employee into a Chinese Van Gogh by slicing off one of his ears. Yang was sued and settled the case by paying the victim $50,000.

Meeting Chef Yang this time, I was glad he was in a good mood. Still, that kitchen incident was very much on my mind and I tried to be especially polite.

"Do me a favor," Yang, a short guy sporting a crew cut, said in Mandarin before my interview. "When you last wrote about my restaurant you recommended too many dishes. There were so many requests that my kitchen couldn't keep up with the orders. This time please limit your recommendations to just one or two." I was more than happy to oblige.

In my previous review I was impressed by his savory Tung Ting shrimp adorned with an egg white sauce; a masterfully seasoned and extremely tender beancurd, accentuated with black beans, scallions, and ginger; and a unique won ton appetizer accompanied by a delicious sauce the likes of which I had never encountered. Now in "Specialties of the House" recipes were included as part of the format. I was eager to get a couple from him but he obstinately refused. I asked him why.

"My recipes are my secrets. I never divulge them to anyone," he said. "Once a customer offered me a lot of money for a recipe. But I turned him down."

"I can't write my column without some recipes."

"No," he insisted.

I was ready to abandon my story. But in a last-ditch effort I said, "Why don't you give me the recipes of some common dishes, even if you have to copy them from a cookbook." Fortunately he agreed.

The article came out around Chinese New Year. As a way to thank me and celebrate this festival occasion, Yang invited me to a private feast at his restaurant. For ethical reasons I normally never accepted any free restaurant meals. But for this celebratory dinner it would be ungracious not to honor his invitation. Besides, I had already written two articles on Szechuan Wok. It was unlikely I would do another and be influenced by any favorable treatment. So, I was looking forward to an incomparable dinner.

On this day Yang closed up for business early and set up two large round tables for his family, manager, servers, kitchen staff, and his only two guests, me and my girlfriend Annie Fung. While we were relishing on such exotica as

305

shark's fin soup, sea cucumber, and jellyfish during the early part of the banquet, Yang followed the Chinese New Year tradition by giving everyone a red envelope. Typically, recipients were employees and offspring. The inclusion of Annie and me made me uncomfortable. I just hoped there wasn't too much money. But since it was considered bad form to open the envelopes prematurely I had no idea what the contents were.

Upon reaching home Annie found $100 in her envelope, which was way beyond my expectations. I was further astonished to find a whopping $500 in mine. I phoned Yang the following day, thanking him for the generosity but saying that I had to return the gift. To make him feel less unhappy I offered to keep $4 for Annie and me.

"Please don't fuss over this," he said. "I wanted to thank you for your nice articles. They improved my business tremendously. The money was just an expression of gratitude."

"I'm a journalist. If I commended your cooking I was just doing my job and reporting the facts. If it increased your business you deserved it. I want to do the right thing and can't keep your gift. Besides, I was grateful enough for your excellent dinner. I'll come over and return the money."

"No, don't do it."

"Yes, I will."

We argued back and forth, and I was getting nowhere. And so, the only thing I could do was to mail him a check, hoping against hope that he would cash it. But days went by, and he never did. When I reported this incident to Goldstein, features editor at the *Courier-Post*, he said: "Don't worry about it. We pay you stringers so little money that you should not feel guilty about making some extra dough." While the *Courier-Post* forbade its writers to accept substantial gratuities, as a stringer I was not bound by such rule. And so, I reluctantly accepted the money.

My next assignment from food editor Ruth Otis was on the subject of chop suey. It was published on June 6, 1979:

"The Chinese may say phooey to chop suey but the mixture, next to chow mein, is probably the best-known Chinese restaurant dish in this country.

"According to folklore, its genesis is attributed to Viceroy Li Hung-Chang (also spelled Li Hungzhang). As China's highest official to visit here over 100 years ago, he received a royal treatment with state functions and dedication ceremonies in his honor (the ginkgo tree he planted at the site of General Grant's tomb in New York still stands). And the press followed his every move—scrutable or otherwise—with the greatest diligence and curiosity.

"Being hungry one day (probably one hour after an American meal) he had his attendants warm up some leftovers of no particular distinction or culinary significance. As luck would have it, a group of journalists dropped in. Naturally they wanted to know what strange looking things he was having. On the spur of the moment he came up with two Chinese words that meant mishmash tidbits and inadvertently coined the name for one of the most famous entrees: chop suey."

"Found at one time in virtually every Chinese restaurant in the U.S., it was a gooey blend of bean sprouts, celery, and onion, topped with meat or shrimp and served over rice. (When served over fried noodles it becomes chop mein.) Curiously, it bore little resemblance to what Li had and was totally unrecognizable in China.

"Over the years, as Chinese restaurants became more sophisticated and authentic, chop suey has acquired a pejorative connotation, especially among the Chinese. A set of chop suey chinaware, for instance, denotes an ill-matched and unaesthetic collection. And chop suey cooking has come to stand for the entire realm of bastardized Cantonese fare varying from butterfly shrimp, egg foo young to egg rolls, which no Chinese or purists would touch with a 10-foot chopstick.

"However, because chop suey cookery has monopolized the nation's Chinese restaurants for so many years and enjoyed such an entrenched popularity, despite the inroads Mandarin and Sichuanese cuisines have made, for a long time few restaurants could survive without chop suey selections.

"The connection between these selections and Cantonese cooking is a historical one. Since the mid-1800s, thousands of Cantonese laborers had come to this country to work in the mines, on the farms and railroads. Subsequently, some of them went into the restaurant business, partially to fill their own needs, being unaccustomed to the strange American diet.

"Discovering that their own cooking did not exhilarate the more conservative and delicate Yankee palate, they began to modify old dishes and invent new ones. Somewhere along, these Southern Chinese apparently needed a name for one of their most successful concoctions and picked the well published words "chop suey."

"In time, they spawned a school of cooking that minimizes the sophisticated and maximizes simplicity and ease of preparation, using relatively inexpensive and common ingredients. One example is egg rolls. They contain mostly celery, cabbage, and a tiny portion of shrimp, whereas the authentic version comprises a good amount of meat and shrimp, and vegetables like bean sprouts and bamboo shoots. Anther distinction is its abundance of gravy (it apparently makes the accompanying rice more palatable). In fact, what separates some dishes from their Cantonese counterparts is little more than the amount of gravy.

"While chop suey cooking still resonates with much of the public today, it gives one a false sense of being full, with its pervasive gravy and gooey mixed vegetables, thereby perpetrating the well-known bromide—and an inaccurate one at that—that one goes hungry one hour after a Chinese meal.

"Chop suey dishes may have also contributed partially to the Chinese reputation of being inscrutable. Since those who christened the dishes were early settlers whose command of English was less than perfect, understandably a great deal of obscurity has resulted, with phonetically spelled Cantonese words like har kew, moo goo gai pan, and wor shu opp. To add to the confusion, some are descriptive dishes in English that contain inaccurate or misleading information. For example, barbecued shrimp is not broiled or roasted but deep fried; there is no lobster in shrimp with lobster sauce, or egg in egg rolls (the proper translation is spring roll), and often the only fowl in chicken chow mein is turkey and not chicken because it is plumper.

"It's a small wonder that trying to decode these dishes or order intelligently is like forcing a camel through a needle's eye. But out of this difficulty, a memorable phrase which has added color to the English lexicon is born: 'One from Column A,' a menu directive intended to help ordering by grouping certain dishes together.

"For the uninitiated, this phrase usually appears under the heading 'Family Dinners'

"For two persons select one from column A and one from column B. For three persons select one from column A and two from column B. And so on.

"But alas, this phrase may be a thing of the past, for after having been the butt of too many jokes, it of late has become 'One from Group A' in certain restaurants."

One unexpected development from my writings was to become the conduit of a secret love affair. The Romeo was the former mayor of a South Jersey town and a man of many accomplishments. I'll call him Bill Wood for purposes of privacy. I interviewed him in connection with his recent visit to China, which had established diplomatic relations with the

U.S. in 1976. Wood struck me as a highly energetic, vivacious, and colorful man. In glowing terms he talked about his wonderful journey and fascination for this developing nation. He was treated like a crowned head and showered with gifts. He also brought back a suitcase full of various factory samples that his Chinese hosts wished him to sell. They included some hobby curiosities. One was a set of "healthy balls," made of two concentric steel balls. By placing two such balls in the palm of the hand and rotating them with the fingers, one could allegedly derive many health benefits: improve blood circulation, counter rheumatism, and develop digital agility. Wood gave me a few sets of the balls, and as a pianist I was glad to receive and exercise with them.

Pleased by my article and spurred by his apparent love for the Chinese, Wood befriended me. He treated me to lunches at his country club and took me to the movies. One day I dropped in to visit him at his residence. There I met his wife who appeared to be a winsome, warm, and kind person. She was hospitable enough to invite me for lunch and cooked a chicken dish.

As our friendship grew Mayor Wood confided in me a well-kept secret: he had a mistress in Taiwan. What made this ongoing affair so unlikely was not only the geographical distance between the two but also the fact that she could not speak a word of English and he not a word of Chinese. Wood at that time was around 60 while she some 20 years younger. But nothing seemed to stand in the way of their torrid liaison. She made him feel young and passionate and gave him great sexual pleasure, he said. The two kept in touch by means of a machine which no longer exists today: telex. Since they had no common language I became the translator. While there were messages of great affection in both directions Wood told me he had such a wonderful, devoted wife whom he would never consider divorcing to marry the mistress, and had so advised her. Nevertheless, the magnetism between the two was over-powering and I ended up going to Wood's office frequently to receive and transmit messages. I felt strange to play the role of a cupid. I could well feel Wood's pain of being torn between his dedication to a loving, loyal spouse and his passion for the Taiwanese woman.

The agony was made worse by Wood's difficulty to get away to see her in Taiwan. To make things easier she flew to the U.S. for a brief visit. I became the go-between, booking a hotel in Philadelphia's Chinatown and going to meet her. She struck me as pleasant and average looking but provided no overt clues as to why she held so much sway over Wood.

After she returned to Taiwan Wood never contacted me again. From time to time she would drop me a note over several years, talking about incidental things but never about her romance, which I suspect ended at some point. Respecting Wood's trust in me, I never revealed his love affair. I tell it now only because he and his wife have both passed away.

Among other people that I wrote about:

- Ken Hom, an American-born Chinese, in connection with his effort to promote his cookbook. He had been teaching Chinese cooking in San Francisco's California Culinary Academy and later achieved international stardom as a TV chef in Great Britain and elsewhere worldwide. He was also a marketer of his highly popular wok and ready-cooked-meals, and recipient of a special culinary award from Queen Elizabeth II. As a fellow cooking instructor, I had a grand time talking to him about our mutual passion. His publication struck me as insightful and informative and I wrote a glowing review. It appeared in not only the *Courier-Post* but also *USA Today*, both members of the Gannett Group.

• Y. H. Ku, an undisputed genius, a giant of the 20th century who was a distinguished professor of engineering at Penn. In addition, he was a gifted writer, poet, political analyst, and art connoisseur. Politically, he served as deputy minister of education and was a member of the national assembly in Taiwan. And amazingly, simultaneously he was confidante to two mortal enemies: Nationalist China's Chiang Kai-shek and Communist China's Deng Xiaoping.

• T. T. Chang was a dynamic character and by far the most famous Chinese in greater Philadelphia. Founder of the Chinatown YMCA (no relation to the national organization), he organized numerous cultural programs and was especially noted for bringing chefs from China featuring a different regional cuisine annually with 10-course banquets that were always filled to capacity. A former Chinese journalist, mayor, and ministry student of literary bent, he was also an excellent calligrapher (he wrote the words "Da Tung" in Chinese as the brand name for my canned won ton soup and sweet and sour pork). Above all he was a public relations expert with few equals. He burst into the Chinatown scene in the 1950s like a colossal shining star, constantly generating news coverage about the community with his PR flair and became its de facto spokesman. Not surprisingly, he was hailed as a hero, a civic leader, and a booster of business. It was Chang who helped organize the first Chinese New Year parade. Other projects included street signs in Chinese, free lunches for the elderly, and training in restaurant cooking.

In subsequent years he lost much of his influence and support when he turned into a controversial figure who was bent on unstintingly promoting himself and the Cultural Center at the expense of community service. One source of resentment was his Chinese New Year banquet. Because it ran several months of the year and garnered a lot of free publicity while the Cultural Center was tax exempt, some restaurateurs were unhappy about the unfair competition. He also alienated the residents, who detested communism, by changing from a highly vocal advocate of the democratic Taiwan to that of the totalitarian regime of China.

I was afraid my article might have offended him a little. While the *Courier-Post* offered Chang a sidebar to tell his side of the story, he seemed to like my piece and asked me if I would consider writing about him in some other publication or pamphlet. But I politely declined.

Toward my fourth year at the *Courier-Post* a big public relations firm in New York approached me to do a story about one of its clients, Tryall in Jamaica.

I arrived there after dark and was greeted with an engrossing sight: pretty reflections of the full moon on the Caribbean Sea, turning the waters into a bobbing chorus of dancing lights. The next day I feasted my eyes on the sun-kissed, pristine white beaches and the inviting turquoise water. There was no lack of other amenities: a world class golf course where major tournaments were held, year-round temperate weather, fine dining, and villas staffed with servants, a chef and a gardener.

To gain some insight I chatted with Tryall's concierge and learned a few facts: saltfish, in particular cod, was the national dish. Also popular was conch (served as fritters, chowder, and salad). Politically, Jamaica had undergone major changes in recent years, having suffered from its leftist, pro-Castro regime to the detriment of its all-important tourism. The current administration was, however, pro-America and happily a growing number of Yankees had been visiting Jamaica.

For a change of scenery, I made a quick visit to nearby Montego Bay, another great resort, known for its excellent beach, bird sanctuary, river rafting, and crafts market, and Ocho Rios where I enjoyed the unusual experience of climbing one of the stair-like waterfalls. Wearing tennis shoes, I didn't mind getting a little wet or the need to be cautious to avoid slipping on the rocky surfaces and found the ascent delightful, refreshing, and invigorating.

I had no difficulty writing an enthusiastic account about Tryall. The PR firm liked it so much that it lined up three more clients in quick succession: a prominent hotel in Seattle, Spain, and Australia.

During my four plus years of tenure at the *Courier-Post* my time and interest increasingly tilted toward acting. Finally, when my aspiration of working full-time for the paper materialized, my priorities had changed and I turned down the offer. Acting, despite all its pitfalls, not least the lack of security and the difficulty of making a steady income, proved to be more alluring. And so in the early 1980s as I decided to make acting my career, I quit my job at the *Courier-Post*—although I did miss the writing.

CHAPTER NINE (1980-PRESENT)

Acting

As an avid theatergoer I used to attend virtually every play that graced the local stage. One turned out to be a catalyst that changed the direction of my life: Arthur Miller's *The Crucible*, a dramatization of the witch hunt trials in Salem, MA. Staged by the Hedgerow Theatre in 1968, it held me spellbound by its unrelenting drive, riveting drama, attention to detail, and especially its compelling acting. Moved profoundly I immediately enrolled in the theater's acting classes.

The oldest residential repertory theater in the U.S., Hedgerow, which was founded by legendary director Jasper Deeter, boasted some of the best-known actors in its company including Paul Robeson, Ann Harding, and Eva Le Galliene, and in its school, such students as Keanu Reeves and Tyne Daly.

Among my teachers at Hedgerow, located near Philadelphia, was Rose Schulman. Having acted with Zero Mostel on Broadway and taught at Brandeis and Boston Universities, she exerted more influence on me than any of her counterparts. Gifted with a supreme sensitivity and perception and a keen observation of human behavior, she had a perfect pitch on what's truthful and would not let the students get away with the slightest deviations.

An obese woman and a heavy smoker who never dressed well, she could be highly encouraging and inspirational, reacting approvingly at good acting and laughing uproariously at something funny. But she could also be extremely harsh in her criticisms. Like with my piano teacher Olga Stroumillo, some students would leave the class in tears, never to return. She could also be a racist. Playing the role of a lowly servant, obviously badly, I aroused a sneering reprimand from her: "You are Chinese. You ought to know what an inferior position is." I was so infuriated that I felt like insulting her back and walked out for good. But for the sake of learning I decided to be humiliated in silence and restrain myself. To be fair, she was otherwise civil and pleasant, complimenting me for my "openness," and after making sufficient improvement I became one of her pets.

My studies, however, were strictly for my amusement and enlightenment no matter how entranced I was by acting. The thought of making it a career never entered my mind, knowing the uncertainty of the profession and the odds against me: my limited ability, my heavy Chinese accent, and my terrible articulation. But I was fascinated by the possibility of inhabiting a character, speaking the immortal words of great playwrights, creating a reality that was true to life and spontaneous, bonding with the audience and moving them in some way. I would be happy to get into some amateur productions.

Around this time my more pressing concern was racism in the theater. It turned me into an activist who participated in two public protests:

> 1. In Murray Schisgal's one act play *The Chinese*, I was revolted by the fact that the title character, a laundryman, his wife and son were all played by Caucasians.

Worse, the lead's portrayal of a Chinese, recalling Mickey Rooney's repugnant performance as a Japanese in *Breakfast at Tiffany's*, was so hideous, demeaning, and humiliating that I complained to the drama critics of the *Evening Bulletin* and the *Inquirer*. Ernest Schier of the former chose not to interview me, but William Collins of the latter did, and wrote a sympathetic article airing my grievances.

2. *Lovely Ladies and Kind Gentlemen*, a musical based on John Patrick's play, *Teahouse of the August Moon* and produced by Herman Levin (*My Fair Lady*). What was reprehensible was his discriminatory hiring practice. He employed only 12 Asians out of 45 such roles. And for the part of Sakini, the Okinawan protagonist, Levin cast a white actor, refusing to audition qualified talents like James Shigeta, Jack Soo (both appeared in *Flower Drum Song*) and Mako (Oscar winner in *The Sand Pebbles*) in violation of Actors' Equity Association regulations.

In a display of solidarity, massive protests were planned in the three tryout cities of San Francisco, Los Angeles, and Philadelphia where the musical was premiered, and I was the organizer. As such, I contacted the media, drummed up support from various Asian organizations, little theaters, human rights and civil rights groups, obtained a demonstration permit from the police, and coordinated with our New York counterparts. On August 17, 1970, the lazy calm of that typical summer evening was shattered by cymbals, gongs, and rhythmic drum beatings in front of the Shubert Theatre, while a Chinese lion dance pranced and a group of Asian actors and their sympathizers picketed with such placards as "Asian-American Actors Want Equal Opportunity" and "End Adhesive Tape Orientals" (an eye makeup that made Caucasians look more Asian). The protest turned out to be a stunning success with extensive newspaper and TV coverage.

Lovely Ladies opened on Broadway in late December but was lambasted by critics and closed after only 19 performances. Perhaps it was also jinxed by our protests, or a matter of poetic justice.

When not preoccupied otherwise, I tried to broaden my theatrical horizon by securing a New York agent, Tony Rivers, whose clients included quite a few Asians and comedian-actress Joan Rivers. In 1970 I made my acting debut on CBS' *Love Is a Many Splendored Thing* as a houseboy with just one line. This job would have qualified me to join the Screen Actors Guild, but I didn't think it would be useful and let the opportunity slip by. When auditioning for a wine commercial resulted in a callback, Tony Rivers told me "you are my rising star." I thought he was exaggerating or just being kind.

Soon, I had an opportunity to be an extra in a TV show called *Jade Snow*. In the midst of a shoot the director asked me to say a few words in Chinese. This amounted to an upgrade, elevating me to a principal and qualified me again to join the Screen Actors Guild (SAG). I jumped at the chance this time and became a member in 1976.

Usually busy with several projects simultaneously, in 1979 I was enjoying a rare period of peace and quiet, having sold my restaurant, the Jade Palace, completed my graduate program in journalism, and stopped teaching Chinese cooking in New York. An avid skier who never had enough time to indulge in this sport, I gave myself a dream vacation: five weeks' skiing in Aspen. In the meantime, I was intrigued by the explosive real estate market in the West and especially in ski resorts like Vail and Aspen. I ended up buying a condo in the latter where one could ski to the door. I thought I had found a gold mine, which I would keep as a rental property for a few years and then sell it at a great profit.

After returning home I landed my first regional commercial pitching for the insecticide Ambush in Mandarin (I also did the translation) with English subtitles. Carrying five business suits as requested, which were a whale of a burden, I flew to Memphis for the job. Shot in a cotton factory, the production went very smoothly and took only a few hours. I thoroughly enjoyed this novel, heady experience, luxuriating in the spotlight as the star and savoring the taste of show biz. The pay was good with residuals to follow.

In 1981 I landed another regional commercial in New York for the Chase Manhattan Bank, which required speaking in Cantonese, one of the five Chinese dialects I knew. It was directed by Steve Horn, who was reputed as one of the four best directors; he was a demanding, methodical, passionate perfectionist who did take after take. But I had no problem following his instructions and again had a memorable experience. However, competition for commercials was always intense. I was convinced getting the job was a fluke and that fortune would not smile at me again anytime soon.

In the early 1980s, I unexpectedly found myself financially strapped. My once flourishing won ton soup business began to lose one customer after another due to the duplicity of my contract packer, who despite our contract, sold to a bigger competition at lower cost. With the sale of my restaurant, my other source of revenue also dried up.

Meanwhile, my Aspen condo turned out to be a terrible investment blunder as it began to decline in value rapidly. Worse, it had a terrible negative cash flow, the expenditure way exceeding the rental income, and soon its mortgage became a great burden. To make my ends meet I was forced to look for a steady job that paid decent wages. While I had been a stringer at the *Courier-Post*, working almost full-time, the pay was unbelievably low. And notwithstanding my interest in a full-time job, there was no opening. Philadelphia had a great newspaper, the *Inquirer*. To be considered I would need sufficient experience with a small paper first, probably at some faraway place as a cub reporter. But it was too much a price to pay. So in lieu of immediate prospects in the fourth estate, I began to consider three alternatives:

1. Copywriting. Ever since I was a marketing executive at DuPont, I developed a fondness and fascination for advertising. And the agency I admired the most was Ogilvy and Mather. My job application resulted in a copywriting test, which consisted of critiquing magazine ads and TV commercials as well as writing original copy for the two media. Ogilvy and Mather seemed impressed by my efforts, saying the test was one of the "few good ones" they had received. But alas, no opening.

2. Public relations. I had been quite successful with my PR efforts on behalf of my won ton soup business and restaurant. I knew how to develop an angle that would trigger the imagination of editors. Furthermore, I found a way to develop personal relationship with key people in the media, and I enjoyed the writing involved. While I managed to get interviews with several large corporations, my background and qualifications did not quite meet their needs.

3. Real estate sales. Because of its easy accessibility and my affinity for selling, I got a sales associate license and joined forces with a broker with much optimism. However, my timing was off for the housing market was in a slump during this time in the early 1980s due to sky high interest rates, and so I sold only a few residential and commercial properties and remained financial strapped.

Luckily, I was saved by an unexpected source: a lucrative national commercial (my very first) for AT&T. It was directed by another well-known professional, Bob Giraldi.[1]

Because landing this commercial seemed relatively effortless I began to look at the world of commercials in a different light and became a little more optimistic about my acting opportunities. Indeed, I soon booked four nationals during one year. Another job won the Clio Award: Stanley Roberts Silverware.

Once looked down by many serious actors as an unworthy way of making money, commercials have since attracted big time actors like Laurence Olivier, George Scott, and more recently, Jennifer Aniston, Matt Damon, etc. Commercials required a different kind of acting but nevertheless still acting and could be challenging, fun, and financially rewarding.

One of the most famous cases was Clara Peller, a Chicago manicurist. She got into the business because one of her customers was a director. Her biggest job was for Wendy's with the line "Where is the beef?" which became a national catch phrase. She reportedly earned some $500,000 that year. A lesser-known case that made history as the longest running commercial involved my actor-friend Calvin Jung. Playing a laundryman for Calgon laundry products, he collected residuals for 12 years making $15,000 annually. I didn't do badly either, my most fertile one being a GE commercial which earned me a total of $60,000 in four years. Generally, if a commercial was aired nationally an actor could earn well over $10,000 annually in 1980s dollars. Considering it normally took a day to shoot, that's a great way to make a small fortune.

---

[1] Later he also directed me in the movie *Hiding Out* starring Jon Cryer, co-star of *Two and a Half Men*. Unfortunately, my scenes opposite him got edited out, but I received residuals for a number of years.

Consequently, the competition was incomparably fierce.

According to a *Wall Street Journal* story about a highly successful commercials actor, it took him 25 auditions to land each job. Odds for me, however, were not as great; I began to average about seven auditions for a booking. A number of factors helped:

- There was a growing demand for Asian actors especially Japanese because of their strong economy fortified by their exports such as automobiles and electronics. Likewise for the Chinese, as their country began to flex its manufacturing muscles. Furthermore, Asian Americans were starting to make a mark for themselves in a number of fields of endeavor other than the stereotypical professions. So they were able to blend more and more into the American scene. In short, they were gaining in visibility in this diverse society of ours.

- There were not too many Asian American actors in the East. In truth, acting was one of the least desirable professions. Fewer competitors meant better chances of success.

- I was considered a good commercial type thanks to the looks and physique my parents gave me. A typical commercial lasts 30 seconds (in real time, only 26 seconds). There was no time to establish or refine a character. One must look—and be recognizable for—the part instantly.

- I seemed to possess some of the requisite acting ability for commercials. It might not require phenomenal talent, but I seemed to have a certain knack. And I am sure my theatrical training helped.

• Some actors could not deal well with rejections. I, on the other hand, having felt I had been rejected during my childhood by the one person whose affection I deeply craved, my mother, was used to the feeling of being unwanted. As long as I tried my best, if the casting director or producer did not like me, it was okay with me; my dignity and self-esteem remained virtually intact.

Commuting to New York to audition was such a drag and could be so unrewarding. Round trip from Philadelphia took some five hours. But the audition itself normally would last just a minute or so. It would be too depressing to return home immediately. Fortunately, my trip always meant something else: an epicurean delight that really sustained me and made it worthwhile. Since New York was blessed with wonderful Chinese restaurants, my auditions always concluded with a subway ride to Chinatown. More often than not I would gorge myself in two restaurants during one meal to capitalize on the specialties of the house. Typically, I would have beef with Chinese water spinach at Sun Luck Kee, 13 Mott Street. It ranked as one of the greatest dishes I had ever had. The meat was succulent, tender, ineffably flavorful, seasoned just right with a faint touch of sweetness, and the vegetable was yummy good and never overcooked, retaining a nice firmness. I would then go cross the street to finish my repast at Hop Lee where the snails with black bean sauce had no equal; the taste was not only inimitable but seemed to linger for a long time. Indeed, the snails surpassed the best French escargot I had ever had.

Philadelphia, where acting jobs were few and far between, had the advantage of being within commuting distance to Baltimore and Washington, D.C., two other cities with greater job opportunities. Again, the scarcity of Asian actors improved my odds. My journeys to these cities also turned into epicurean excursions as in New York. I had developed an unparalleled love for blue point crabs, and I always looked forward to making side trips to Baltimore's Inner Harbor where I would feast on crab soup, crab cakes, imperial crabs, crab au gratin, and whenever possible, soft shell crabs.

Soon my show biz ventures extended to other areas. One was voice-overs. English being my second language, I always had to struggle with some enunciations. But after taking voice lessons with Laurie Wing in Philadelphia and much hard work I began to make progress and my Chinese accent, which had become much less pronounced, actually helped me get jobs that required such an accent. With my first gig doing a radio commercial I opted to join SAG's sister union, the American Federation of Television, Radio Artists (AFTRA). Once in a while there was a call for a Mandarin speaking actor. Again, the lack of competition helped me succeed.

Another area that opened up for me was modeling, better known as print jobs in the trade. I was at the right age with the right look. The few top New York modeling agencies would submit me, and I became relatively successful, getting bookings for AT&T, Citibank, NYNEX, AC Nielsen, and numerous others. But I did not enjoy the casting calls since models were picked mostly on the basis of their appearances and very little on their acting ability.

There was yet another source of income for me: industrials. These were mostly in-house training films utilized extensively by larger organizations. Federal agencies like social security, the CIA, and Medicare, corporations like Coca-Cola, Cigna, and Applied Science, and institutions like National Education Association and AARP were among the dozens of my employers.

Strangely, all these endeavors gradually nudged me into a new career I had never dreamed of before: professional acting.

But with my success in the various above-mentioned areas and especially in commercials, I was able to make a very modest living. And when the *Courier-Post*, where I had spent four plus years as a stringer, finally offered me a full-time job I turned it down; the taste of show biz was more gratifying.

But the precariousness of the acting business had its fruitful and lean days. To make sure I had better chances of meeting my expenses, I was forced into doing extra work. Now in the West, serious actors tended to look down on extra work—and still do today. As a matter of fact, for a long time there was a separate union, SEG, or Screen Extras Guild. However, in the East, except for the top professionals, many actors would make a living by doing both principal and extra work. There was plenty of need for the latter and a good number of actors were able to rely on that as their sole source of income.

A notable extra job for me was the TV series *Sex and the City*. I played a pedestrian at Columbus Circle in Manhattan just as a bus was pulling by. That scene became the opening that accompanied every episode of the popular show. Because I was highly visible with my full face on the screen, all my friends recognized me. That should have been an upgrade, or so I thought (in an identical case I was so upgraded in the TV series *Mathnet*). But producers did not think so, and I received not a penny in residuals. Today, ironically some of my friends fail to associate me with the innumerable principal roles I have had but always remember me for my appearance in *Sex and the City*.

The most endearing word for extras was "upgrade" or being "bumped up." That materialized when the director decided to elevate them into a principal—usually on the spur of the moment. As a result they became entitled to residuals. I was lucky enough to be so upgraded in half a dozen commercials such as Levi's Jeans, Land Rover, Capital One, and movies including *If Lucy Fell* (starring Sarah Jessica Parker and Ben Stiller) and IMAX's *Across the Sea*.

In the latter I was to play a Chinese chef stir-frying with a gigantic wok. Because of the importance of that scene and my background as a professional chef I ended up not only getting bumped up as an actor but also as a de facto director. To do justice to the scene the wok must be heated to just the right temperature. If it was too hot, the food would be burned. If not hot enough, the cooking would not be effective. So the director deferred to me to call the shot. The scene lasted several minutes. After editing it was reduced to just a few seconds. Nonetheless, I had my fleeting moment of glory. And I have been collecting residuals for the past 30 plus years—and still continuing—albeit in dwindling amounts.

As my pursuit of an acting career started to gain traction I was keenly aware of the need to take classes; there was so much to learn, and I resolved to continue. Initially I considered returning to Hedgerow. At my meeting with my Hedgerow teacher Rose Schulman, 15 years after we last met, she was 75, still overweight, stopped smoking on doctor's orders but looking much older. But her mind and memory were still sharp as a tack. She told me: "When you last worked with me in *All My Sons*, you were getting somewhere." In fact, I did that scene well with tears streaming down my cheeks but was utterly surprised she still remembered it after so many years. Though I loved her teaching I eventually decided what I really needed was to explore diversified areas of acting. Hence, I enrolled in the following:

- The Stella Adler Conservatory and the Riverside Shakespeare Academy to learn classical acting.

- The Wilma Theater in Philadelphia as a Method student of Gordon Phillip, who was once the right-hand man of Lee Strasberg, director of Actors Studio.

- The Weist Barron commercial classes.

- A 10-week accelerated Sanford Meisner method taught by John Roderick (not to be confused with his namesake, the musician.)

- An improvisation class taught by John Stinson.

- Scene study. My teachers included actors Richard Fancy and George DiCenzo, who was best known for starring in *Helter Skelter*, a movie about Charles Manson's murder trial.

All these studies proved helpful in my career. But I did not need any of them in my most unusual and literally the most painful and bloody commercial audition for KFC. It called for a Chinese chef. Because of all the years I had worked as one, whenever an advertiser needed such a specialist, I was in my element, finding myself virtually with no competition and almost always getting a booking. For this type of audition, I would bring a little chopping block, a few stalks of celery, and a sharply honed Chinese cleaver, sporting a chef's uniform and hat. That was how I auditioned for the KFC commercial in midtown Manhattan.

When the auditor said "action" I started to cut the celery in a very dramatic way with lightning speed. In the midst of my cutting the auditor asked me some questions. Now, as a cooking teacher for many years, I always told my students that a Chinese cleaver was a lethal weapon; when using it, one must take extreme caution and pay strict attention to the process of cutting, or else one might get hurt. On this occasion, I ignored my own advice. I should have stopped my cutting when talking to the auditor. Instead, I continued my rapid chopping while turning my eyes away to look at her. Suddenly I felt an acute pain and I knew I had cut one of my left fingers. I tried very hard pretending nothing unusual was happening even though blood started to flow. Fortunately, the audition came to a quick end. I gathered my props and hurriedly headed for the men's room.

On the way there I was leaving a trail of blood on the floor. Inside the men's room I was horrified that blood was rushing out like the Johnstown flood. The reason: I had been taking a very high dosage of Coumadin for an arthroscopy for a torn meniscus in the knee. Since Coumadin was a powerful blood thinner, my blood would not coagulate. I tried everything I could think of to stop or slow the bleeding: rinsing the finger with cold water, soaking it with paper towel and raising it high above my head. But nothing worked. While suffering persistent agony I was making a bloody mess all over the sink and floor. I knew I had to get out of the men's room soon to avoid monopolizing it and to get some medical help. It would be unconscionable to leave the place without cleaning up. But without a sponge and with the continuing throbbing I couldn't do an effective job with a paper towel. As I stepped out, I did not forget the bloody trail leading to the studio. I again was doing a lousy cleaning job. I then dashed out of the building. Luckily there was a pharmacy just across the street. I asked the pharmacist for help. He sterilized the finger and wrapped it with layers of bandage. By this time the bleeding slowed down considerably but seemed to take forever to stop. After reaching my Philadelphia home I continued to feel pain for a long time. The second day I called on a doctor. He did not think stiches were required but gave me a tetanus shot.

Soon the good news came. I got the booking for this hard-earned national spot. But there was an ironic end. My scene was shot in a New York studio in April 1989. It didn't involve any cutting of ingredients, only stir-frying. Featured in this commercial was also an actual KFC restaurant in Beijing located very near the famed Tiananmen Square which was KFC's biggest in the world then. It was on this very plaza on

June 4, 1989, that a massive student democracy protest was crushed by the government with hundreds of fatalities. So KFC decided to kill the commercial after paying me $500 in residuals, a tiny fraction of what I would have earned otherwise.

I booked another job again as a Chinese chef in a Pabst beer national commercial with unexpected results. In anticipation of lucrative residuals, I planned a ski vacation in Alta, CO, with a friend. However, just two days before the trip, I was invited by a public relations firm to spend 14 days as the guest of the Australia government to do a travel story. I opted for skiing.

This decision turned out to be a tragic one. During the ski trip one day Alta had its worse snowstorm in history and it was first closed. By noon I saw ski patrols coming down the slopes awkwardly, struggling with the terrible conditions which locals called "glue" as it had such a strong adhesive effect. Alta was finally opened around noon. I should have just skipped skiing that afternoon since the snow conditions were still perilous. Instead, I decided to make one run before taking a lesson. I did, however, take the precaution of loosening my bindings so that my boots would pop out in case I found my knees in a slow, twisting position. Stupidly, I picked a double diamond trail and was skiing badly. At one point as I was turning right turn my left ski was buried deep into the snow and glued to it. So my body was turning one way but the left ski would not budge without being released by the bindings. I ended up tearing my anterior cruciate ligament.

I hurried home with a heavy heart and spent six long weeks doing physical therapy. I eventually was able to ski and play tennis again but had to wear a knee brace. In the interim I was shocked to hear more bad news: the Pabst commercial initially contained five segments. Unfortunately, they were deemed too long and mine was excised.

Yet another surprise was with Triscuit Bits. The advertising agency was Young & Rubicam which picked me for the job because I had a "rubbery face," meaning complimentarily that my facial expressions were highly variable and flexible like a rubber. It was a humorous commercial poking fun at Japan for its remarkable ability to miniaturizing everything. The tiny crackers were made by General Mills. At the time it was planning to borrow a few billion dollars from Japan. After the commercial was shot General Mills had second thoughts about airing it, thinking that the humor might offend Japan thereby jeopardizing its chances of borrowing. The result: General Mills paid me a holding fee of $366 for the first 13 weeks before canning the commercial.

I had better luck doing a commercial in Canada for which I was treated like a VIP. By SAG contract, the advertiser, McCann Foods, picked me up from my Philadelphia home in a limousine, flew me first class to Toronto, paid $50 at the airport to allow me, a non-Canadian citizen, to work, ensconced me at a plush hotel, the Sutton Place, and paid my per diem in advance.

The set of the commercial was a Chinese restaurant where I, along with a few other Chinese, played waiters. As the scene opens, we are just closing shop, settled on a table and waiting eagerly for our well-deserved midnight snack. A colleague brings us an ornate Chinese bowl with a lid. When it is removed the contents are not some delicious Chinese delicacies but French fries. We all dig in with chopsticks as if we have not eaten for days. It was a highly successful, funny commercial.

But after it was aired for a year, I was stunned that the Canadian counterpart of Screen Actors Guild decided to withhold all my residuals unless I joined the union. Fortunately, SAG interceded and for over 25 years I have been receiving residuals every now and then.

I learned from fellow actors that a common trick for an out-of-town job was to try to make some extra money by a little ruse. Since producers were obligated by SAG contract to fly actors first class and there was of course considerable disparity in costs between first and economy classes, many actors would exchange the former for the latter and pocket the difference. So when I got a job to do a milkshake commercial in Miami I tried this trick. But by that time producers had wised up, so the airline told me that yes, I could change to an economy class but the difference in prices would not go to me but to the producer.

If I loved doing commercials my heart was still set on television shows, motion pictures, and particularly the stage. I got my first break in the movie *Sweet Lorraine* in 1987. Directed by well-known stage director Steve Gomer, it boasted an all-star cast that included Maureen Stapleton (*Reds,)* Lee Richardson and some of the most talented rising young New York actors such as Edie Falco (*The Sopranos*), Giancarlo Esposito (future winner of two Obies), and Evan Handler (Harry Goldenblatt in *Sex and the City)*. The movie involved multiple days in intermittent weeks for me and was shot in a Catskills hotel during the summer.

The setting was a borscht belt lodge, the former Heiden Hotel. More than a few Catskills hotels had Chinese chefs because of the profound Jewish affinity for Chinese food and my role was that of such a chef, Tony. In one scene with Evan Handler, who played a waiter and my tormentor, I exacted my revenge in the kitchen by pouring hot soup over his shoulder while smiling broadly. Initially he remained motionless and without reaction. As soon as I finished pouring he screamed in pain and said: "I just had my first Zen experience." With a sharp Chinese cleaver nearby, I had the upper hand and the waiter had the good sense of not fighting back.

In another scene on a baseball field my job was to hit a single. A terrible player, miraculously I delivered beautifully on the first pitch, but in the excitement and jubilation I forgot to run to the first base and ruined that shot. In subsequent takes, my bat would not connect no matter how I tried and that scene had to be done by intercuts.

One day when I didn't have to work I played real chef by cooking a multi-course Chinese dinner for the entire cast and crew with the help of two of our regular caterers. Though I was handicapped by not having some essential Chinese cookware, I was able to improvise and prepare a meal that was extremely well received.

More memorable was the wrap party at the Plaza Hotel in Manhattan right after *Sweet Lorraine* was previewed. I had attended other wrap parties but nothing approached the scale and grandeur of this one with food and drinks galore. The cast was introduced in a grand ballroom individually to the guests who applauded as if we were Oscar nominees, and I felt vicariously like a star.

Reviews for *Sweet Lorraine*, however, were not too enthusiastic. Some of the kinder remarks: "It has a cheerful, good feeling . . . Maureen Stapleton has a kindly authority (as the hotel proprietor) as does Lee Richardson," and "the young actors cast as staff members are an attractive bunch. The hotel is the real star and Mr. Gomar (the director) does make it as sweet as it is." To me, *Sweet Lorraine* was my very first feature film. It gave me great fun, and will always have a special place in my heart.

As I got into different facets of show biz, the most rewarding but also the least profitable was the theater. Other than Broadway plays and musicals, pay elsewhere under Actors' Equity Association contract was less than living wages. But theater was what motivated me to acting in the first place and I longed for such an opportunity. While film is considered a director's medium, theater an actor's medium, where he can hone his craft and grow, luxuriate in leisurely time to develop and refine the character, work out other details and enjoy communion with the audience.

My first taste of performing before an audience was in Philadelphia in the Annenberg Center's inaugural production of *St. Joan of the Stockyards*, based on Upton Sinclair's *The Jungle*, concerning inhumane working conditions of the Chicago stockyards. This epic drama starred Obie winner Laura Esterman (*Marvin's Room*) in the title role and involved a large cast. I played three minor roles including one as a meat packer, adored the experience, and often wondered when I could act in the Big Apple.

In New York, Pan Asian Repertoire had long attracted my interest. It had done some marvelous work and its productions were reviewed by numerous publications including the *New York Times*. Tisa Chang was the founder and artistic producing director. A person of great accomplishments and vision, she was a professional dancer, had Broadway credits, championed the cause of Asian playwrights, and provided acting opportunities for Pacific Asian actors. Pan-Asian had an open-door policy whereby an actor could request a general audition. I did a monologue from *Teahouse of the August Moon*, and Chang seemed much taken.

When casting for *The Imposter* she called me, and I was exhilarated to land a job. Based on a true story, *The Imposter* is the chronicle of a young man, who by pretending to be the son of a high Chinese Communist official, is able to get all kinds of special favors and privileges, and in the process, exposes the corruptions of the government. The law eventually catches up with him, and he is brought to justice. The play had only a few performances in Shanghai before it was banned by the totalitarian regime. A copy was smuggled out to Hong Kong and translated into English. My part was that of the high official, the Venerable Comrade Zhang, of whom the young man pretended to be the son.

Not surprisingly I was filled with elation and eagerness to

be in this production. However, there were logistical problems to cope with. I was living in Philadelphia. I couldn't very well commute when the play called for six days' performances weekly with a morning show on Wednesday and a matinee on Saturday. I certainly couldn't afford a hotel from this off-Broadway play. So my first order of business was to find a place to stay. Sometime before I had become acquainted with Bernie Hurwood. I was a stringer for the *Courier-Post*, and we met as fellow travel writers on a trip to Spain. We hit it off and became like brothers, and his wife, Marcy, was like the sister I never had. Knowing that I came to New York frequently for acting jobs, he told me he had a sofa bed in the living room and that if I needed a place to crash overnight I would be welcome. Gratefully I had taken advantage of his offer quite a few times. But to do *The Imposter* would mean staying with the Hurwoods for an extended period and an extreme stretch of our friendship. But they generously welcomed me. I repaid their kindness with an offer of some cash and cooked dinners for them on a number of occasions.

The play was well received. Richard Hornby in the *Hudson Review* had kind words for the cast: "As Oriental Americans, they are not likely to be big commercial stars in our theatre, but they are fully professional . . . The director, Ron Nakahara, staged the play deftly. As a result of careful attention to detail and an easy, sincere acting style throughout, we always felt that we were actually in contemporary China, which seemed both strange and familiar." Hornby also had generous words for me: "Zhang, superbly played by Ben Lin, a mature actor with dignity and power, speaks movingly of the ideals of the revolution, and the need for bureaucrats to be answerable to the people."

My next Pan Asian Rep play was Kitty Chen's comedy *Eating Chicken Feet*. By this time to my great sadness Bernie Hurwood had died of prostate cancer. He was a gracious person, a talented raconteur, and a prolific author who had penned some 68 books. His wife Marcy, after a period of mourning, found a new companion, Steve Kursh (whom she later married). Living in a four-story house on 107th Street, Kursh proved to be as generous and warm as Hurwood and gave me his apartment key. Since Kursh was a rich man, the only way I could repay his hospitality was to occasionally cook for him and Marcy and invite them to Chinese dinners.

Eating Chicken Feet, directed by Kati Kuroda, is the story of a comatose young woman whose medical condition is at the heart of this frothy comedy. I played Dr. Sung, the young woman's father, and Wai-Ching Ho played her mother. In one scene, we fought furiously, and she savagely knocked me down with the back of my head seemingly hitting the floor. This was carefully choreographed, and we two practiced enough times to ensure no injury would occur. But the unexpected happened: Once she pushed my head so hard that it actually banged on the floor, almost knocking me unconscious. As I lay there I was worried not so much about the extent of my injury—if any—but the distinct possibility that I would not be able to say the lines following. Thankfully I was not hurt seriously and able to continue.

Otherwise, things were going well. I realized how much I enjoyed doing comedies, and laughter from the audience was really music to my ears. But after a Wednesday morning show, Pan-Asian's business manager gave me horrible news: "Your brother Henry just died. I got word earlier but thought I'd better tell you after the performance." Henry was undergoing chemotherapy treatment for colon cancer and succumbed to it. Just a few days before, Henry's wife Lydia told me he had been in pain and had difficulty breathing but I didn't anticipate the end coming so soon.

I was thunderstruck and tears soon welled in my eyes. Ironically, because of this brother, I had suffered a most debilitating inferiority complex that lasted many years well into my middle age. But his passing made me realize how much I had loved him. All through lunch and during part of the afternoon I was sobbing. Henry, an engineer, was not only my kid brother (just one year younger) but also the last surviving one (my two older brothers had both died prematurely). We also shared a profound love of music; he was an avid cellist and I, a pianist, and we last played together at my older brother David's funeral service. His death at the age of 57 made me mourn almost as much as the passing of Mother.

When 8:00 P.M. was approaching I had an insurmountable dread to go on stage and do a comedy no less. But the saying "the show must go on" never struck me so closely and tragically. How do you make people laugh when you are crying inside?

Just before the play began I asked our stage manager to announce the news of my brother and requested a brief moment of silence from the audience. In between my scenes I was still crying. It was my most difficult experience in acting!

I attended the memorial service three days later on a Saturday in Philadelphia at 9:00 A.M. I wept during hymn singing but restrained myself when reading my eulogy. An excerpt:

"As the baby of the family, Henry may well be the best loved brother. He won affection from others as well with his artistic disposition. An avid cellist, he graced his playing in many a church service and social gathering. He could also do a mean cha cha, fancy foxtrot, and elegant tango.

"He had a special way with dogs. When he volunteered for the Air Force he worked with German Shepherds. Later, he cared for one of his own at home and kept it to this day.

"Last but not least, Henry was a deeply religious Christian. This abiding faith gave him a direction in life, made him a loving person, aided him in times of crisis, and surely sustained him during his darkest hours and suffering.

"As we bid farewell to you, Henry, words fail to express our full sentiments. The world is a little less and we shall miss you very much."

Right after the morning service, I hurried back to Manhattan by driving, the fastest way, and made the 2:00 P.M. performance of *Chicken Feet* just in time.

For a change in pace and venue, I got a part in the play *The Wash,* staged by the Studio Theatre in Washington, D.C. The most dramatic moment occurred not on stage but off. In one of the final rehearsals, Earnest Abuba, an Obie winner (former husband of Tisa Chang, Pan-Asian Rep's founder), and the lead, got into a fight with Joy Zinoman, the director. During previous weeks, I knew Abuba had been unhappy because she would not let him "follow his impulse," an acting dictum. I thought things would work out somehow since artistic differences often happen in the rehearsal process and eventually they would come to some resolutions. But not this time. The firestorm that erupted that day took everyone by surprise. The character Abuba played, Nobu, was a Nisei. The argument began when Zinoman wanted him to be "more Japanese." Disagreeing with her, he started to protest. Normally Abuba was a very soft-spoken, mild-mannered man, but now became angry as he exchanged heated words with Zinoman, with increasing volume and intensity, culminating in shouting with four-letter words, reaching an irreconcilable climax, and storming out.

With opening only one week away in this highly complicated play in which the character Nobu appears in some 90% of 33 scenes, everyone involved thought for sure there would be no opening and the play would be shelved.

But Nobu McCarthy (not to be confused with the character Nobu) who played Marsi, Nobu's estranged wife, thought of a last-minute replacement, an acting colleague of hers from Los Angeles, Alberto Isaacs. Zinoman immediately flew him over.

With only five days of rehearsals, Isaacs not only saved the opening but did a brilliant job.

Notwithstanding this nerve-wracking experience, *The Wash* turned out to be one of my favorite gigs. Written by Philip Gotanda, it's one of his seminal works. I played Sadao, Marsi's new love interest, and it was a wonderful part.

At one point, Sadao is heartbroken reminiscing the death of his wife. To enact his heightened emotion I turned weepy. Now shredding tears on demand was never easy—especially when it's replicated in eight performances a week. But with careful preparation, concentration, personalization, and emotional recall I was able to manage. And ironically almost every time I cried I would instantly experience a wonderful sense of catharsis, uplifting of the spirit, and joy.

The production won unanimous encomiums from the critics: "Graceful and moving, *The Wash* is a quiet winner . . . (playwright) Gotanda tells it with such tact and indirection that it's much more powerful than an evening of Strinbergian fireworks. At times you almost wish someone on the stage *would* scream—but the tension is destined to remain silent, unspoken. Sadao (Ben Lin) is an easy going fellow, a good-hearted man who truly loves Marsi, who warms in his presence and even gets a little girlish and silly," commented the *Washington Post*'s Lloyd Rose. From the *Washington Times*: "Mr. Lin and Miss McCarthy's scenes of new love at a mature age are genuinely affecting."

"Ben Lin's Sadao is the perfect embodiment of assimilation. Both traditional and modern, he radiates easy charm. His appeal to Marsi is easy to see," remarked *The Review*.

Because of its popularity, *The Wash* extended its scheduled one-month run to four. Sometimes people would recognize us actors on the streets and told us how much they had enjoyed the play. Further enhancing my enjoyment was my accommodations: a hotel suite complete with a kitchen so that I could do my Chinese cooking; my access to a grand piano owned by a Studio Theatre board member and acting teacher who had heard me play and graciously offered me her house key. My routine during the four-month run: I always started the day by playing the piano. During lunch, I would often feast on raw clams, oysters, and soft-shell crabs at the Waterfront; play tennis in the afternoon with Keenan Shimizu, a cast member who masqueraded as my son in *The Imposter*; do the soul satisfying play in the evening. Afterwards we would occasionally have a party.

If I was satisfied with the way my career was progressing, I, however, was dissatisfied with my protracted bachelorhood, especially at a time when my age had approached the half century milestone. Not having the right prospect and my initial aversion to the institution of marriage were two factors, but the chief reason had to do with my debilitating psychological disorder and emotional trauma stemming from sibling rivalry.

During the 1970s I had overcome enough of my psychological hang-up to develop—and enjoy—close relationships with two women: Verena Lagutt, a Swiss physical therapist, and Ellie Wood, a publisher's reader. But I was not quite prepared to make a commitment.

I was finally ready in 1982, when my former girlfriend Annie Fung traveled from Hong Kong to visit me. I had first met her there nine years prior when she was an 18-year-old student nurse. She became enamored of me but without reciprocity. Subsequently she had an unhappy marriage and was estranged from her husband. When we re-met in Philadelphia she was still carrying a torch for me. This time I responded in kind and decided to take the plunge as we moved in together while waiting for her divorce to come through. Ironically, when it did materialize, she lost interest in me (but kept it a secret) worsened by the combined impact of her inability to pass her nursing certification and my financial insecurity as a fledging actor. To my upmost sorrow, she abruptly left me without even saying goodbye when I was working out of town; just a note stating untruthfully she was returning to Hong Kong.

Still grief-stricken three years later, I was glad another woman entered my life—and not a moment too soon: a 22-year-old college senior, Lily (for privacy reasons some facts are altered). I fell under her spell not only for her exuberant youth but also her baby-faced beauty, bubbling personality, and sweetness. Moreover, we happened to be fellow pianists who at different times studied with the same teacher: the renowned virtuoso Natalie Hinderas. Gifted with strong musicality and wonderful facility, Lily could master pieces easily, including a beautiful rendition of Chopin's "B Minor Ballad."

When we first met I was 53 years old and wasn't sure about her possible interest in an older man like me. But she volunteered that she didn't have any social life because "nobody is taking me out." Happy and grateful for the hint, I promptly asked for a date.

Soon we fell in love. A very sensitive and overly jealous person, she insisted I destroy all the photos of Annie Fung, my previous girlfriend, but I refused for old time's sake. One day while secretly reading my journal she was so offended by some of the pages, in which I mourned the loss of Fung, that she tore them to smithereens, though they were written three years prior, just after Fung had deserted me. Lily was under the impression I could never break away completely from my emotional ties to Fung and threatened to break up with me instantly. It took me a monumental effort to convince her that I had an absolute affection for her and what had happened in the past was history and no longer relevant.

As we resumed our relationship we began to broach the

subject of marriage. But a big hurdle stood in the way. First, her mother in Macau not only objected but demanded that she stop seeing me, which she refused. Then, her father, a very successful businessman and about my age, came to visit her and forced the issue. Lily was the youngest sibling and the apple of his eye. She was torn between her filial piety to him and devotion to me. Reluctantly choosing the former, she promised to be an obedient daughter and sever our relations. But after her father left she continued to see me every chance she had.

Nevertheless, dismayed by the inevitability of our doomed affair, one day she weepingly told me she would stand by her promise to her father and shortly leave for Macau for good. When we held close to each other, she discovered some of the tears on her face were mine. As our tears mingled, words failed to express the profound sorrow and agony we were experiencing.

Upon her graduation and before departing for Macau, she asked me never to get in touch with her ever again to avoid complications. I respected her too much to contradict her. The only exception was when our beloved teacher Hinderas died of cancer, I sent her a newspaper clipping without my name or address.

For a period I had no female companion let alone a life partner. I began to suffer the pang of loneliness and was determined to end it. But how and where to find a mate was difficult. As a professional actor, I spent most of my time away from home auditioning and working. While I used to be active in the Chinese social circle and had plenty of opportunities to meet the opposite sex, I was out of circulation and no longer had the right connections. Concerned friends tried to match me with half a dozen prospects, but things did not work out for one reason or another.

In 1990, to abate my solitude and fulfill my longing for the old country, which I left in 1949 and had never returned to, I joined a small touring group of seven including a chef on his fifth trip seeking a wife. On the eve of my departure I chanced to remember the words of Dr. Li Qi Tang, a good friend and a former tenant of mine in Philadelphia: "My mother is the deputy director of a Shanghai hospital and knows many nubile women. If you want to, she can help." And so, I advised him of my trip.

Our first stop was Shanghai. Dr. Tang's mother helpfully introduced me to a Dong Hao Feng, a member of the People's Liberation Army and a student nurse. She was attractive, vibrant, and appealed to me. During that time in the 1990s many Chinese women were known to be more than willing to marry American citizens as a means to have a better life in the U.S. Apparently this was the case with Dong. She was 18 and I was 57. But despite our age disparity, she reacted favorably toward me. After my return home, we began to correspond and soon with the understanding—and her mother's approval—I was going to bring her here to tie the knot. At one point, I casually wondered in my letter if she might have some difficulty coping with life in America without speaking a word of English. She became absolutely furious, thinking errone-ously that I was looking for an excuse to dump her. She returned the photos of me and unceremoniously severed our ties. It was another setback for me but it really happened for the best. She was way too young for me, indeed, young enough to be my granddaughter, and I doubt we would have had a bright future together.

Luckily, Dr. Tang, a research scientist, came to my aid again after relocating to Chicago. He urged his wife Lisa to join his effort. By coincidence, she was acquainted with a divorcee by the name of Serena Wei. Graduated first in her class from Beijing's top art institute, she was an award-winning fashion designer working in the Windy City and not averse to Lisa's attempt to play cupid. Although I was 63 and 21 years her senior, we were married in 1996. She proved to be a wonderful match as we both felt we had the right karma. She is bright, resourceful, and energetic, blessed with a keen sense of observation, an abundance of common sense, and a surprising talent for cooking. In fact, despite my professional background, Serena outperforms me in the kitchen, having better versatility, instinct, originality, and imagination (she started cooking at the age of seven), and often cooks better than the restaurants we visit. To my gratitude, this Beijing native always places my interests above hers and takes care of me in every way imaginable. Of special help to my career, she edits my English-Chinese translations, which I did frequently as part of my acting or voice-over jobs (she was a published author in China), and coaches my Mandarin when needed. Realizing Serena's fervent wish to unite with her 17-year-old son Mo Zhang, who was living in China with his father, I sponsored his immigration and welcomed him to live with us.

Finally settled down, I was looking forward to my next project: Pan-Asian Rep's production of *The Joy Luck Club*. It was based on Amy Tan's celebrated novel and adapted for the stage by Susan Kim. I loved the original masterpiece and adored the movie version directed by Wayne Wong. When auditioning for Tisa Chang, director of this play, for the role of Canning Woo, the male lead, I was well prepared. At the end of my scene I noticed Tisa was shedding a tear or two. Within a few days she offered me the part.

It's a given that actors need to go to numerous auditions before getting a part. Earlier that day I had another audition for casting director Todd Thaler for the movie *Night and the City*. Subsequently, when I got booked to do a scene opposite Robert De Niro as a martial arts emporium owner, I knew the incredible had happened: I succeeded in both auditions by scoring two victories on the same day.

To do *The Joy Luck Club,* I would have the same problem of finding a place to stay. Tisa Chang had a guest room in her uptown apartment and cordially offered it to me. Moreover, she generously granted my request to reimburse my weekly traveling expenses for going home. Initially I was overjoyed that she had a grand piano in her spacious living room. My fingers were still itching to play whenever possible. But that was impossible because Tisa had a tenant who was cramming for her Ph.D. studies, and she did not want to be disturbed.

This was to be my fourth New York play. The cast comprised 16 playing multiple roles in this complicated drama that involved several generations of four Chinese families. The best-known member was Tina Chen, who had a ton of credits including co-starring roles with Robert Redford and Charlton Heston. The older actors—including myself—had one thing in common: the worry that we might have a memory lapse. At the time ginkgo biloba was considered a memory booster because it allegedly increased blood flow to the brain. So we all religiously took this herbal supplement daily, and one actor doubled the recommended maximum dosage just to be safe.

In addition to Woo, I also played Water Melon Man, and the wicked Wu Tsin who raped a young woman, forced her to be his third concubine, and eventually drove her to suicide. As Woo, husband of Suyuan and father of June, my big scene came toward the end of the play when I mourned the loss of my beloved wife on my journey to China with June, climaxing in meeting her twin stepsisters. It was one of the play's most moving scenes, which challenged me to dig deeply into my emotional well.

Under the inspiring, sure-handed directing by Tisa Chang, this sprawling drama achieved an admirable level of clarity, coherence, and theatricality. Not surprisingly it opened to a highly enthusiastic audience. While some reviewers faulted Susan Kim for her less than perfect adaptation of the novel, there were plenty of kudos for the production. For example, DJR Bruckner of the *New York Times* wrote: ". . . often impressive efforts by the director, Tisa Chang . . . a very energetic cast . . . they bring the characters distinctly to life." The success of this production was certified by the capacity audiences and frequent sold-out houses. By popular demand the play extended from its scheduled one-month run to a record four-month marathon.

Near the end of our first month's run, Amy Tan flew to New York from her West Coast home to attend the play. A reception was held in her honor. It was such a thrill to meet this superb talent, who had written several other bestsellers since *The Joy Luck Club*. There were just a handful of prominent Chinese-American writers and to me, none soared to the heights Tan did (two native Chinese, however, won the Nobel Prize in literature: Gao Xingjian in 2000 and Mo Yan in 2012). Lauding our production, she warmly shook hands with the cast. When reaching me she said smilingly, "You lecherous man!" referring approvingly to the wicked Wu Tsin character I played. For much of the evening she enthralled us with the writing of this first novel and revealed that some parts were based on her own family history.

During the early part of *The Joy Luck Club* run, I got an unexpected call from Johnson-Liff Associates, one of the greatest Broadway casting directors (*Phantom of the Opera, Oklahoma, Les Miserables, The Producers*). They wanted to see me concerning a new version of Rodgers and Hammerstein's *Flower Drum Song,* with book by David Henry Hwang. At my meeting with Geoff Johnson, he told me they were casting for a development staging of this musical and would like to consider me for the part of Chin, one of the eight principals, at the suggestion of David Henry Hwang. I had a passing acquaintance with Hwang, having taken a playwriting course with him years earlier, and I doubted if he remembered me.

But Johnson said Hwang liked me in *The Joy Luck Club* and thought I might suit the part of Chin, a newly created one as an assistant theater manager. I was completely flabbergasted and humbled. I knew several cast members of *The Club* had auditioned for this new musical and all got rejected.

While I long had a profound love for musicals, I had never trained for this uniquely American art form. To get a high recommendation from a famous playwright and an interview with a top casting director was beyond my wildest dreams. But being practical, I told Johnson I would not be equal to the task because of my limited vocal studies and had to respectfully decline. He said he would keep my headshot/resume for future reference, but I thought I would never see him again.

A few days later I had a change of heart. I went back to see Johnson without an appointment. I said my singing perhaps was not as inadequate as I had thought, but that I had studied for about three years with two teachers including Philip Cho, an operatic star and protégé of Jan Peerce. He said I had a good voice and that it was "better than Tony Bennett's."

Johnson was happy I reconsidered. In the interest of time, he asked me to immediately arrange an audition for David Chase, music director of *The Flower Drum Song*. Chase told me he would like to see me that very afternoon. I had just a few hours to prepare for the audition and frankly thought it would take a miracle to make a favorable impression. It's said that a tenor needs six years of training to fully develop his voice. Mine was far from maturing. My last lesson with Cho was some 15 years prior, and I had done no singing—not even in the shower—since. But I was determined to give my best effort. Lacking a pace to vocalize and practice, I did not want to waste any time to get ready. As I was walking on Broadway near Times Square towards Central Park, I started to sing loudly, totally oblivious to the pedestrians who probably thought I was crazy. When reaching the park, I let myself go even more and sang at the top my lungs and nobody paid any attention to this seemingly demented fellow.

When I called Chase to confirm our appointment, he asked me what my music background was. I told him about my studies with Cho, performing as a chorus tenor in Handel's *Messiah* with an orchestra, singing in the choir at Columbia University's St. Paul Chapel, and studying with a Juilliard piano teacher. To my utter surprise and relief, Chase said "You don't need to audition for me; you are in."

With rehearsals beginning in some three weeks, I knew I had to take a crash course in voice lessons. Through the recommendation of an actor friend I became a student of Joyce Hall, whose most famous pupil was Julie Andrews. A walking encyclopedia of musicals, Hall had virtually every score in her library. She was a pianist to boot, so she could easily accompany me on whatever pieces she assigned me. I left my first lesson with a plethora of vocalizing exercises.

However, I had one big problem: where could I practice? I was still in *The Joy Luck Club*. I continued to stay in Tisa Chang's guest room and her tenant was still cramming for her Ph.D. exam. The only place I could find was the shrubbery area between Riverside Drive and Westside Highway near Chang's apartment. I thought it would be a safe sanctuary and certainly nobody would notice me. I began to spend several hours daily in the morning hiding among the bushes. But to my surprise I apparently attracted the attention—and interest—of a female, for she left a name and telephone number on a piece of paper glued to a leaf on the spot where I practiced. If I were single this could have been the beginning of an amorous adventure. But I was a married man and a loyal husband and so I took no action. Soon the paper was removed.

No matter how hard I worked on my voice, I knew I could not progress much in three short weeks. As the first rehearsal for *The Flower Drum Song* approached I was deathly worried about one thing: If I were called upon to do some solo, the director Robert Longbottom (*Sideshow*) and the music director David Chase would discover my deficiencies and might well fire me as soon as I opened my mouth. It would be a most humiliating and horrible disgrace.

Meeting the seven other principals, I found myself in distinguished company: several of them were endowed with beautiful voices, and two were leads in *Miss Saigon*, then on Broadway: Dee Dee (Kim) and Lo Yung Wang (the engineer). Fortunately, my fear of doing any solos was unfounded for all my requisite singing was in the ensemble. The rehearsals proved to be one of the happiest times in my life. I had a boundless love for music and acting. To be able to do both was sheer heavenly.

David Henry Hwang came to every rehearsal, taking copious notes and making change after change. His job was not easy. He had to stick to the original characters and their relationships to one another. Within these narrow confines, he was trying to create a slightly different and more updated story without deviating too far from the original plot. And whatever changes Hwang made had to be approved by the custodians of the Rodgers and Hammerstein musicals. It was a daunting task and he proved to be an exceptional adapter.

Almost all of the original songs were retained and there were some truly beautiful tunes with ingenious and humorous lyrics, including "I Enjoy Being a Girl," "Don't Marry Me," "Grand Avenue," "Gliding through My Memories," and "You Are Beautiful." After a few weeks' rehearsal we presented a concert reading at the Juilliard School of Music. The performance went exceptionally well, and the response was quite enthusiastic. After further revisions the new *The Flower Drum Song* opened on Broadway over two years later. I was disappointed at not being cast but not surprised; vocally I was not ready, and as it turned out the Chin character did sing a solo. The production won three Tony nominations for the book, choreography, and costumes, and it ran for 169 performances. I attended one of them and felt I was performing vicariously.

Knowing I was an actor who had a deplorable weakness for raunchy jokes, my then girlfriend Sharon posed a Shakespearean riddle: try to match an appropriate play title with each of the puzzles:

1. Abortion
2. Wet
3. Dry
4. Three inches
5. Six inches
6. Nine inches

The clues: highly sexual in connotation and even graphic, with references to men's scepter of passion.

The respective answers:

1. *Love's Labor Lost*
2. *Midsummer's Night's Dream*
3. *Twelfth Night*
4. *Much Ado about Nothing*
5. *As You Like It*
6. *Taming of the Shrew*

My academic association with Shakespeare began with my enrollment in Shakespeare classes, the Riverside Shakespeare Academy, and the Sella Adler Conservatory. If I found the language difficult initially, once I got past the iambic pentameter and obscure words, my appreciation for the bard grew by leaps and bounds. Indeed, I could well appreciate Laurence Olivier's sentiment of "supping on his caviar." I also found my earlier difficulty memorizing the lines and especially the monologs abating, and reciting the latter aloud aided me in my articulation. Today I keep three of his monologs as part of my repertoire: the prologue from *Henry V*, the famous lamentation from *Richard II* by the king (act 3, scene 2), and Shylock's "a pound of flesh" speech from *The Merchant of Venice*.

As much as I loved to do Shakespeare, regrettably I had just one such opportunity: *Much Ado about Nothing*, staged by All American Artists of Philadelphia. Although my part of the sexton was tiny, it represented a breakthrough of sorts, a non-traditional casting of which I was the only Asian in its all-white company. The real joy came from rehearsing and performing the play when Shakespeare's characters came vividly alive and his words resounded beautifully.

I never had the good fortune of doing a Broadway play; there were far too few parts for a Chinese actor like me. Indeed, all this time I had only a few such auditions. While movies and TV shows were more accessible, all too often Asian American actors were consigned to stereotypical roles. For men, they were waiters, houseboys, laundrymen, chefs, and bad guys like gangsters and drug dealers; for women, sleazy characters, prostitutes, dragon ladies. Worse, when there were decent Asian roles they were often played by white actors, giving rise to the term "whitewashing."

I was lucky enough to experience a rare exception to this odious policy, indeed, to transcend and cross the racial barrier. In 1990, my agent Paul Felipo of the Hartig Agency got me an audition to portray a character named Tsongas in the TV series *True Blue*. Since I did not look the least Caucasian, I was reluctant to go but was persuaded otherwise because "Hollywood was not always close-minded and that non-traditional casting sometimes did happen," rationalized Felipo. At the callback there were two other actors; both seemed to look

Greek. Because I did better I got the part. Accordingly, the producer changed my character's name from Tsongas to Chong.

I also managed to cross the age barrier. Casting director Joy Todd initially asked me to audition for an Italian TV show called *Little Italy* for the part of a taxi driver. When I showed up, she said that the estimable Eli Wallach had already been cast for the part. To make me feel better for wasting a trip to New York, she asked me to audition for the part of a Chinese restaurateur a few days later. She did admit it would be a long shot because I was too young for the role.

At the audition, there was just one other candidate: my good friend Kim Chan, whose age was just right. But Todd and the director, John Pepper, an American who flew from Italy to audition us, liked me better and cast me.

I landed two other substantial roles on TV: *John Updike* and *Kay O'Brien*. For the former, a BBC production, the director and the producer flew to the U.S. and gave me the ultimate luxury of auditioning in the privacy of my living room. Shot in Reading, PA, the story was based on one of Updike's writings. I played the lead as a tough Japanese Toyota executive who comes to repossess its auto dealership from its American dealer. He goes on to deliver a scathing but humorous monolog contrasting a disciplined Japan with an undisciplined America, the simple life and pleasure of the one against the materialistic indulgence of the other, with a manner and tone that reverses the role of a servile Asian with that of a bossy Yankee.

In the TV series *Kay O'Brien*, directed by Michael Caffey and shot in Toronto as a stand-in for New York for economic reasons, I was the lead as Tom Woo in the Chinese segment of one episode as a gift shop owner. Faced with two gangsters, Chong (Mike Chin) and Lee (Jusak Bernhard) who try to extort money, Woo ends up with a gun fight, killing Chong and seriously wounding Lee but gets shot in return, resulting in two failed kidneys. In a plot that can happen only on TV, surgeon O'Brien (Patricia Kalember) comes to save Woo's life and the only way to do so is to get approval from the Chinese Godfather (Kim Chan) to transplant kidneys from the brain-dead Chong to Woo in exchange of treating the wounded Lee. Against all odds, O'Brien successfully makes the tradeoff and saves the lives of Woo and the extortionist.

To do my shooting scene, a gun expert was brought to location to advise me on safety and the ropes of firing with a Colt 45. The blanks were making so much noise that I had to wear earplugs. It was with a mixture of excitement and fear that I made my practice shots and did my scene. I was reminded of a tragedy elsewhere: when an actor playfully pointed at his temple with a .44 magnum handgun containing a blank and pulled the trigger, he was killed because the impact was so powerful. Another accident involved super star Bruce Lee's son, actor Brandon Lee. He was fatally shot by a real bullet mistaken for a blank.(In a similar mishap in 2021, Alec Baldwin accidentally killed the cinematographer in the movie *Rust*.) My scene with the hooligans entailed just one take which went well with no incidents.

Kay O'Brien did not prove to be a successful series. Of the 17 or 18 episodes produced, only half of them—including mine—were aired.

One movie that nearly cost my life was *Cadillac Man*. It was directed by Roger Donaldson (*No Way Out*), starring Robin Williams and Tim Robbins and shot mostly in Queens, NY. Robbins played a crazed, jilted husband who crashes into an auto dealer showroom in a motorcycle with an assault rifle and a bomb and threatens to kill everyone including all the customers (I played one of them). Luckily, Williams, one of the salesmen, is able to smooth talk to Robbins and delays his drastic actions till the cops arrive and arrest him.

Happily for me, *Cadillac Man* meant a six-week engagement. But again the question of where I would stay for this extended time arose. I thought of my actor friend Kim Chan. We first met doing the award-winning Stanley Roberts Silverware commercial together. He had once been manager of his family-owned restaurant, the House of Chan, in Manhattan. Having never studied acting, he had such fine instincts and imposing personality that eventually he became a very successful actor, starring in the TV series *Kung Fu* and such movies as *Lethal Weapon 4*, and *The King of Comedy.* One highlight was SAG's lifetime achievement award. Gregarious, congenial and charismatic, Kim befriended me right from the start. He had a spacious, three-bedroom apartment in the Bronx and would welcome me to use his guest room. But he also warned me that he lived in a very dangerous neighborhood, not far from the subway at 178th Street and Grand Concourse and that he had been robbed a few times. But the rent was so cheap he would never consider moving elsewhere.

"If you stay with me, you must come before 10:00 P.M.," he warned. "After that time you might get mugged." He also cautioned that when entering the elevator I should make sure there were no suspicious characters no matter what time of the day.

During my stay with him, my game plan was to go daily to Chinatown for dinner at the end of the shoot. Since few restaurants there accepted credit cards, I carried $300 in cash. Afterward, I would head for Kim's apartment, arriving most likely well before 10:00 P.M.

The first two days went by exactly according to plan. I didn't think Chan's neighborhood looked particularly threatening at night. There were people walking and no signs of danger anywhere. Chan was nice enough to give me a key to his apartment.

On the third day Chan, who was working as an extra in

another movie, *She Devil,* told me he had left his wallet and key on the set and asked me to return the key. He assured me he would return home early enough to let me in.

As I headed for his apartment around 9:30 P.M. he was not home. So I went to a bar near the subway. I ordered a beer and tried to kill time by watching TV. It was June 4, 1989, and the small screen was filled with images of protesters on Beijing's Tiananmen Square. Mostly students, they had been protesting for about one week. Many were emaciated by hunger strike. Some spoke passionately about their yearning for democracy, the symbol of which was a facsimile of the Statue of Liberty. This was followed by soldiers indiscriminatingly firing into the crowds, killing hundreds, and turning Tiananmen Square into a river of blood. As an ethnic Chinese, I was deeply moved and saddened.

I tried to phone Chan every 30 minutes or so to no avail. When my watch ticked close to 11:00 P.M., I became increasingly concerned. By that time, the phone in the bar was not working too well. So I went to a phone booth outside but there was no dial tone.

Meanwhile a Latino approached me asking me if I could exchange a dollar for 10 dimes. This should have been a serious warning. But without thinking I reached for my wallet in my right pocket and made the exchange. He thanked me and disappeared. Looking for a working phone, I went down to the 178 Street Subway station where I again tried to phone Kim. He finally answered. As I was hurriedly walking toward the stairs, I was suddenly knocked down from my back. It happened so fast I was totally dumfounded but instantly realized I was mugged. Indeed, the definition of mugging was "to be assaulted from behind with the intent of robbery." Working as a team, there were two muggers. One, standing about 5'7," held a knife. To terrify me he flashed it in front of my face to show me how lethal the blade was, and even in the dimness of the subway I could tell it was extremely sharp. He then made a gash on my neck. Had he wanted to, he could have easily pushed it just an inch deeper so that there would be no witness. The other mugger, a taller guy, the one who had asked me to exchange money to find out where my wallet was, took it out immediately.

They were so efficient that within seconds they took off. Stupidly I ran after them. When I reached the surface, there was no sign of these criminals. It was just around midnight and the streets were totally deserted.

When I entered Chan's apartment he never told me where he had been all evening and offered no words of sympathy or apology for putting my life in peril. Instead, he said sternly: "You should have been more vigilant."

In no mood to argue, my immediate concern was the loss of my credit and bank cards. So I spent the next 20 minutes canceling them. When I finally went to bed, I could not fall asleep. The overwhelming sensation was that I was most horribly violated. And for the first time I could identify myself with a female rape victim. She and I no doubt share the same sense of violation, that it invades our innermost privacy and sanctity, and that nothing we could do to undo what has happened, and it would stay with us the rest of our lives. This feeling was so pervasive that I stayed awake all night.

When I reported this crime to the police I was shown the pictures of a number of suspects. Never very good in remembering faces, I could not identify my assailants. The police did tell me that the area around 178th Street and Grand Concourse in the Bronx was one of New York's worst crime locations and that on a "good" day there were some 15 muggings.

Since I had another five weeks or so for the movie shoot, I desperately tried to find accommodations elsewhere. A very good friend and former high school classmate from Shanghai kindly agreed to put me up for a couple nights. But when I asked if I could stay longer, I discovered the truth of Ben Franklin's observation that after three days, fish and sleepover guests both stank. Sure enough, this pal denied me any further courtesy and sent me packing. So I went back to Kim Chan with a small difference: I brought my car from Philadelphia so that I could drive to work in *Cadillac Man* and tried to park as close to Chan's apartment as possible in the evening. And luckily, for the remaining shoot there were no further incidents.

The movie itself went very well. It's quite a pleasure to watch two Oscar winners at work: Tim Robbins (*Mystic River*) and Robin Williams (*Good Will Hunting*). I first met the latter in the movie *Moscow on the Hudson* in which he played a Russian musician seeking asylum in the United States and I, a Japanese tourist. Then he was a different actor, keeping close to himself, seemingly an introvert, sitting quietly, sulking and talking to no one. When I tried to converse with him, he replied with a Russian accent. I realized he was staying in character. In *Cadillac Man* he became a totally different person: vivacious, outgoing, and in between takes he made no effort to stay in character. Instead, he tried to entertain everyone. Gifted with the fastest mind and the greatest vocal facility of anyone I knew, he would be joking right to the last minute with no trouble getting into character. Among his more memorable clowning, he imitated a chipmunk, John Wayne, Linda Blair, and Toshiro Mifune, the Japanese actor. He also knew something about tai chi and added some comic routine to it. I taught him a little Chinese, and he learned it immediately, with just the right inflections. In doing his scenes, he was full of vitality, offering a wide range of vocal shadings, and he was highly spontaneous— even after the 10th take. He also ad-libbed like crazy and never seemed to do the same take twice. And yet he was able to hit all the crucial points. (As widely reported, this comic genius took his own life in 2014.

The suspected cause was due to depression, but according to his wife, Susan Schneider, he was also suffering from the debilitating brain disorder Lewy body dementia).

After the film was finished a fellow actor sued the producer for violating the Screen Actor Guild contract. He was cast as a principal but to save money the producer started him off as an extra and then weeks later made him a principal as if he was upgraded. The upshot was that this actor won the case and was compensated. I found out about this too late afterward, which was quite unfortunate because I was an identical victim. I was submitted by my agent for the part of a principal, a Korean customer turned hostage. After auditioning for director Roger Donaldson, I was booked for a six-week engagement. But on my first day I was also told I would start as an extra and be bumped up to a principal at some point later. The second day I was upgraded to a silent bit (slightly higher pay than an extra but no such category exists today). Only after some five weeks' work, when I did a scene opposite Tim Robbins was I elevated to a principal. Though I got credits as such, I should have been paid for the entire six weeks as a featured actor and not just the last few days of the shoot.

In another film a production assistant asked me if I spoke any language other than English. I said my native tongue was Chinese.

"How about German?"

"I had two and a half years of German in college."

"Good. How would like you to audition for the part of a German-speaking Chinese?"

"I'd love to give it a try."

When she sent me the sides I was stunned by the obtuse language, for the German was East Berlin dialect. I called a couple of German-speaking friends for help but got very little, for they too found the language difficult. Nevertheless, with the help of a German-English dictionary and sheer determination, I was able to learn the part. Since I seemed to have an affinity for languages and the sides comprised only a few lines, I did well in the audition. The director of this short film, *Sausages*, Philip Farha hired me on the spot.

I played the part of Hans, a Chinese who lived in Germany a number of years before moving to New York where he became a street vendor and was thrilled to find two German customers who were his pals back in Germany.

I was under the impression that Hans was a small part and that there were not too many lines which I could somehow manage. But much to my surprise Hans was a substantial part, a co-starring role with some 50 lines of obscure East German. My initial reaction: this may be way beyond my ability. Instead of disgracing myself, perhaps I should back out. Nonetheless, I decided to meet the challenge. By drilling the lines repeatedly into my brain I slowly learned. But I couldn't simply recite the lines like a robot; I had to add meaning, emotion, and nuance. Moreover, since Hans had dialogues with two German friends I had to learn their lines too. The producer flew two actors from Germany and the three of us began our scenes in Times Square where I had a hot dog stand.

Using my limited German, gestures, and guess work, I found out that the two actors, who could not speak English, were seasoned professionals and were doing a little better than I for this job: They were to be paid, and I was not under a special SAG experimental film contract. During the four days of filming we became friends. As I started to talk in their native tongue, amazingly many of the German words that I had learned some 20 years prior came back. I told them I was a pianist and that I had studied with a great German teacher, Lonny Epstein. I also recalled my travels to Germany and enjoyed my stay in Munich where I relished its "schweinshaxe." The Chinese also have an affinity for a similar Shanghai dish called "red cooked shank" in which the pork is seasoned with wine, soy sauce, sugar, and spices, and slowly cooked until the meat is chopstick tender and succulent.

Director Farha used a straightforward approach. There was no soul searching, painful struggling over unnecessary details. He knew what he wanted and the three of us delivered with few takes. My memory was good, and I did not once mess up my lines.

Sausages was eventually distributed in some 200 theaters in Germany and in Switzerland. Henning Molfenter was the screen writer and one of the two producers. His other producing credits later included some 46 movies, such as *Inglourious Basterds* and the Oscar winning *The Pianist*.

Having never received a fan letter, I was most gratified to get one from Alain Chuat of Kloten, Switzerland. He said in part: "I am one of your certainly numbered fans. I think you are a great and wonderful actor. I love to watch your movies. From those I have seen which have been shown here in Switzerland I especially liked *Sweet Lorraine, Night and the City,* and *Sausages.* But also great: *Gardens of the Night.* I hope to see you in many more movies. To receive your autograph would mean a lot to me."

When I tried to meet with him during my vacation in Switzerland in 2015, unfortunately, he had moved.

I also have fond memories of a 1977 TV movie titled *Love-Struck.* My part was a comedic one. I thought I did a pretty good job in the audition, and I was well complimented. But I had also learned not to trust the words of casting directors, since their comments were invariably "very good," "excellent," even though the performance might be execrable. Since I did not hear from my agent right away, I assumed the worst. But all was not lost: I had planned a one-week ski vacation in Aspen and was happy I didn't have to give it up. But a couple of days into my skiing my agent told me that I got the part and asked me to travel to Richmond, VA, immediately. I was really torn between accepting the offer and staying on in Aspen.

Opting for the latter, I told my agent that I had already incurred expenses and so very reluctantly I could not accept the booking. The agent soon called back saying that the *Love-Struck* director would not take "no" for an answer, that he had auditioned numerous candidates but liked me the best and would compensate for whatever monetary loss I might suffer from cutting my vacation short.

So I promptly flew home and proceeded to drive to Richmond. I brought my wife, Serena, along to keep me company, and in the hope that she might work as an extra. She was a member of both SAG and AFTRA and had done extra work in a number of movies. Happily, she got cast and both of us got two days' work.

In *Love-Struck,* Emily (Cynthia Gibb) is a young woman disillusioned in an affair of the heart after a failed relationship. To remedy that, Venus (Suzanne Somers), goddess of love, dispatches her son Cupid (Costas Mandylor). However, being an inept archer, he aims at Emily but gets hit by the arrow himself and falls in love with her. In a subplot, I, as a green grocer, am annoyed that an obese African American shopper (Cynthia Webb) keeps squeezing the tomatoes. A heated argument ensues with mounting vehemence. Just then, Cupid is trying to instill love in a quarreling couple nearby and misses his mark again. As recipient of this errant arrow I become a Romeo instantly, hopelessly in love with the shopper. As I pour out my heart in impassioned English and improvised Chinese, she is totally stunned and disgusted. Undeterred, I persist in my heightened emotion.

In our next scene together she returns to shop, thinking since I am her love slave she may get some special favors. In fact, my fervor is still strong. But the magic of my passion suddenly wears off. I instantly detest her. "No more buying on credit," I rudely tell her. "You'll have to pay cash." Thus ends a beautiful romance.

There is nothing sadder for an actor to see a seeming victory snatched away. Mine had to do with the movie *The Last Emperor*. Casting was done by noted actress and casting director Joanna Merlin. She had the reputation of being knowledgeable about the more prominent Chinese actors not only in the States but worldwide. I thought my audition for Merlin went exceptionally well and she seemed genuinely pleased. Next Merlin told me that the director of *The Last Emperor*, Bernardo Bertolucci, would be flying from Italy to New York for one day to finalize his choice of actors. "You don't have to audition for him; he just wants to meet with you," said Merlin. She sounded quite encouraging, giving me the impression that getting a part was within reach.

The meeting took place in a New York midtown hotel attended by Merlin, Bertolucci, and me. The Italian greeted me warmly and told me about his recent visit to Shanghai, my birthplace. We chatted about the city during the time when it was partitioned into differed territories controlled by foreign powers and in particular a park which had the sign No Chinese or dogs are allowed. We laughed at the irony of how China was bullied by European countries once and now was beginning to flex its muscle as a fledging superpower.

As our conversation flowed smoothly, suddenly Bertolucci said, "Let me hear you do some reading with the Mandarin accent," contradicting Merlin's promise. I was not given any time to look over the sides and had to comply with his request instantly. Now the word *Mandarin* was—and still is—used loosely. Theoretically it means standard northern Chinese dialect virtually identical to Beijingese and is China's official language. But in this country Mandarin has never been precisely defined. When Chinese restaurants say they specialize in Mandarin cooking, they can mean food from Beijing, or other parts of Northern China, or at times all regional cookeries other than Cantonese. So Bertolucci's perception of

English with a Mandarin accent meant simply speaking with hints of Chinese accent, and John Lone, who was cast as the Last Emperor, actually spoke with distinct traces of Cantonese accent, his native tongue. Since I had a natural accent it could and should satisfy the director. But just then I got confused and thought mistakenly I had to speak differently. On the spur of the moment I put on an affected accent that prompted both Bertolucci and Merlin to ask, "Is that Mandarin accent?" Consequently, I was rejected and lost the chance to go to China to do this film which won seven Oscars including the best picture and the best director.

Obviously, an actor's ability to speak English with an authentic foreign accent can be invaluable. But it took me a while to find my voice and make it an asset. Shortly after my fiasco with Bertolucci I had an audition to speak with a Korean accent. While my Chinese accent could be passed as generic Asian accents I was blind—or deaf—to this fact. And again I put on an affected accent, having absolutely no idea what I was doing. To my surprise and humiliation, the three auditors broke out laughing; especially after one of them said "You sounded Jewish!" I knew I again made a fool of myself.

From the two painful lessons I learned to capitalize on my natural accent. In time I got dozens of jobs requiring an Asian or a Chinese accent including radio commercials like L'eggs, Skippy, Georgia Lottery, TV shows like PBS' *Savage Earth* and *Sea Power,* and Acoustiguide for the San Francisco Museum of Art.

In two other memorable voice-over jobs: 1. I played a Thai, one of the two title characters, in National Geographic's *Bird-nesters of Thailand*, which was nominated for a documentary Oscar. 2. Discovery Channel's *Forbidden City*, in which I voiced three persons including two Chinese emperors.

One well-known fact about accents is that the Chinese and Japanese have trouble pronouncing "l" and "r," often reversing the two. In other words, "l" is pronounced as "r" and "r" is pronounced as "l." Thus, the song "Fly Me to the Moon" comes out as "Fry Me to the Moon;" an order of fried rice becomes an order of flied lice. This recalls a crude joke: When Mrs. Franklin Roosevelt asks the Chinese ambassador at a social occasion, "How was your election?" He replies: "I have not had an erection since Fliday."

I had a real experience of pronouncing this "l" and "r" reversal in the TV series *The Thorns* starring Tony Robert. I auditioned as a Chinese caterer for Mike Nichols. He was, of course, one of the most talented directors. But I heard about him way before he became famous in the early 1950s when I was a student at Penn. A fellow pre-med by the name of Bob Nichols often told me about his director/brother Mike, and that the two could whistle an entire overture from a Wagner opera. So, at the audition I asked Mike if he was the brother of Bob. Yes, indeed, he said. "He is a doctor now practicing in California," seemingly amused at the irony that instead of being a practicing doctor like his brother I ended up choosing one of the world's most insecure professions and was now facing him as an actor.

In my audition at one point I angrily shouted at my neighbor (Kelly Bishop) with the word "violation" for the unsanitary way she was disposing her garbage. For comic effect I purposely mispronounced it as "vioration." I doubt if most people caught on this funny twist of accent. But Nichols laughed at this and my other lines and hired me.

For quite some time I had been toying with the idea of relocating to the West. I was getting tired of the same old acting scenes and where else would an actor go to but Hollywood, the show biz capital of the world? More importantly, my commuting was taking too much toll on me. I was travel weary, especially with jobs or auditions that required an early appointment. For far too many times I had to get up in the middle of the night. I was sleepy all the time and started to lose my memory. I would see a movie and forget every scene, read an article and could not recollect its contents, and see a familiar face and have trouble identifying the person. I also worried that extreme sleep deprivation would be detrimental to my health and life span.

Toward my goal of exploring acting scene in the West, I finally took the big step, albeit a tentative one initially. Of no small help was encouragement from my friend Joan Ruggles,[2] a standing offer that Serena and I could stay in her L.A. house before settling down. It was a generosity for which I could not be more grateful, for it really paved my way of going to a strange land, easing the pain of relocation and uncertainty.

In October, 1999, shortly after Serena and I vacationed in China, we became her house guests. I kept my Philadelphia home so that if things didn't work out I would have a place to return to.

My first two orders of business were finding an apartment and securing an agent. As guests of Joan, I didn't want to overstay our welcome. After diligent searching we found an ideal place in Burbank: The Royal Equestrian. Rent was reasonable and it was furnished. But to my astonishment, our application was rejected because of our "negative credit rating." To my best recollection I had always paid my bills on time. But we discovered that Serena had an outstanding telephone bill of less than $60. When she moved from her Chicago residence to Philadelphia, it was never forwarded to her. By the time the problem was resolved, regrettably I had stayed at Joan's house longer than expected, although she graciously disagreed.

---

[2] I met her in Philadelphia in a yoga class many years ago. A highly successful freelance photographer, she later married Bob Young, a TV screenwriter (*My Two Dads, Joey and Melissa*).

In L.A., no actor freelances; one has to work exclusively with just one agency. If it is good, meticulous with casting breakdowns and has good connections, an actor is truly blessed. The bigger agencies would not consider any new talent without industry recommendations. Smaller agencies are more accessible, but finding the right ones has never been easy. In contrast, in the East, where I freelanced as most actors did, I had no problem hooking up with top notch agents. And I almost never missed any auditions that matched my profile. Here in L.A. I've eventually worked with a good number of agencies with varying results, some excellent such as CESD, some inattentive, missing casting calls that I should have gone to, and some terrible, including one, a bi-coastal agency that I fired for absentmindedly failing to notify me of two bookings and making me lose money. Another agent would never return my calls, no matter how urgent, and was similarly axed.

As I set out to try my luck in L.A., not unexpectedly I discovered getting a part was far more difficult because Asian actors were a dime a dozen, including many who spoke Mandarin. Indeed, I got just one commercial booking during my first year and ended up doing extra work which I was hoping to avoid. But I did get a few callbacks, giving me the hope that Hollywood might not be too inaccessible. I turned out to be right in the years that followed.

I did much better in San Diego. Shortly after my relocation, through the referral of an actor friend, Kathy Oh, I signed up with an agent. By chance, Elegance immediately got me an audition, my very first in the West. It was for Mastercard and an Asian couple were needed. I brought Serena along. But she has had no training whatsoever and had never auditioned. So her tryout went very poorly. And as expected, casting director Barbara Shannon bluntly told her: "You are not an actress, are you?" Consequently, Serena was absolutely dumfounded—and thrilled—to be cast, along with me.

Subsequently, San Diego proved to be a very friendly place as I landed several other jobs including an episode of *The Chronicle,* two casino commercials, and a print job. Ironically, I found myself spending hours commuting long distance again as in the East. In time, I gave up San Diego; I valued my sleep too much.

In L.A., as in New York, commercials proved to be my forte as I continued to progress. I was especially successful in 2006 when I did five: Time Warner, FedEx, Safeway, and two Pacific Gas & Electric (one in Mandarin and one in Cantonese). To date I've done a combined total of some 80 bi-coastally.

The most competitive audition was for HSBC, a London-based bank. In addition to notifying all commercial agencies it also posted notices on the Internet to entice all possible candidates, professionals (one was big-time actor James Hong), and amateurs. As expected the audition was a cattle call, a mob scene the likes of which I had never seen. After three callbacks I was one of the six Chinese chosen to play businessmen. One of them, Bill Yee, had never acted before. He was an attorney who went to the audition on a lark, survived the three callbacks, and landed this exceptionally humorous commercial.

A British businessman is being entertained by his Chinese counterparts in a restaurant. He is shown a small, live snake just before cooking. (Many Cantonese consider this scaly species a great delicacy.) Despite his great horror and revulsion, the Briton pretends he thoroughly enjoys the dish to be polite or seal the deal. His seeming appreciation brings about an unexpected reaction. Thinking he really has an affinity for snakes, the hosts show him an even bigger, live one some 10 feet long weighing about 80 pounds as an encore. The poor man has to try even harder to pretend that he is not eating poison but the most delicious dish in the world. This hilarious commercial turned out to be a big hit. It was critically acclaimed and aired internationally, and in Hong Kong it won one of the ten best advertising awards.

This commercial had an expected irony for me. After being on the air for one and half years it paid me a tiny six-month holding fee—without residuals—with the option to renew. In my experience once a commercial ended up being on hold, it would never run again. By a strange coincidence, just before the end of this holding period, I nailed a Citibank commercial. The pay would have been phenomenal: triple the SAG scale. While actors were not allowed to have two competing commercials on the air or two on hold simultaneously, I thought I could safely accept the Citibank job, since the burden was on HSBC to renew the contact if it so desired, and it didn't on the last day of the holding period. But my agent (not CESD) was far too timid and cautious. He took it upon himself to contact the bank in London to determine its intentions. The bank informed him that it had already engaged another ad agency to do its commercial but decided to extend me another holding period. As it turned out, the original commercial never ran again.

Among my theatrical endeavors, one of the more challenging was for *Six Feet Under*, Alan Ball's critically acclaimed series on HBO. Against very stiff competition during a two-day casting session I played a Thai dying of heart attack. So realistic was my performance that I heard gasping sounds and approving words from the auditors and earned a co-starring role. In one scene I played a corpse lying in Fisher and Sons funeral home, but alas, my Method Acting did not prove useful.

Some of my other credits: TV's series such as *Robbery Homicide Division* (now defunct), ABC's *Fresh off the Boat*, and TBS' *Angie Tribeca;* films including *Gardens of the Night*, *Revenant* (directed by D. Kerry Prior and produced in 2009, not to be confused with the 2015 *The Revenant*), and *Ping Pong Playa* (directed by Oscar winner Jessica Yu). I also did looping (post-production sound effects or dubbing) which, like all principal roles, paid residuals, for movies like *Rebel, Mummy 3*, and *The Great Wall*. The combined total of my TV shows and movies—including those from the East—number several dozens. Among the luminaries I have worked opposite: Robert De Niro (*Night and the City*), Kathleen Turner (*Friends at Last*), Lou Gossett (*Gideon Oliver*), Tracey Ullman and Blythe Danner (*Tracey Ullman Takes on New York*, in which I also taught the latter to speak Chinese).

Meanwhile, there were dramatic improvements in my quality of life: sleeping seven full hours a day, seven days a week; playing tennis all year round; never worrying about breaking my back shoveling snow and putting chains on my car as in Philadelphia during the frigid winter, or suffering the sweltering, humid summers; enjoying frequent skiing at the superb Mammoth Mountain Resort, delighting in the wide choices of regional Chinese cuisines of every description—all within close proximity. Moreover, many of these restaurants charge very reasonable prices, especially the ones offering "luncheon specials" that may vary from a low $5.95 and up.

Adding to our appreciation of this area was Serena's rising star as a professional. Having been a top fashion designer in Melbourne, Australia, and Chicago, she easily found a job as a fabric/print designer at Citroen. Among her prodigious out-puts, some 50,000 units were sold at Nordstrom. At Harari her designs graced such stores as Neiman Marcus, Macy's, and J.C. Penney. Moreover, she often saw women wearing her designs on the streets, at Disney Concert Hall, in her church and elsewhere, including an actress on Chinese TV and an American tourist in Naples, Italy, where we vacationed. Thanks to these developments I decided to spend the rest of my life in Southern California, sold my Philadelphia home, and bought one in an L.A. suburb.

In 2008, I got a proposition to act in Mandarin in the title role of *China's Andy Rooney,* an Onion News video to be produced in New York City. *China's Andy Rooney* is a barbed satire making fun of China's harsh judicial system. The pay was not great: AFTRA scale, plus agent's fee and per diem. But only one day's hotel accommodations when two were really needed to allow for a little breathing room. And no reimbursements for airfare.

There were other negative factors. Though I had nothing to do with the text, what if China was offended by the satire and decided to "kill the messenger" by denying my visa applications, or heaven forbid, charging me with the crime of "revealing state secrets?"

Adding to my worry was that fact I had done an earlier satire on *Jimmy Kimmel Live.* It was during a time when China was producing shoddy toys that contained toxins, gaining worldwide publicity and condemnation. To remedy that, I played the Chinese Minister of Trade at a press conference to assure everyone that China had mended its ways and now was offering the safest toys, so safe that one could eat them with impunity. To prove that, I proceeded to gorge myself on some of the toys like trains and cars on display in front of me. They were, however, made with chocolate.

Mitigating my apprehensions about doing *Andy Rooney* were the facts that it would be an honor to play a Chinese version of this iconic TV writer and commentator, especially when the producers told me they had spent months nationally in search of a suitable actor and failed; my frequent flying mileage would allow me to travel for free; and my great friends Steve and Marci Karsh offered to put me up (despite the fact Steve was dying of cancer).

After deliberating the pros and cons I accepted the Onion News offer, hoping Beijing's sense of humor would override a little ribbing.

Because the Chinese translation[3] was horrendous, I redid the whole thing, making it more conversational, accurate, and illuminating. The production, which had great time constraints, was done in a little over one hour, and I felt unreasonably rushed. Nevertheless, the Onion News coordinator Cody Beke told me the management was highly pleased. Indeed, the video received over 147,800 viewings as of this writing. It provoked over 500 comments, debates, and even heated dialogue among the viewers, most of which centered on the larger issues totally unrelated to the video itself (e.g. discourse on totalitarianism, social reform, economic planning, etc.). Of the ones directly related to the contents, the overwhelming majority was favorable. Some examples: "It has me rolling upon the floor." "I speak Mandarin and I assure you that this is translated perfectly." "Very funny." "He does a good Rooney." "The facial expression on that guy is pure gold."

A small minority hated the video: "This is shit compared to other Onion videos." "Not funny at all." "So stupid." Others attacked my Mandarin, including: "They can't even speak chinese (sic) properly, grammar and syntax problems all over the place."

For the record, YouTube has been banned in China.

One year after this gig at the age of 75 I got shocking news:

---

[3] In my experience, translated scripts all too often used words or phrases that were too florid and obscure and therefore lacking in lucidity. Sometimes the translation would miss the subtlety and nuances, even making unthinkable mistakes. (Two such examples: in a Broadway-bound play, the word *ground* meaning the earth on which we stand was initially translated as the past tense of *grind*. And in a Baltimore Port Authority text the word *knot* meaning ship's speed was translated as the knot in a cord.) As a result, almost without exception I found myself retranslating when doing a Chinese role or voice-over.

prostate cancer. While my PSA (prostate specific antigen) had always remained constant around 3.4, considered acceptable, my primary care physician Mark Weissman discovered in 2009 in his digital examination that my prostate felt hard and suspected the worse. Indeed, a biopsy revealed that half of my prostate was more than 90% cancerous. Dr. Mathew Bui, a urologist, told me I would have eight more years to live if untreated. Of the few possible treatments such as hormone and radiation, I opted to remove the damned thing; anything else would feel like living with a time bomb. And in January 2010, Mark Kawachi, who specialized in what's called "robotic surgery," also known as the Da Vinci System, performed the operation. Making five small incisions, he used high resolution cameras and micro-surgical instruments to remove the prostate. While some patients experienced no ill effects after the procedure, I suffered the terrible problem of incontinence. To counter that I had a "sling operation." It was partially successful, decreasing the leakage dramatically but still requiring changes of diapers daily. More importantly, my PSA has been negligible for over 11 years and I continue to monitor it. (Today, prostatectomy has become highly controversial and many doctors recommend non-surgical treatments or observation.)

While there are no proven cures today, I take PectaSol, or modified citrus pectin (pulps and peels of citrus fruits), initial studies of which have demonstrated anticancer activity, reducing tumor growth and metastasis. My other supplements include lycopene, pomegranate, reishi mushrooms and beta-sitosterol (containing zinc and selenium).

I have another health issue: acute knee arthritis. This was totally avoidable had it not been for the corruption, greed, and dishonesty of my insurance company when I suffered a skiing accident in 1989. It resulted in a minor tear on my left knee meniscus with minor pain. Diagnosed by Dr. Joseph Torg, a top sports medicine specialist, he recommended sewing up the tear via arthroscopy. But my insurance company required a second opinion, who by nature was a crooked doctor on its payroll for the sole purpose of dissuading any operations, no matter how dire. That was what happened as a hand specialist—and not an orthopedic surgeon—assured me that my knee was in good shape; not unexpectedly, I bowed under the pressure.

When I twisted the same knee again playing tennis and enlarged the tear, the pain at times became almost unbearable. But despite the urgent need for surgery, the dishonest insurance company forced me again to seek a second opinion. The doctor this time was as unethical as the first, for he incredibly also counseled against any operation. By overruling him I finally had surgery by Torg who found the tear too big to be repairable and had to remove most of the cartilage. But I slowly developed arthritis which became progressively worse, culminating 27 years later in my inability to walk without excruciating pain.

My orthopedic surgeon, Randall Farac, advised knee replacement. But because of the alleged horror stories associated with this invasive operation, I decided to try an expensive stem cell prolotherapy (almost $10,000 and not covered by any insurance) by Dr. Peter Fields. But my pain persisted, and I eventually resorted to knee surgery after all. Luckily, I found an award-winning specialist, Dr. Andrew Yun, who was director of St. John's Replacement Service Center in Santa Monica, CA. He told me his success rate was 99.3% and that I did not need a total knee replacement, only a partial one. Medicare would pay 80% of the costs and my SAG-AFTRA health insurance the balance. The surgical procedure consisted of resurfacing the knee damaged by arthritis and then using metals (alloys of cobalt-chromium and titanium) and plastic to cap the thigh bone (femur) and shin bone (tibia).

The operation on January 24, 2017, which entailed a four-inch incision, was totally successful, taking only one hour. About five hours later a physical therapist made me walk 300 feet with a walker. After a few months recuperation and rigorous physical therapy, I felt like a new man, able to play tennis and looking forward to the ski season.

Otherwise, I have been in relatively good health as an octogenarian. I still go out on auditions, though they don't come my way too often, and my betting average has declined significantly. Nevertheless, I did do a few ingratiating jobs:

- I reprised my role as Canning Woo in East West Player's production of *The Joy Luck Club*. One reviewer said, "Lin delivers a profoundly moving monologue." Cici Lau, who played my wife, told me she cried every time I did the final, emotional scene, and David Standbra, another cast member, observed on occasions "there wasn't a dry eye" (in the audience).

- In the short film *Paper Lotus* I was winner of the 2013 Los Angeles Movie Award as the best supporting actor. This noteworthy movie by Tiffany Wu won other categories as well, including best screenplay, directing, actor, and cinematography, and was screened at major international film festivals.

- For *Touch* (based on a true story) I was 2014 NBC UNIVERSAL Short Film Festival's best actor nominee. I played an unwitting sex offender caught in the cultural clashes and misunderstanding between the East and the West. Written and directed by Lulu Wang (*The Farewell), Touch* was screened at the Palm Springs International Film Festival and won Asians on Films' best drama award.

Now in the sunset of my life, I have outlived my brothers (the oldest, Dave, died at 63; an older one, Harry, at 29; and a younger one, Henry, at 57). I am blessed with a loving, dedicated wife and grateful for whatever God-given talents I am endowed with and for having lived a fulfilling life. No mortals can ask for more.

EPILOGUE

Of my myriad professions, acting stands out as the most enduring. After a span of 30 plus years, my passion for it never dimmed. Whether facing a live audience or camera I've never failed to get a thrill. Despite my advancing age as a performer who is pushing 90, as long as I am physically able and mentally sound I will never retire.

I find equal joy playing the piano. Unlike acting in which one cannot indulge without the process of being cast first, factors that are beyond one's control, I am free to exalt in my Steinway whenever my mood moves me. Indeed, if I have one life to live I opt for that of a piano virtuoso.

ACKNOWLEDGEMENTS

My mother, Priscilla. Gentle, gracious and giving, she nurtured me, educated me, and loved me as only a saintly mother could.

My father, Peter. As thoughtful and caring as my mom, he supported me in every way possible, including ventures of which he had great misgivings. I am especially grateful to him for bringing me to the U.S. where I was able to pursue and live my American dream.

My wife, Serena. She is my soulmate, best friend, and indispensable companion. To put up with my narcissism, temper, and indolence she requires—and possesses—boundless patience, diligence, and understanding. Furthermore, she took care of me, who is twenty-one years her senior, in every imaginable way and beyond the call of duty. She is an especially talented culinary artist, consistently turning dishes that pamper the palate. And during my infirmities including my prostatectomy and knee replacement operation, she tended to every detail and my every need.

My stepson, Mo Zhang, an electrical engineer and college professor, taught me much about computers and solved many of my problems large and small. (I was—and still am—a high-tech ignoramus.) He is also a wizard with his hands, tackling not only chores that challenge a good handy man, but complicated jobs like assembling a home gym, building a gigantic storage shed, and erecting a porch.

Joan Ruggles, a former Philadelphia freelance photographer. When I tangentially considered relocating to Los Angeles to further my acting career it might not have materialized without her encouragement and generous offer to be her house guest.

King Chen. He was my former business partner who got me started in my won ton soup enterprise. Without his initial support and especially his assistance in supplying the large labor force to hand roll the thousands upon thousands of won tons for canning, I might not have become an entrepreneur. While our partnership did not last too long, I will never forget his contribution.

My friends who gave feedback to my memoir, with their valuable critiquing, helpful suggestions, and encouragement. They include George Wong, my high school classmate; John Bull, former managing editor of the *Philadelphia Inquirer*; my nephew Lester Lin, an enterprising businessman; Mai Hsu, an artist and a friend from way back; Dennis Chan, a writer/ director; and my godsister, the late Lee Wei.

Jeffery Smart, U.S. Army historian, provided the names of key people during my tour of duty in the Army Chemical Center in Edgewood, MD.

ABOUT THE AUTHOR

Ben Lin was born in Shanghai in 1933. His father was a banker and mother a teacher. They immigrated to the U.S. in 1950. A Penn graduate, he researched with micro-chemistry at DuPont where he also had a stint as a marketing executive. Dubbed "The Won Ton Wizard" by the *Washington Post*, he commercialized America's first packaged won ton soup and sweet and sour soup, was owner-chef of the award-winning Jade Palace in Philadelphia and taught cooking at the China Institute in New York. He may be one of the few researchers able to unveil the mystery of MSG and arrive at a definitive conclusion. Holding a master's degree in journalism from Temple, he contributed occasionally to *Philadelphia* magazine, wrote for South Jersey's largest daily, the *Courier-Post*, and published elsewhere including the *USA Today*. He has been an actor since 1980, having amassed some 80 commercials and acted opposite such luminaries as Robert De Niro, Kathleen Turner and Lou Gossett. Critically acclaimed for his performance in the play *The Wash*, he was Los Angeles Movie Award's winner as the best supporting actor for the short film *Paper Lotus*. Ben is married to Serena Wei, a former fashion and graphic arts designer.

CPSIA information can be obtained
at www.ICGtesting.com
Printed in the USA
BVHW042137310822
646046BV00003B/21